FAITH FITS THE FACTS

Dr. David J. Carlson

FAITH FITS THE FACTS

© 2021 Rev. Dr. David J. Carlson | ISBN: 979-8-500-01783-3
This handbook is independently published by Case Ministries Int'l (CMI) to help financially support all CMI apologetics/charity-focused initiatives and to actualize CMI's vision to globally impact 1M+ for Christ by 2050.

Copyright Provisions

Biblical References

Work Contributions

The handbook's organizational "Diamond of Truth" diagram, depicted on the front cover, was digitally produced by the author and his brother, Mr. Jonathan S. Carlson. The back cover image of David and spouse, Kristen, was photographed by Mrs. Jennifer A. Dashner. The 3-D charts shown on pages 81-83 were designed by Mr. Remus Escoto. All other charts, sketches, maps, and photos were produced or purchased by the author, with exception of the images shown on pages 59, 62 and 63, which are properly documented in the Endnotes.

Author Accessibility

Readers who have pressing apologetics questions for Dr. Carlson and/or who desire to schedule him as a guest lecturer can connect 24/7/365 via the "Bookings" tab of the Case Ministries Int'l website: www.caseintl.com.

Dedication

Published in Honor of Rev. Harold S. Carlson

1922 – 2000

Devoted husband to Jane (1923-2021) and loving father to Jim, Ron, Julie. Beloved grandfather to David, Jon, Candace, Jason, Jared, Patrick, Kristin. Esteemed Baptist General Conference (BGC) minister for over six decades. Beloved preacher, church-builder and humble servant of Christ whose oft-quoted life motto also sublimely captures this book's ultimate aspiration.

 To God Be the Glory

Three generations of evangelists, Rev. Harold S. Carlson (left), his eldest grandson, David J. Carlson (middle) & eldest son, Dr. James H. Carlson (right), are traveling from San Francisco to Manila to serve on a short-term mission in the Philippines during the month of Feb. 1983. The Carlsons were ages 61, 12 & 36, respectively.

Book Theme Verse:

"But in your hearts
set Christ apart as holy and acknowledge him as Lord.
Always be ready to give a logical defense
to anyone who asks you to account for the hope that is in you,
but do it courteously and respectfully."

— I Peter 3:15
(Amplified Bible)

Contents

"Faith is built on reason and knowledge. We should have good reasons for thinking that Christianity is true before we completely dedicate ourselves to it."

~ J.P. Moreland

"A reasonable faith is not only possible, it's necessary, for the heart cannot embrace what the mind regards as nonsense."

~ David K. Clark

Foreword

As the headmaster who hand-picked David for his first administrative post at Brent Int'l School in the Philippines, I have developed a close relationship with David that spans many years. He is one of the most multi-talented educators and pastors with whom I have had the privilege of working.

When David asked if I would write the Foreword to his book, *Faith Fits the Facts,* I must confess that I felt humbled to be offered the honor of this literary task, particularly since my name and viewpoints (on pages 9 & 25) are alluded to with such kindness. Yet the fraternal friendship I have for David, as well as my great respect and admiration for his God-given talents as a writer, his extremely intelligent mind, his professional experience, and his contagious enthusiasm, persuaded me that I should accept David's request. I have thus crafted here four personal observations regarding the high caliber and practical value of David's publication:

(1)   I believe the originality, organization and methodology of David's work make it a model textbook in Christian apologetics. David's concise and clear exposé will not only be useful to high school and university students who desire to study apologetics, but it will be valuable to all people interested in deepening their understanding of facts pertaining to the basic Christian world view — facts often contested by a culture of postmodernist thought that embraces agnosticism, moral relativism and/or philosophical naturalism.

(2)   In cogently reminding us that our personal response to God must include our whole being, body, soul and mind, David rightly emphasizes that "solid believers must also always be sound thinkers." Yet David is also realistic about the nature of absolute Truth and the person-relativity of human knowledge. Although he convincingly shows that the core beliefs of the Christian world view seem to be corroborated by 21st-century science, history, archeology, and other disciplines, he also wisely notes that we must be very humble whenever we make truth-claims, that we must keep an open mind to wherever cumulative evidence leads, and that we must be careful not to become so rigid and dogmatic in our faith that we cease to consider new warranted insights.

(3)   In the tradition of the world-renowned ecumenist, the Right Rev. Charles Henry Brent (1862-1929), an Episcopal Church Bishop whose vision for church solidarity inspired my own ministry, David also captures the beauty of an ecumenical perspective, since his compendium of evidence focuses on the universal truth-claims which bind all Christians. The book should thus serve as an ideal trigger for ecumenical discussion groups, as it upholds the ideal of Christ's John 17 prayer, "that all [believers] may be one."

(4)   Finally, David's work bears an important personal invitation. He asks us to turn away from the paths of skepticism and agnosticism and to follow a path of personal faith, to embrace Christ and his great love for us, and to understand, as Paul poetically writes, "that neither death nor life, neither angels nor demons, neither the present nor the future, nor any powers, neither height nor depth, nor anything else in all creation, will be able to separate us from the love of God that is in Christ." (Romans 8:38).

As one who has sought to serve Christ most of my life, I pray this well-written, user-friendly handbook, *Faith Fits the Facts*, will greatly impact many for Christ in the 21st century, and that God will indeed be glorified as people encounter the undeniable truth of Christ within these pages.

Rev. Canon Gabriel P. Dimanche
Canon for Int'l Education — Episcopal Church in the Philippines

Preface

Christian apologetics, the art of defending the Christian faith, is certainly one of the most important academic subjects to which a person can ever be exposed, since it deals directly with the question of Truth (with a capital "T"). We all desire to be in possession of Truth, or that which corresponds to reality, and Christ claims he is it. But many have never studied or even heard of the term apologetics. This digestible handbook was written to help change that reality, since it offers an accessible, yet scholarly compendium of the best of 21st-century Christian defense. It is a utile apologetics treatise.

Given that this handbook articulates facts and insights progressively mastered, with the help of many mentors and experiences spanning more than four decades, I feel it is fitting and appropriate, in this opening Preface, to offer an explanatory autobiographical memoir regarding exactly how and why this practical opus originated, with particular emphasis on how specific individuals and past life experiences helped to shape the content and organization of the work.

To begin, it is necessary to offer a snapshot of my early upbringing. As the son, grandson and nephew of well-known Christian pastors, I was exposed to Christianity ever since I was born on 28 February 1971. I accepted the lordship of Jesus at age seven and was baptized by my father, Rev. Dr. James H. Carlson, in the Pacific Ocean in Hawaii. Growing up a PK (or preacher's kid) I was exposed to thousands of Bible lessons and potent sermons, most of which were preached by my father, an expert communicator. As a result of this exposure, I was able to grow as a young Christian. By age 18, I could claim that I was not only a high school valedictorian and U.S. Air Force Academy appointee, but a biblically-literate believer. Looking back, I am grateful for the Christian heritage that my parents so wisely passed on to me. They surely "trained me up in the way of the Lord" (Proverbs 22:6). Yet, despite this solid Christian upbringing as a youth, I had yet, like many Christians today, to be exposed to a scholarly digest of Christian apologetics. That is, I had yet to learn how to construct a cogent, "intellectual" defense of the faith in Christ I professed.

After high school, although I stumbled through a period of rebellion, I felt a distinct "call" to become a pastor so, in 1989, I decided against attending the U.S. Air Force Academy and instead went to Bethel College in Arden Hills, Minnesota. As a sophomore in 1990, majoring in philosophy and theology and serving as the chaplain for the renowned Bethel Choir, I decided to enroll in a course entitled Apologetics 101. It was here that I gained my first substantive exposure to the discipline of Christian defense. Looking back, I realize it was fortuitous for me that this course was taught by Dr. Gregory A. Boyd, a genius professor who, since that time, has authored many award-winning apologetics books, including *Letters from a Skeptic* (an ECP Gold Medallion Award winner) and

BETHEL
UNIVERSITY

Cynic Sage of Son of God. Interestingly, in the Preface to *Letters from a Skeptic*, Dr. Boyd thanked his apologetics class at Bethel College for "their insightful comments and editorial suggestions."[1] I am proud to say I was a member of this memorable class, a class where Dr. Boyd showed his students the vital importance of studying apologetics. It thus did not surprise me when I saw that Dr. Boyd was chosen in 1998 as one of 12 world experts interviewed by Lee Strobel for his award-winning book, *The Case for Christ*. Since 1998, in addition to authoring dozens of bestsellers, Dr. Boyd has founded Re|Knew (see reknew.org) and pastored Woodland Hills, a mega-church in St. Paul, MN.

Motivated by my studies under Dr. Boyd, I began "practicing" apologetics during my summer breaks, particularly as I worked as a Head Lifeguard supervising 10 lifeguards on a Lake Michigan beach (in 1991), toured 12 U.S. states with a professional vocal/drama sextet (in 1992), and backpacked through 10 nations of Europe (in 1993). I learned a key lesson from these varied experiences, namely, that nearly all people are open to discussing the truth-claims of Christianity.

In the fall of 1993, after earning a B.A. in Philosophy/Biblical Studies from Bethel College, I decided to attend Bethel Theological Seminary, a seminary from which both my father and grandfather (see page 3) had graduated in 1945 and 1972, respectively. In 1994, I enrolled in an advanced apologetics course taught by Dr. David K. Clark. In his book, *Dialogical Apologetics*, Dr. Clark argues that apologetics should be both rational and personal, that real-life apologetics should always be about "presenting the case for Christianity, by the Spirit's power, with rational force, cultural appropriateness, and personal sensitivity in the context of relationship,"[2] and that success in dialogue is not dependent on whether my dialogue partner agrees with me, but rather when, "in addition to making the case, I understand his views better, develop a relationship with him, or grow intellectually."[3] Dr. Clark's exemplary tutelage made a profound impact on my thinking about apologetics. In establishing a sound person-centered approach to Christian defense, Dr. Clark taught me the importance of being a person-centered apologist — of presenting the best case I can for the truth of Christ, for the benefit of others, with the recognition that, although I should use clear, concrete and cogent reasoning, I must also always consider the worldview, culture, personality and attitude of the individual(s) to whom my case is made.[4] I must tailor my approach to effectuate maximal impact.

During the mid-90's, along with academic training at Bethel, I also gained invaluable "hands-on" exposure to mission work in Europe, Asia and South America, and to pastoral ministry in three church denominations. Serving as a youth pastor for Trinity Evangelical Free Church in Lakeville, MN, then for First Baptist Church in Coon Rapids, MN and, after a 1996 move to the Philippines, for the Cathedral of the Holy Trinity (an Episcopal church in Manila), I not only saw how apologetics is often useful in ministry settings, but I learned from the Christ-like examples of Reverends Don Reigstad, David Johnson and Bob Tiling, my three respective senior pastors, that a Christ-like character is really the best apologetics case one can ever present to others.

My 1996 move to the Philippines (mentioned above) took place when I accepted a job to teach at Brent International School Manila, the largest of a conglomerate of PK-12, international schools affiliated with Episcopal Church in the Philippines. For two years in Manila, in addition to teaching high school courses in History, Religion and Philosophy, and serving as youth director for the Episcopal church above, I began to conduct church seminars on basic apologetics. In 1998, I was asked to be an Administrator at the Brent located in Subic Bay, so I transferred. Over an eight-year span at Brent International School Subic (98-'06), a timeframe where my firstborn son, Joshua, was born on 29 June 2000, I was able to serve as Brent's chaplain, guidance counselor and activity director and teach numerous K-12 classes. As I preached for student chapels and taught religion / history / philosophy courses, I observed that using "acrostics" worked well in helping students to memorize academic facts, so I have incorporated this practical principle into this work. Specifically, I have created 12 easy-to-memorize acrostics to help readers better remember all pivotal handbook points presented. In addition to this mnemonic approach, the  diverse atmosphere at Brent also inspired me to adopt an ecumenical approach to teaching apologetics, meaning that all Christians worldwide can benefit. Brent Subic's founder, Rev. Canon Gabriel P. Dimanche |1927-2013|, made a tremendous impact on my thinking regarding the beauty of an ecumenical perspective. While serving as the Canon for Int'l Educational for the Episcopal Church in the Philippines, Fr. Dimanche agreed to author the *Foreword* to this book (see page 7), a gift of prose for which I was eternally grateful. Fr. Dimanche's eloquent sermon commentary on Jesus' John 17 ecumenical prayer "that all [believers] may be one" also appears on page 25.

Having observed the wisdom of an ecumenical mindset, I decided, in crafting this book, that it would be judicious to focus my apology exclusively on the four ecumenical truth-claims which define universal Christianity, namely, (1) the reality of a personal Creator God, (2) the historicity of the biblical Gospels, (3) the divinity of Christ, and (4) the life-saving power of the Christian kerygma (or the original gospel proclamation), since these four "non-negotiables" are common to everyone in Christendom. To construct an easy-to-use defense of these four truth-claims, I designed a unique baseball-type diagram which I call the Diamond of Truth (see pages 26, 35 and 167).

Regarding the Christian truth-claim that the Bible is God's Word, note that, like the four truth-claims above, I do not "assume" this from the outset, for apologists should not dogmatically hold to this assumption. We can demonstrate the cogency of Christianity (through science and history) without presupposing the "holiness" of the Bible. This is not to say we should not defend the Bible. I provide potent evidence that the Bible *is* God's Word (see page 144), but only *after* making the case that Jesus was God. If we can show that Jesus was who he said he was, then we can construct a sound case for Scripture, since Jesus spoke to this critical issue. It is vital we never presuppose *any* belief to be true. We must start from a blank slate and examine where all evidence leads. This is the only sound way to build a defense. And using sound argumentation is vital (see page 42). I have found this to be true in thousands of dialogues held in every corner of the planet.

The reason I was able to travel so much, specifically to 82 nations/territories spanning all seven continents, was due to a career transition I made in 2006 to become an active-duty U.S. Navy  chaplain, a career that spanned eight global commands and saw the birth of my second son Caleb on 24 December 2009. While serving as a chaplain (LCDR), I made a concerted effort to talk to as many as possible about Christ. In fact, I was able to dialogue, in non-proselytizing ways, with thousands of U.S. Marines & Sailors who inquired about Christ, and the seed of these dialogues saw many come to know Christ. Regarding military highlights, in addition to earning a 2011 Doctor of Ministry (DMin) degree from Bethel University (summa cum laude) and a 2015 JPME Diploma from Naval War College (with highest distinction), I was able to conduct over 4000 confidential counseling sessions, 800 Christian worship services, 500 Christian baptisms, 400 military training seminars, 200 community service projects, 150 military funerals, 100 military nuptials, 50 intra-command athletic tournaments, and four humanitarian initiatives, namely, (a) the running of the #1 U.S. Feds Feed Families program globally, (b) the rescuing of sex trafficking victims in the Middle East, (c) the founding of an Emergency Family Assistance Center (EFAC) in Japan and (d) the overseeing of a USN ship foc'sle mission where I cared for 49 Somali refugees rescued-at-sea in the Gulf of Aden. These were formative experiences.

Re my non-military life, on 17 October 2020, I married the love of my life and best friend, Kristen Kaye Carlson, a seasoned R.N. who now helps me run Case Ministries Int'l (CMI), a 501(c)3 apologetics/charity-focused org with a mission motto of "Championing Christ & His Agape Love" (see caseintl.com). In 2021, to raise CMI revenue, in addition to publishing *Faith Fits the Facts*, I recorded a seven-song a cappella album entitled "Faith & Freedom Favorites" and invented a one-of-a-kind laundry product called Faith-Forged Locks-4-Socks, a device forged using Bible numbers which binds 12 sock pairs in the washer/dryer so that users "Never Sort Another Sock Again" (see locks4socks.com). All three products bear one "telos" (or purpose) — to honor and champion Christ.

Speaking of championing Christ, in ruminating on past conversations, whether these took place during past mission-trip excursions, academic pedagogy, military deployments, doctoral studies, or 501(c)3 ministries, I have come to see that sound reasoning *for Christ* can often lead many *to Christ*. In fact, in considering all the encounters I have had with others from various world religions — e.g., from Muslims in Egypt to Buddhists in Thailand to atheists in Romania to Jews in Australia to agnostics in Panama — I am convinced that apologetics is essential to evangelism, as it reveals the "intellectual" cogency of Christianity. I am also convinced that, if one is properly exposed to apologetics, he or she will conclude that Christ is 100% credible, that faith fits the facts. In fact, in considering all the life memories above, I now view apologetics as the most vital domain / bailiwick a Christian can study. I also believe, given the divinity claims of Jesus and the undeniable evidence he is alive, agnosticism is *not* a valid option. That is to say, we cannot remain precariously neutral forever about Christ's identity. Jesus forces us to ultimately make a choice. Allow me to explain.

Although, epistemologically speaking, it appears we, at best, can only reach *undeniability* and never 100% certainty regarding truth (see pages 28-32), since truth is absolute but our human knowledge (our grasp of truth) is always to some degree person-relative and limited, we must nonetheless always neutrally investigate where all evidence leads and then wisely consider what *personal verdicts* we should formulate from exposure to such evidence. Although we should always refrain from being so rigid that we cease to be open to new insights, we must also realize that faith demands a "yes" or "no" response; we cannot remain neutral forever about Christ given his claims. Agnosticism may possess the virtue of being intellectually open to all truth-claims, but, at the same time, diehard agnosticism forces me to be forever stagnant in neutrality, for if I always say — "I don't know if Christ is real"— then I forever put myself in a position that lies outside of personal faith, which, in turn, keeps me forever outside of God's saving grace (which may be vital). Consider it this way. If faith is required for God's grace to be operative (see Eph. 2:8-9), yet agnosticism forever prevents me from embracing faith, then I will never possess the grace that I need. In the divine-human synergy God set up, faith is mandated (see Rom. 10:8-13). Thus, it is vital for agnostics to weigh the claims of Christ and choose: He is either Lord OF ALL or not Lord AT ALL. He does not allow any middle ground. He did not intend to.

Path #1: No Jesus, No Life
Path #2: Know Jesus, Know Life

That said, as you study this handbook's powerful evidence, my sincere hope is that you will indeed consider a personal verdict of saying "yes" to Christ, that, in reading this text, you will either solidify an already-present faith, or conclude for the first time, that Jesus is indeed humanity's loving Creator and risen Redeemer, and that he deserves our genuine love and unselfish devotion, both now and for eternity. After all, eternity is really the bottom line regarding our existence. Think about it! At death, an endless future lies on the horizon for all of us. This is a cold fact we cannot ignore. Consider the biblical options. We will either (1) experience "eternal destruction" apart from God (see 2 Thess. 1:9) or (2) we will live forever in a heavenly realm where God will "dwell with His people" (see Rev. 21:3). These are the two after-death alternatives Christianity presents. Although, in the Christian worldview, God lovingly desires that "none should perish" (see 2 Peter 3:9) but that all enjoy life with him forever, he does not force heaven upon us. We have been given the power to embrace his love, the power to choose a future path. It is thus essential we choose the right path, the path of abundant and eternal life offered by the Way, the Truth and the Life — Jesus himself.

Since the person of Christ is what Christianity is all about, this compendium of evidence offers not just a case for ecumenical Christian truth-claims, but ultimately for *Christ himself*. For Christ, in a very real sense, *is* the gospel. As my late grandfather (see page 3), Rev. Harold S. Carlson, once wisely noted, "Christ came not so much to preach the gospel as that there might be a gospel to be preached!" Consider Jesus' words as recorded in John 3:16, a verse which not only succinctly summarizes the Christian *kerygma*, or gospel proclamation of the first apostles, but one which encapsulates an essential truism toward which all apologetics should ultimately lovingly lead:

For God so loved the world that he gave his one and only Son [Christ], that whoever believes [trusts] in him shall not perish but have eternal life.

My sincere prayer is that, as you digest this practical handbook, you will not only enjoy mastering the book's 12 acrostics re: Christ, but that you will indeed desire to place your trust in Christ, the true Creator and Redeemer of this world, for he surely desires to share eternity with you.

— David J. Carlson

"God is not intimidated by hard
and testing questions, nor is he unable to answer them. But
we must come with the right kind of skepticism—not the kind that
refuses to believe anything at all, but the kind that is committed
to believe only what is really true."

— Philip Graham Ryken

Introduction

When this book's title asserts that "faith fits the facts," we of course are talking about faith in Jesus Christ. But is Jesus worthy of human faith? This is an all-important question, for it demands an explanation as to why Christ, the supposed God-man, is true. He either is or he is not. We must decide.

To show why Christ is truly divine, and thus why Christianity is the only ontologically accurate worldview, we must probe the field of apologetics, the art of defending the Christian faith. I have compiled this handbook to serve as a practical compendium of the best of 21st-century apologetics.

Yet before we examine specific apologetics arguments and facts, it is essential, by way of introduction, that we first consider the following six foundational questions: #1 – What does the term "apologetics" mean precisely? #2 – Who are the most well-known Christian apologists? #3 – What are the benefits of studying apologetics? #4 – What is unique about this particular handbook? #5 - How has this book been pragmatically organized? #6 – What do apologists need to understand about Truth? So, before we address the plethora of cogent reasons why faith in Christ fits the facts, let us consider each of these requisite introductory topics.

#1 – What does the term "apologetics" mean precisely?

To provide a precise definition of the word apologetics, let us first consider the term's etymology (or origin). The word is derived from the Greek word *apologia* which meant to speak in defense of a belief or concept. Today, the modern term is reserved exclusively for Christian defense. Consider these three examples: #1–The Random House Dictionary defines the term as a "branch of theology concerned with the defense or proof of Christianity."[1] | #2 – Dr. Ron Carlson (1950-2011), my late uncle and an expert who lectured on apologetics in over 90 nations/territories, defined the term as "systematic argumentative discourse in defense of Christian doctrine."[2] | #3 – Dr. David K. Clark, for whom I worked as a Bethel Seminary teaching aide (TA) in 1995-96, offers a person-centered definition in his erudite book, *Dialogical Apologetics*, deftly arguing that "apologetics is best defined as the art of the reasoned defense of the Christian faith in the context of personal dialogue."[3]

Of these three options, we will hereafter use this last definition, since it captures the sound notion that we should indeed attempt to cultivate a personal and dialogical approach to apologetics if we want this discipline to be impactful, instead of being an abstract practice buried in academia. People must be our target. And our method must vary with every individual. As Clark puts it, "apologetic practice must take into account the person to whom an argument is offered. Apologetics must be audience specific."[4]

The apostle Paul is one individual who knew well the necessity of doing apologetics well among real people. We see an early example of Christian apologetics "in action" in Acts 28:23. Luke writes these words concerning Paul's personal apologetic tactics and tenacity:

From morning until evening, Paul explained and declared to them the kingdom of God and tried to convince them about Jesus from the Law of Moses and from the Prophets. Some were convinced by what he said.

Here we see Paul persistently, from sunrise to sunset, trying to convince others that Jesus was the promised Messiah. By speaking in "defense" of Christ, Paul engaged in one of the first recorded acts of apologetics. Did his day-long effort yield fruit? Yes. Some in the crowd were indeed convinced. Ultimately, this should be the #1 goal of every apologist — to attempt, as Paul did, to passionately and with sound reason, convince others of the truth of the lordship of Christ.

#2 – Who are the most well-known Christian apologists?

Although thousands of erudite apologists, like Paul, have existed across history to "contend for the faith" (Jude 3), ever since Jesus gave the great commission to "make disciples of all nations" (Matt. 28:19), a few figures stand out as exceptional and influential. To be concise, I have selected the names, timeframes, and contributions of 12 of history's most impactful ancient & modern apologists, given their unique contributions. Consider this impressive list of Christian faith defenders:

(1)   **Justin Martyr,** in 138, wrote an apology (a defense) re: Christ to Greek philosophers, and Emperor Pius, saying Christ was the pivotal Reason (or Logos) behind the cosmos (cf. John 1:1) and, as such, was the foundation of wise reasoning, such as that found in Greek sages.

(2)   **Irenaeus,** Bishop of Lyons, wrote between 170 and 220 to refute the views of Gnosticism, a heresy perpetuated by Marcion & Valentus that said that all matter is evil and, thus, Jesus could not have been human.

(3)   **Tertullian of Carthage,** in 194, wrote a concise apology against the combining of pagan Greek philosophy with Christian doctrine, and thus crafted his most famous quotation: "What has Athens to do with Jerusalem, the Academy with the Church?" Tertullian was, fascinatingly, the first Latin writer to use the term "trinity" (trinitas).

(4)   **Origen of Alexandria** crafted, in the early 200's, an apology called *Against Celsus*, where he defended orthodoxy against the Roman writer, Celsius, who vehemently attacked Christians, saying Christianity was a religion of the uncultured. Origin responded by showing that Christianity was actually the key to the perfection of the intellect, which is "what all souls are in their pure form."

(5)   **Athanasius**, Bishop of Alexandria, was present at the first ecumenical council at Nicea in A.D. 325, where he was instrumental in helping to refute the widespread heresy of Arianism, created by Arius, a man who denied the co-eternality of Jesus with the Father, claiming (and often singing), that "there was a time when the Son was not." For Arius, Jesus was a created being, not God. The Nicene Creed (see p. 124) counteracted this early heresy.

Well, I think Jesus is not really God.

Arias' Theology Paraphrased

(6)   **Augustine**, a fourth century Bishop of Hippo and rhetoric expert considered to be one of Christianity's greatest philosophers, wrote many apologetic works, including a classic, 10-part autobiography called *Confessions* — between 398 to 400 — in which he retraces his wild, sexually-indulgent youth, his doubts and questions about faith and religious truth, and his sudden conversion to Christianity.

(7)   **Thomas Aquinas**, a Dominican monk & quintessential theologian, is best known for his erudite *Summa Theologica*, a text which, written in 1272, contains not only an encyclopedic digest of theological doctrines, but five classical "proofs" for the existence of God.

(8)   **Blaise Pascal** (1623-1662), one of the world's math geniuses, inventor of the barometer, and the father of hydrostatics, is equally famous for his theological musings. In his best-known apologetics work, *Pensees*, he offers what is now famously called *Pascal's Wager*. In this wager, Pascal says it is always best to bet for Christ, for we cannot lose. If, when we die, Christ turns out to be false, then we lose  nothing. But if we choose Christ, and he is real, we gain eternal life. Of course, the flipside to the wager is that, if we do not bet for Christ, and he turns out to be true, we end up losing everything.

(9)   **Francis A. Schaeffer** was an erudite *philosophical* apologist who crafted, during the 20th century, sound philosophical arguments for the Christian worldview. Schaeffer argued that only a God who is both *infinite* and *personal* could provide real meaning to life. His most influential work was *The God Who is There* (1968).

(10) **C.S. Lewis** (1898-1963) was not only an Oxford/Cambridge scholar, but popular author of 30+ books, including both children's novels, e.g., *The Chronicles of Narnia*, and apologetics classics, such as *The Case for Christianity*, *The Four Loves* and *Mere Christianity*. Lewis' theistic argument from desire is featured on page 69 and his apologetic views on Christ appear on pages 116, 120 and 166.

(11) **Billy Graham** (1918-2018) was a spiritual advisor to nine U.S. presidents and preached the gospel to more people than anyone in history, thus profoundly defending the Christian kerygma. In addition to a lifetime radio/TV audience of over 2.5 billion, Billy preached live to more than 215 million at over 400 crusades held in 185 countries and territories. Evangelism-related quotes from Dr. Graham can be seen on pages 27 and 170.

(12) **Josh McDowell** (1939-) focuses on evidential apologetics and has authored many best-sellers, such as *Evidence that Demands a Verdict* (1972), *More Than a Carpenter* (1977) and *The Resurrection Factor* (1981). McDowell quotes appear on pages 116, 140 and 146.

#3 – What are the benefits of studying apologetics?

Although each of the apologists above brought augmentation and enhancement to the field of apologetics, this fact alone does not help us determine *why* apologetics is a valuable discipline to pursue. Suffice it to say, studying apologetics carries with it three main benefits:

Benefit #1: APOLOGETICS OFFERS A COGENT DEFENSE

First of all, apologetics offers *cogent reasoning* for those who have yet to adopt Christian beliefs. Since the term "cogent" is used consistently throughout this handbook, let us define it clearly. A truth-claim becomes cogent when it is logical and convincing by virtue of a clear presentation. This is what Christian apologetics seeks to offer humanity: a clear, logical and convincing defense. Indeed, the principal appeal of the Christian worldview is not because it makes us feel good, but because *it is true*. That said, the ultimate aim of apologetics is not victory, but verity. We as humans instinctively desire verity, which is the Latin word for truth. Jesus even claims he alone is the truth. But is he? Is trusting Christ a cogent act?

Yes. I have found that the presentation of a cogent defense of the Christian worldview can often convince "many" not-yet-Christian people to embrace Christ as truth. I say "many" here simply because I have also observed that many non-apologetic factors such as a Christian's life choices, personal testimony, or unselfish acts of agape love, can often be more powerful than any evidence-based argument. Nonetheless, evidentiary apologetics cannot be ignored; it can and does convince many skeptics and agnostics and, thus, when appropriate, should be aptly articulated by Christian witnesses in the context of personal dialogue.

Benefit #2: APOLOGETICS FORTIFIES FAITH

Secondly, by presenting cogent reasons for faith, apologetics fortifies the intellectual side of faith, helping a Christian's mind gain confirmation of what the heart has already trusted. Blaise Pascal, the famous 17th-century French mathematician and philosopher (cf. page 15), once wrote in piety that, when it comes to faith in Christ, "the heart has reasons for which Reason knows nothing." This may well be true, but Pascal also knew that, in choosing to believe

"The Thinker" by Rodin

in Christ, Reason also has many solid reasons of its own. Yes. The mind is integral to faith. Solid believers must also always be sound thinkers.

That is, faith and reason are allies, not enemies. They function reciprocally; reason enhances faith and vice-versa. In fact, Christian faith only finds its meaning in its *truthfulness*. We are called to faith not because Christianity will solve all the world's problems or make us feel good, but because *it is true*. Faith fits the facts! Thus, as a Christian, I do not check my brains at the door when I choose to follow Christ. When I take a "leap of faith" toward Christ, to borrow a phrase from famous 19th-century Danish philosopher, Soren Kierkegaard, my leap is by no means blind or unreasonable; I do not leap into a dark abyss. I have compelling evidence that Christ is standing at the ready to catch me.

Benefit #3: APOLOGETICS PREPARES BELIEVERS

Thirdly, in 1 Peter 3:15, we see an important mandate issued to believers, for the author instructs his first-century Christian audience to always be prepared to give an answer to anyone who asks about their faith — all the while making sure to do this with courtesy and respect. The Amplified Bible (1987) offers an excellent translation of 1 Peter's mandate:

But in your hearts set Christ apart as holy and acknowledge him as Lord. Always be ready to give a logical defense to anyone who asks you to account for the hope that is in you, but do it courteously and respectfully.

What a bold order. It is not easy to always be ready. Yet perhaps at no other time in history has the Christian duty to "be ready to make a logical defense" been more pressing than in the 21st century, particularly since, in the previous century, non-Christian ideologies, such as postmodernism and philosophical naturalism, gained traction and numerous adherents.

As someone who has dialogued with others in 82 nations/territories spanning all seven continents, including thousands of agnostic university students, I am convinced that, indeed, one of the greatest quandaries facing the global church today is that believers do not know how to effectively defend their faith. My sincere hope is that this pragmatic handbook will equip many believers to possess a ready defense. Although being prepared to "give an answer" is a personal duty, the practice of  apologetics has far too often centered on the philosophical to the exclusion of the personal. Yet real life does not take place inside of textbooks. Life occurs among real people who engage in real conversations. Christians thus need to get back to what the apostle Paul did daily, to cogently defend Christ in the context of respectful personal dialogue.

Presenting a logical defense of Christianity, in authentic real-life dialogues, is vitally important, since, in making such a case, Christians can not only reveal compelling evidence for Christ, and thus potentially impact lives for his kingdom, but they also show that faith never stands contrary to human reason, that mature faith seeks to embrace all truths to which evidence points. Apologetics may indeed state bold truth-claims, yes, but it does so welcoming all truth investigation. That is, apologetics does not shy away from any knowledge area, whether it be logic, science, archeology, or history, because the Christian worldview, if it is to be truly credible, should seek to line up with all that is correspondent to ultimate reality! As Arthur Holmes famously said, "All truth is God's truth."

#4 – What is unique about this particular handbook?

Given that dozens of erudite publications on Christian apologetics already exist to boost and instill faith, to help believers think better and thinkers believe better, what is unique about this particular handbook? How does it bring enhancement to the art of apologetics? Is it a valuable tool for Christian defense? To answer these important queries, let us examine the book's intentional characteristics. The book is meant to be:

Concise ♦ Easy-to-Memorize ♦ 21st Century

If we examine the meaning and rationale behind these three motifs, we will see why this handbook is unique to this specific theological genre, for unlike other apologetics works, these three characteristics have been consistently kept in mind so as to be profitable to a 21st-century audience. To explain how and why this is true, let us consider each motif separately.

Characteristic #1: A CONCISE DEFENSE

To be concise is to cover much in a few words, to state things simply, not simplistically, but simply. Why is conciseness desired? Three reasons: (1) Conciseness avoids clutter. In the 19th century, Henry David Thoreau saw the beauty of avoiding a cluttered life, famously offering these three words to describe how he wanted to live: "Simplicity, simplicity, simplicity!" (2) Simplicity can be especially desirable in a data-overload environment. Consider our 21st-century media world where we are bombarded by dozens of magazines, hundreds of cable TV programs, thousands of new books, and millions of websites. It is no wonder that people want information to be concise. We are overloaded with data! If you ever watched Fox News Channel in the 2000s, U.S. news anchor, Bill O'Reilly, daily asked his television viewers to write response emails that were pithy (or short and to the point), since such emails, if  ever re-read on the air, were the most digestible and efficacious for a mass TV audience. (3) Seminaries have also long known that keeping ideas concise is a key to effective communication. The acrostic K-I-S-S is thus taught to seminarians who want to become effective preachers. It reminds them when they preach to: Keep It Simple Seminarian. As an author, I have sought to practice the K-I-S-S principle throughout this text.

Characteristic #2: AN EASY-TO-MEMORIZE DEFENSE

Being concise is helpful but it doesn't necessarily entail practicality, so I have endeavored to make this book as practical as possible in two ways. First, I have added easy to follow headings and subheadings so that the flow of thought can be easily found and followed at a quick pace. Second, I have created unique mnemonic "acrostics" to structure the book so that all apologetic arguments can be easily remembered. In fact, the entire handbook revolves around an easy-to-memorize acrostic defense. A total of 12 acrostics, four major and eight minor ones, have been incorporated into the work to help readers better memorize all arguments presented. For easy reference, I have summarized each of the book's 12 acrostics in a useful schematic diagram shown on page 35.

Acrostics are nothing new; these mnemonic devices have been around for thousands of years. Consider the acrostic K-I-S-S (alluded to above) or the contemporary acrostic, Every Good Boy Does Fine, which is taught to beginning piano students so that they can better memorize the treble clef — E-G-B-D-F. Acrostics are used widely simply because they work. They help us to better remember things. Even in ancient times, acrostics were well known and adopted. The Old Testament contains 14 Hebrew-based, acrostic poems, the most notable being Psalm 119.[5]

The most famous Christian acrostic originates from the ancient Greek word ICTHUS. The word simply means "fish." The acrostic has a truly fascinating origin. The fish symbol was used by second century Roman Christians due to its significance in the Gospels (e.g., see Mark 1:18 where Jesus proclaims that he will make his disciples "fishers" of men), and, primarily, because the five Greek letters of the word spell out an acrostic for Iesous Christos Theou Uiou Soter, or in English, Jesus Christ, God's Son, Savior. This five-word phrase captured in a concise way the true identify of Jesus. Roman  government officials, who were at this time trying to exterminate the Christian religion, were actually unaware of the acrostic meaning of the fish image, since early Roman Christians were able to maintain it as a secret code — often used in catacombs — to secretly identify one another. Since, during this era, followers of Christ were often killed for their faith, it was important to keep this fish acrostic secretive, because any outward symbol of faith could lead to certain execution.

Since it was simple to draw in the dirt or sand, the fish image was also utilized by early Roman Christians as a type of covert password. This is fascinating: If two strangers met on the road and were unsure whether each was a Christian, one would draw an arc in the earth. If the other person were a Christian, he/she would complete the secret symbol with a reverse arc, forming the image of a fish and thus confirming a shared faith in Christ. Suffice it to say, the fish image, and the clever ICTHUS acrostic it represented, gained a  meaning of precious significance for these early Christians. It is no wonder that, years after the Roman persecution, Christians were often referred to as Pisciculi; the root of this Latin title stands for "fish".

The ancient ICHTUS "secret code" has always fascinated me. Having had opportunities to travel to Rome and Vatican City on three separate occasions, I always tried to visit not just the tourist sites of Rome, such as the Colosseum and St. Peter's Basilica, but also the Roman catacombs where the first ICTHUS images were carved by first-century believers. These visits inspired me to invent the 12 acrostics found in this practical handbook. These acrostics are obviously *not* meant to be secret codes (as ICTHUS was) but each does bear the same purpose, namely, to encapsulate and help believers better remember Christ-related truths. Indeed, all Christians should be able to remember *why* the Christian faith fit the facts. ICTHUS was the first Christian acrostic to do this, and do it well.

Shown below is a 1993 photo I took of one of the earliest known ICTHUS images created by Christians on the walls of Rome's catacombs. The history of the artwork associated with the ICTHUS symbol is fascinating.

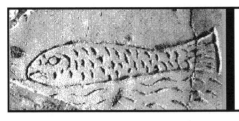

The I-C-TH-U-S Acrostic

Iesous Christos Theou Uios Soter

Jesus   Christ   God's   Son   Savior

Even in the 21st century, the fish image is recognized around the world as a symbol of Christianity. Often with the ICTHUS acrostic embedded inside, the fish image can today be seen on all types of Christian jewelry, Bible covers and car bumper stickers. It is personally my favorite acrostic, since it represents a concise, early Christological creed invented by early Christians to describe the true identity of Jesus Christ. Interestingly, the fish symbol was actually used in a "covert" manner in recent modern history as well, just like it was in ancient Rome. Consider this unsung fact: During the U.S. Great Depression, a chalk fish-mark was used as a "secret code" by homeless wanderers to mark the houses of people who could be depended on for charity or for food? Pretty clever!

Why are acrostics popular anyway, both today and in ancient times? These are invented because they help people remember things better and faster. Or as psychologists would say, acrostics are powerful mnemonic devices proven to enhance memory recall. Let us provide here a quick memory test to  prove this point. Imagine going grocery shopping for these items: fish, lettuce, onions, watermelon, eggs, raisins and soup. With no pen handy, how might one rapidly remember these items? Read each again quickly, then eyes closed. State each one fast. Can it be done? For most, no. Now utilize the seven-letter acrostic: F-L-O-W-E-R-S. Ready? Go! Was it easier? Definitely! Why? It is because this simple seven-part acrostic enhanced the mind's recall speed and ability. By using the acrostic, one could easily restate the seven grocery items — no pen, no paper. Ergo, acrostics serve as extremely powerful memory devices.

What Groceries?

Recognizing this practical insight, I have outlined this handbook by creating four basic acrostics — R-E-A-L, T-R-U-E, F-A-C-T, L-I-F-E — not only to succinctly organize the book's contents, but to help each reader memorize, and/or utilize in dialogue, each of the book's core arguments. These acrostics not only construct a cogent case for Christ, but they add practicality to a believer's repertoire of apologetic skills. My hope is that many Christians will be able to use these acrostics as they seek to share the truth of Christ with others who have yet to embrace his salvific redemption.

Characteristic #3:   A 21ST-CENTURY DEFENSE

Finally, in the interest of holding to the highest standards of academic excellence, I have, in addition to conciseness and practicality, endeavored to champion not just a cogent and compelling defense, but a completely modern, up-to-date, 21st-century defense.

Although, as a result of this 21st-century standard of excellence, the reader must, of necessity, be exposed occasionally to some complex terminology, such as the concept of *irreducible complexity* (discussed at length in Ch. 1) or the idea of an *amanuensis* secretary (probed in Ch. 2), every effort has been made to explain all "daedalean" concepts in a clear and concise manner. I believe it is essential that complicated, yet critical, apologetics ideas be made digestible to every reader, as long as lucid clarity is never sacrificed in the process.

Readers will notice that all of these scholarly concepts originate from a variety of academic disciplines, such as biochemistry, physics, history, astronomy, archeology, etc. But such a multi-faceted investigation is essential. If the Christian worldview is to be truly cogent, it must be able to correlate with all knowledge areas. For example, Christianity should never stand opposed to current scientific findings. Remember the axiom we alluded to earlier: If a Creator God truly exists, then all Truth is His.

Although "Truth" (with a capital "T") is often difficult to detect, particularly since we in the 21st century are bombarded with a plethora of "Truth-claims" from a variety of mutually exclusive worldviews, we are not left helpless. That is because there are critical approaches of reason that can help us sort out fact from fiction. Specifically, what we need to do whenever we seek to construct a defense for a particular world view, if we desire to be truly erudite thinkers, is to adopt a cumulative case approach, an approach which offers a sound strategy for assessing all worldview truth-claims. A worldview indeed becomes more credible when it can explain a wide range of cumulative evidence gathered from a broad range of knowledge disciplines. The most cogent worldview is the one that makes the best overall, most compelling, most evidenced cumulative case. Invoking a cumulative case approach is really the only sound way to practice Christian apologetics in the 21st century.

In *Dialogical Apologetics*, Dr. David K. Clark demonstrates what a typical, cumulative case approach looks like. He does this by outlining facts from five disciplines, namely, cosmology, anthropology, ethics, religious experience, and history. In so doing, Dr, Clark provides a basic cumulative case to show that the Christian worldview carries with it a sound, multi-faceted explanation for reality. Dr. Clark's case is as follows:

Cosmology: the existence of a universe that is not eternal; its order and structure, especially its capacity to sustain life.

Anthropology: the existence of humans with incredible potential for thought, creativity, and beauty; their thirst for ultimate meanings.

Ethics: the nearly universal experience among humans of obligation to others and of outrage at injustice, cruelty, and undeserved human suffering.

Experience: the nearly universal human desire for self-transcendence and connection to a higher reality; the sense of duty to this reality.

History: the life of Jesus, his character, teachings, and works, especially his miracles and resurrection.[6]

The cumulative case cited here is meant only to be a sample, yet it is already compelling. As an avid rock climber (see adjacent military photo), I consider this type of reasoning being analogous to a climbing rope. Imagine the statements above are like strands of a rope. One strand may be weak, but if we put many strands together, they form an extremely powerful rope which can support a climber. In the same way, in a cumulative case, isolated facts can be intertwined to form an extremely compelling, overall case for a particular worldview or belief system.

Chaplain (USN LT) Carlson rappelling down training wall at USMC boot camp in San Diego, CA in 2007.

In the interest of being fair-minded and receptive to all truth-claims, we will follow a cumulative case approach throughout this handbook. By examining with an open mind the totality of 21st-century evidence present in all relevant fields of academia, we will carefully construct a case that is totally up-to-date and comprehensive, a case which will rationally demonstrate that, indeed, the Christian worldview provides the best explanation for reality vis-à-vis all competing worldviews.

#5 – How has this book been pragmatically organized?

In building a cumulative case for Christ, I have tried to keep the organizational structure of this book as basic and pragmatic as possible. Hence, as alluded to in the Preface, I have chosen to focus exclusively on the four "ecumenical" truth-claims which define universal Christianity.

What are ecumenical truth-claims exactly? Dictionaries define the term as any concept or practice that applies to the whole Christian church. The word is thus closely related to the Christian term "orthodoxy," which means widely-accepted doctrine and the term "catholic" which means universal or, literally, according to the whole. Like the term catholic, Christian scholars use the term ecumenical as a synonym for universality. As such, the term is often invoked to describe the universal councils of the early church, such as the Council of Nicea (AD 325) that occurred in what is now Turkey.

In fact, Nicea is now referred to as the First "Ecumenical" Council. Interestingly, the Nicene Creed (see page 124), which was painstakingly crafted at Nicea to counter-attack the growing Christological heresy of Arianism, became, and continues to be, the most widely accepted creed of Christianity. In fact, many recite this creed at every worship service.

From these definitions, we see ecumenical beliefs are core beliefs universally accepted by the global church, which today includes nearly two billion members spanning four branches of Christendom, namely, (a) Roman Catholicism, (b) Protestantism, (c) Eastern Orthodoxy and (d) "Other." The adjacent chart offers a breakdown of the main geo-regions and population of each branch:

> **Roman Catholic**
> - About 50% of all Christians; over one billion people.
> - Dominant in Western and parts of Eastern Europe, Latin America, parts of Africa and Southeast Asia.
>
> **Protestantism**
> - About 24% of all Christians.
> - Dominant in Northern Europe, North America, Australia and Africa.
>
> **Eastern Orthodox**
> - About 11% of all Christians.
> - Dominant in Eastern Europe, Russia, and in parts of the East Mediterranean.
> - There are also several other Christian groups (Coptic Church, Ethiopian Church, Armenian Church, etc.) that are usually included in the Eastern Orthodox group.
>
> **"Other" Christians**
> - About 15% of all Christians.
> - Huge variety of denominations, including Oriental Orthodox Churches, Christadelphians, Mormons, Nestorians, Unitarians, etc.

In studying apologetics, the main reason that we should first focus on ecumenical truth-claims, e.g., such as the reality of a personal Creator, the historicity of the Gospel portraits, the divinity of Jesus Christ, or the salvific power of the Christian kerygma, is because these beliefs define universal Christianity and, as such, represent the essential *non-negotiables* of the faith. If these beliefs are false, then Christ is false, and if Christ is false, then Christians need to find a new religion. But if these beliefs are true, Christ becomes the only option. A second reason to focus on core truth-claims when studying apologetics is that, when done, Christian unity and solidarity is promoted. On that point, we see Jesus himself passionately prayed for Christian unity. Consider his words in John 17:20-21 (Amp). After praying fervently for his 12 disciples, Jesus then prays for all future believers:

Neither for these alone do I pray [it is not for the disciples' sake only that I make this request], but also for all those who will ever come to believe in (trust in, cling to, rely on) Me through their word and teaching, that they all may be one, just as You, Father, are in Me and I in You, that they also may be one in Us, so that the world may . . . be convinced that You have sent Me.

What a beautiful prayer. Jesus asks that just as he and the Father are one, so all believers may be one. But what does this mean? The author

of this book's Foreword, Rev. Canon Gabriel P. Dimanche [1927-2013], an Episcopal priest who for more than six decades served as a parish rector and/or headmaster of K-12 international schools, once gave a potent sermon on Jesus' John 17 prayer to an inter-denominational audience. Fortunately, I was able to record his words. He summarized the homily as follows:

As followers of Christ, then, we fulfill Jesus' beautiful prayer for "oneness" in John 17 when we, despite our denominational differences, are pragmatically willing to proactively minister, worship and pray together in the spirit of love and ecumenism, with the recognition that, as global Christians, we possess one Father who created us, one Spirit who empowers us, and one Christ who saved us, a Savior who desires that none should perish, but that all come to repentance, that all come to embrace the universal forgiveness he offers, and the one baptism he established, for new and unending life in Him.[7]

So, according to Fr. Dimanche, the ecumenism of John 17 begins with pragmatism. That is, Christians need to be willing to proactively minister alongside fellow believers and celebrate Christian commonalities with a mindset toward Christian unity in ministry, worship, and prayer. Having ministered and worshipped in ecclesiastical settings in dozens of denominations across 82 nations/territories spanning all seven continents, I have come to agree with Rev. Dimanche's words of wisdom. Christians indeed need to strive to cultivate a pragmatic mindset of cooperation, despite the doctrinal disagreements which exist among denominations. Christians have so much in common, especially ecumenical truth-claims. Note that Jesus prayed for "oneness" of the Church *in order* that the world might be convinced

The symbol for ecumenism shows the cross of Christ operating as a mast above a boat, the Church, sailing together in solidarity over the (rough) waters of life.

he was sent by God (see verse 21). Thus, part of persuading others of the truth of Christ, according to Christ himself, is the promotion of Christian solidarity. Focusing on ecumenical apologetics does this well.

As seen on the back cover, ecumenical apologetics champions forth a fervid "YES" to these four foundational questions which collectively define the non-negotiables of the universal Christian worldview:

(1)   Did an eternal, personal **CREATOR** engineer this universe?   YES
(2)   Are the biblical **GOSPELS** historically accurate & reliable?   YES
(3)   Was Jesus a divine & resurrected **CHRIST** for all humanity?   YES
(4)   Is the Chrisitan **KERYGMA** an eternal-life-giving message?   YES

To offer a unified defense of these four ecumenical truth-claims, I have created a practical diamond diagram that I call the Diamond of Truth. This diagram serves as a unifying design for organizing this book's main apologetic acrostics, R-E-A-L, T-R-U-E, F-A-C-T, L-I-F-E. It is worthwhile to take a moment, at this point, to turn to the acrostic diagram located on page 35 to see how each letter of each acrostic is utilized. These acrostics can help Christ-followers more effectively present the cogency of the Christian worldview whenever chances to do so arise.

The Diamond of Truth

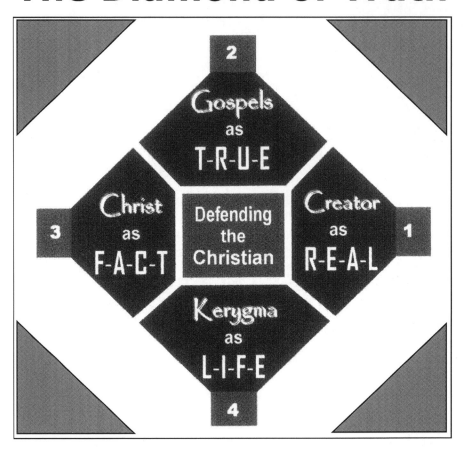

To better understand how the Diamond of Truth (shown above) operates as an organizational tool and practical guide to ecumenical apologetics, consider this helpful sports analogy: Think of the Diamond of Truth like a real-life baseball diamond, a place where a baseball player has to run around the bases, in sequence, in order to fulfill the main goal of the sport of baseball, namely, to score runs and win the game.

Most people have seen or played baseball, so they know there are certain basic rules to the game, such as, when a player hits a fair ball, he or she must touch each of four field bases in sequence in order to score a run. The Diamond of Truth works in a similar fashion to establish organizational guidelines for how ecumenical apologetics should best be studied and presented. Just as a baseball runner must touch a precursor base before moving on to the next base, so in apologetics we must touch on certain prerequisite truth-claims before we can progress further.

Theologically-speaking, this means that, in traveling through the Diamond of Truth, it is important that I first touch on and defend the reality of an eternal, personal Creator (first base), since any talk of theology or personal faith would be meaningless if the Christian God did not exist. If I can indeed show, through rationally convincing arguments, that an eternal, loving, personal 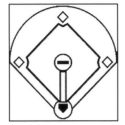 Creator most probably exists, this would, in turn, help me to better defend the four biblical Gospels (second base) as reliable & trustworthy documents, which would, in turn, significantly help me to better understand and defend the historicity and deity of Jesus Christ (third base) about whom the Gospels were written, which would, in turn, help me, in an evangelistic way, to present a sound case for the Christian kerygma, or early Christian proclamation, which held that genuine repentance and trust in Christ as the risen Lord yielded forgiveness and eternal life. If I can progressively, base by base, make a cumulative case for each core truth-claim in the Diamond of Truth, I should be able to successfully fulfill the main goal of apologetics, that is, to present a compelling case for universal Christianity.

As a 21st-century apologist, once I present all, or even parts of, the Diamond of Truth's acrostics, I may even get a chance to engage in evangelism, that is, to get  someone to travel past home plate to accept Jesus as the risen Lord. In other words, if my dialogue partner has already fully intellectually accepted each of the four truth-claims in the Diamond, and if they are now willing to take a genuine faith-leap to trust in Christ as their Savior & Lord, then I as a Christian witness have a duty to help them. Such is really the final aim of apologetics, to lead people into the kingdom of God, where they will be able to reside with and enjoy God in his forever family.

And this aim is not just for the calling of the professional minister, but the shared duty of all Christians. Consider the firm admonition of Rev. Dr. Billy Graham on this point. In the Foreword to Dr. Bill Bright's 1993 evangelism-strategy book, *Witnessing Without Fear*, Graham writes these thought-provoking words regarding the necessity of Christian evangelism:

The world is more ready for the gospel of Jesus Christ today than ever before. More men and women than you ever imagined would say "yes" to the Savior if only someone would tell them how... With a world so ready, the Christian community cannot afford to sit back and hope that the relatively few full-time ministers of the Word accomplish the task alone. The fulfillment of Christ's great command to "Go into all the world and preach the gospel" is the shared responsibility of every individual who calls Christ Savior and Lord.[8]

#6 – What do apologists need to understand about Truth?

Finally, in order to aptly close this Introduction, it is vitally important, before we move to Chapter 1, that we articulate three key points regarding the relationship of this handbook to the field of epistemology, or the branch of philosophy which investigates the origin, nature, methods and limits of human knowledge and particularly its relationship to absolute Truth. The philosophical terminology may get a bit abstract here, that is, it will be arduous for me to follow the K-I-S-S principle in this section, but it is essential, if we are to be truly sound apologists, that we possess a correct mental grasp of the following three key explications regarding epistemology, especially before we craft apologetics. So please read this section carefully. Taken together, these points erect a stable philosophical foundation that will solidly undergird our case for ecumenical Christianity.

EXPLICATION 1: Since this is meant to be a digestible handbook, I have, unlike other apologetics works, decided it prudent *not* to offer a verbose critique of how the topic of "knowledge and truth" is dealt with by 21st-century epistemological paradigms, views such as agnosticism, rationalism, soft rationalism, classical foundationalism, experientialism, fideism, evidentialism, combinationalism and postmodernism, mainly because to deal adequately with virtues and vices of each option would force us to venture beyond the scope of this introductory resource. However, since the idea of truth" is a vital one for apologetics, we cannot simply ignore the concept either. It is essential that we are absolutely clear about what we mean when we say something is "true." So what we need to do here is to construct a lucid definition of truth and conduct a proper analysis of our possible knowledge of it. If we do this well, then we will see that a critique of the above options is really unnecessary.

So how can we ever know when we are in possession of the Truth? In John 18:38, Pontius Pilate is said to have posed a unique question to Jesus after Jesus told him that "everyone on the side of truth listens to me." In

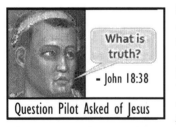

Question Pilot Asked of Jesus

response, Pilate then (sarcastically?) asked Jesus: "What is truth?" It is a crucial question, Most experts would say that, if a statement corresponds to reality, then it can be said to be True (with a capital "T"). The key question, though, is how can we know for certain when our beliefs *about* reality actually "line up" *with* reality? As Immanuel Kant once aptly noted in his classic, *Critique of Pure Reason*, the world *as it appears to be* (the phenomena) is, logically, a much different category than the world *as it actually is* (the noumena). In other words, the world we observe around us is not necessarily ontologically equivalent to ultimate reality.

For example, I may assume that I am in a house now; it appears to me as if this proposition is true. In reality, however, my mind is locked inside a hologram generated by an A.I. supercomputer. I think I am in a house, but, similar to the plot of the Matrix movies, I am actually floating in water and being used as a "human battery" to generate power for this A.I. Of course, that sounds absurd. But such a notion is not far-fetched for Kant.

Noumena: World As It Really Is | Absolute Truth (A.T.) | **GULF** | Human Grasp of A.T. | Phenomena: World as Perceived

For Kant, citing the above distinction between "noumena" and "phenomena" led him to a position of agnosticism with regard to absolute truth and our knowledge of it, since he concluded that only appearance can be known, not ultimate reality. Since for Kant the "stuff" of knowledge is provided by the senses (via empiricism) and the "structure" of knowledge is provided by the mind (via rationalism), one can only know what something is *to-oneself* but never what it is *in-itself*, and hence one must remain agnostic about reality. In Kant's words, we can know the phenomena but not the noumena; there is an impassible gulf between the real world and our knowledge of it.[9] See the diagram above. But is Kant's agnosticism valid? Is it correct to claim that we can only know that reality is somehow *there* but that we can never know what *reality itself* is? I would argue no, for what Kant asserts catches him in a logical quagmire. That is to say, logically speaking, Kant's agnosticism is self-defeating, for it claims that all knowledge about ultimate reality is impossible, and yet this statement itself is offered as a truth about reality, in which case it defeats itself. I am convinced, however, that we can *know*, with undeniability, much about the reality around us *as it really is*. Allow me to explain why.

EXPLICATION 2: In meticulously studying issues of epistemology over many years, I have developed a thesis regarding human knowledge and its relationship to Truth which is entirely cogent, since it draws upon the most up-to-date insights of 21st-century science, history and philosophy. It is important that we, in this introduction, correctly grasp this thesis since it provides us with a solid philosophical foundation for studying and practicing apologetics! Consider these five key thesis points (A to E):

(A) Although I disagree with Kant's form of agnosticism, I do nonetheless agree with Kant (and with all postmodernists) that, other than analytic truths that add nothing new to reality (e.g., such as tautologies), we can never actually attain 100% certainty regarding any truth-claim about reality, since, in our post-Einstein world, our human knowledge, or our apprehension of absolute Truth, can always be shown to be to some degree person-relative and limited. In other words, no finite mind will ever be in possession of all facts, nor will any finite person ever be able to comprehend completely all the relationships between facts.

(B) Ergo, what we should mean when we say a proposition is "true" is not that we are certain the proposition corresponds to *absolute Truth* (or Truth with a capital "T"), but rather that we have solid reasons to believe it is warranted, substantiated, and justified. That is, it is the best human truth (i.e., truth with a small "t") we can formulate about reality, given all the evidence. This means Truth and knowledge are different ideas. Truth is linked to propositions that correctly portray objective reality as it *actually is* (and is thus not subject to correction), whereas knowledge describes one's best percipience of Truth (whereby erroneousness is possible).

(C) Ergo, a proposition which has "knowledge" status is best defined as a "justified true belief" regarding reality, a belief wherein the adjective "true" means not *absolute* Truth, but our most *justifiable grasp* of absolute Truth. I call this human truth. A human truth, in turn, can find justification (i.e., be defended) through five distinct, yet interrelated, epistemological truth tests. That is, we can test this human truth-claim's veracity through (1) *a priori* (non-experience-dependent) reasoning that shows the belief to be entirely coherent and logical, (2) *a posteriori* empirical data (e.g., scientific observations) which confirm the belief squares with sense perception, (3) the fact the belief perfectly "fits" with other credible truth-claims in a coherent, interdependent web, (4) the fact that the belief produces pragmatic results (i.e., it works), and (5) the fact that a credible authority (a recognized expert) claims that the belief is indeed justified and credible.

Let us provide an example of a justified "true" belief by running it through the five truth tests above. Consider the ubiquitous belief that "*a Sun exists which allows humans to survive*": (1) Does this belief make logical sense? Yes. It is not incoherent; (2) Does it square with daily sense perceptions? Yes. We see and feel the Sun; (3) Does it "fit" with other beliefs like photosynthesis? Yes. Plants use sunlight as a source of energy to synthesize organic material; (4) Does it work? Yes. Plants produce oxygen and we survive. (5) Does it match what credible experts say? Yes. Astronomers tell us the belief is true. Is there a Sun then? Undeniably. That said, we still cannot rule out the minute possibility of being locked in a fake reality. such as the *Matrix* reality alluded to above.

(D) Ergo, we can make sound belief statements (or truth-claims) about reality, especially if all five, or at least many, of these truth justifications are found to be fulfilled. Although each truth test by itself would be insufficient to completely justify a belief, when taken together, these tests help humans to possess, at high tide, undeniability that a belief is True, and at low tide, at least a good probability that a belief is True, despite the likely reality that absolute certainty will forever evade us.

In other words, concerning any given truth-claim, we have a hierarchy of confidence levels present (just beneath certainty), wherein we can, many times, be monumentally confident, beyond any rational doubt, that we are in possession of Truth as we construct a certain belief statement. For example, when the philosopher Descartes came up with his now famous proposition "cogito ergo sum" or "I think, therefore, I am" (see page 41), he was confident that he had crafted an undeniable truth about reality. And most agree. To unpack this hierarchy further, consider the below chart of epistemic hierarchy, one modified from Dr. Roderick M. Chisholm's original version found in *Theory of Knowledge*.[10] This chart lists 13 possible stages where a human truth-claim about reality can fall in terms of how confident a person can be that their belief is *actually* True and, therefore, correspondent to ultimate reality (i.e., Kant's noumenal realm). Except stages 6 and -6, where unobtainable 100% certainty is required, each stage is able to be occupied by countless propositions.

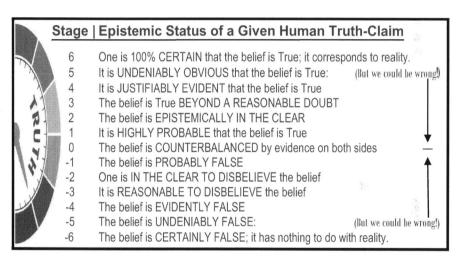

Stage	Epistemic Status of a Given Human Truth-Claim
6	One is 100% CERTAIN that the belief is True; it corresponds to reality.
5	It is UNDENIABLY OBVIOUS that the belief is True: (But we could be wrong!)
4	It is JUSTIFIABLY EVIDENT that the belief is True
3	The belief is True BEYOND A REASONABLE DOUBT
2	The belief is EPISTEMICALLY IN THE CLEAR
1	It is HIGHLY PROBABLE that the belief is True
0	The belief is COUNTERBALANCED by evidence on both sides
-1	The belief is PROBABLY FALSE
-2	One is IN THE CLEAR TO DISBELIEVE the belief
-3	It is REASONABLE TO DISBELIEVE the belief
-4	The belief is EVIDENTLY FALSE
-5	The belief is UNDENIABLY FALSE: (But we could be wrong!)
-6	The belief is CERTAINLY FALSE; it has nothing to do with reality.

(E) In considering this chart, although I have justifiable reasons (as shown above) to believe that is likely impossible for humans to arrive with certainty at level 6 or level -6, due to our intrinsic limitedness, I do believe we can arrive at level 5 or level -5, and, for all practical purposes, this is sufficient in describing truth. If a truth-claim has reached stage 5, most would be willing to bet their life or fortune on it, for, at stage 5, we are totally convinced of a belief's Truth. In short, I would contend that Level 5 refers to truth with a small "t" and that is simply the best humans can do.

To sum up EXPLICATION 2, although it is indeed a valid objection that we cannot claim 100% certainty about Truth (which is absolute), since our human knowledge (or our apprehension of Truth) is always person-relative and intrinsically limited, this does not mean that we cannot be certain that many "truth-claims" are undeniably obvious (level 5), given all available data, and that, at minimum, some truths are most probably true (level 1), such as facts regarding historical matters or parts of reality we cannot directly observe (like atoms). In short, we can often propose a "human truth-claim" and be *supremely confident* this claim really does correspond with *absolute* Truth, especially if many experts can collectively agree that the claim passes many, if not all, of the five tests above. Raising a doubt then about such a truth-claim would be irrational, even if we can never possess 100% certainty. A reasonable probability is the only certainty.

> "A reasonable probability is the only certainty."

EXPLICATION 3: This epistemological insight regarding the definitions of small "t" truth (human truth) and big "T" Truth (absolute Truth) is a fact we must always bear in mind when doing apologetics. We can indeed talk about Truth. We simply need to back up what we claim with proper justifications. Logic, sense experience, coherence, pragmatism, authority — these all must be considered every time we say something is True. And we must never forget to be humble about our Truth-claims; none of us has all the answers. We should always be open to all possibilities. That is, we should never hide from knowledge progression if such happens to come about as a result of new insights that better shape our understanding. For what we believe to be True, even in the sciences, has often been progressive throughout history. Often a scientific theory might explain many facts for a while, but the constant presence of anomalous data, which the theory cannot explain, forces us to forge a new, illuminative, revelatory hypothesis.

Consider, for example, the plethora of major paradigm shifts of understanding that have occurred in the history of science, e.g., Ptolemy to Copernicus re: planetary motion, Newton to Einstein re: space-time relativity, etc. Even the best scientists in history have gotten it wrong and/or did not see the whole picture on occasion. Indeed, one generation's so-called "fact" becomes a future generation's fiction. On that point, I argue in Chapter 1, for example, that "Darwinian macroevolution," a theory that gained prominence in the 19-20th centuries, now warrants total repudiation and replacement with a credible scientific theory, one which *can explain* the vast variety of life and the existence of the irreducibly complex bio-machines which saturate our planet. In short, a paradigm shift in biology is now warranted, for macroevolution has totally failed as a scientific theory. Ironically, scientific theories are like species in one area the theory got right: only the fittest survive. And macroevolution is clearly no longer fit to survive. Is Christianity as a worldview fit to survive? That is what we will determine as we examine all the cogitable evidence.

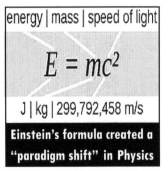

energy | mass | speed of light

$$E = mc^2$$

J | kg | 299,792,458 m/s

Einstein's formula created a "paradigm shift" in Physics

A Brief Summary

To encapsulate all the critical concepts that have been covered in the last six sections of this work's foundational Introduction, we can construct the following six summative points:

(1)   Apologetics is best defined as the art of the reasoned defense of the Christian faith in the context of personal communication.

(2)   This art was mastered, in various ways, by many erudite apologists throughout church history. We briefly looked at 12 ancient and contemporary examples. Each one of these scholars can inspire Christian witnesses to become better defenders of the faith.

(3)   Apologetics not only offers a cogent defense for skeptics and agnostics, but it can help fortify the faith of Christians, since reason confirms what the heart has already trusted. The practice of apologetics is also clearly mandated as a duty for every Christian, that is, a duty to present a "logical defense" (I Peter 3:15) to all who may be curious about Christ and Christianity.

(4)   Apologetic evidence should be practical. Evidential apologetics should ultimately be used for dialogical apologetics — i.e., real-life apologetic conversations. Therefore, this book offers data that is concise, practical and up-to-date to help Christians to be well-equipped to engage in effective dialogical apologetics.

(5)   A useful diagram for organizing and dialogically sharing the best of Christian apologetics is the Diamond of Truth, a practical diagram (unique to this handbook) which offers four easy-to-memorize acrostics specifically designed to champion a cogent case for the four ecumenical truth-claims of universal Christianity.

(6)   Before engaging in apologetics, particularly apologetics which seeks to champion Christian truth-claims, we must first understand the key difference between ultimate Truth and our human knowledge about Truth. Truth (with a capital "T") is indeed absolute but our human knowledge — i.e., our grasp of Truth — is always to some degree person-relative and limited. Therefore, we need to make sure that any proposition we propose as "Truth" is fully justified by: (a) a priori reasoning and/or (b) solid empirical observations and/or (c) coherent inter-connectedness and/or (d) pragmatic utility and/or (e) the viewpoints of experts in the discipline to which the proposition relates. In applying these tests, we can indeed construct "true" propositions. These "truths" can never be absolute (in terms of 100% certainty), but they certainly can be *undeniable* to any rational human. Undeniability is the key.

In sum, as we, base by base, examine the best apologetic facts and evidence currently available and, in so doing, construct a cumulative case for each of the four ecumenical truth-claims found in our Diamond of Truth, we will indeed see a compelling case become actualized, a case that will champion a persuasive "defense" of universal Christianity.

Three Prescient Predictions

Since this defense is sound, I can offer here a prescient prediction, that the case we will examine will be extremely convincing to anyone with a critical mind. In fact, I am confident that its cogency will not only compel many non-yet-Christian skeptics to consider Christ as a credible option but will effectively equip many 21st-century Christians to be able to convince others of the truth of Christ, helping them navigate the maze of Christian attestations.

So let us now get about the task of constructing a cogent case for Christ. As we do, I can offer a second prediction, namely, that all readers will be embarking on the most important reading adventure of a lifetime, for as we trek through the labyrinthian maze of 21st-century apologetics, finding Truth will be our sole objective. And what could be more vital? All humans desire to Truth. The Gospels have Jesus saying "I tell you the truth" 77x. Jesus even says he himself is the Truth! Consider his audacious claim as recorded in John 14:6:

> Jesus answered, "I am the way and the truth and the life. No one comes to the Father except through me."

We cannot hide from this exclusive claim of Christ to be Truth. We must determine if it is cogent and credible. In fact, as we will see later, "neutrality" is not a valid option given the other claims of Christ. So, I invite each reader to put on their best thinking cap and, with a critical, open mind, carefully consider this concise defense of ecumenical Christianity.

No matter what one's age, gender, culture, or background, I can offer a final prediction, that each reader who probes this work seriously will absolutely become a more intelligent and well-equipped scholar after digesting this compendium of the best of 21st-century apologetics. Moreover, each serious reader will also ultimately be able to explain why all Christ-followers possess rock-solid credibility to unashamedly assert the undeniable truism (and title of this practical opus) that "faith fits the facts."

Twelve "Diamond of Truth" Acrostics

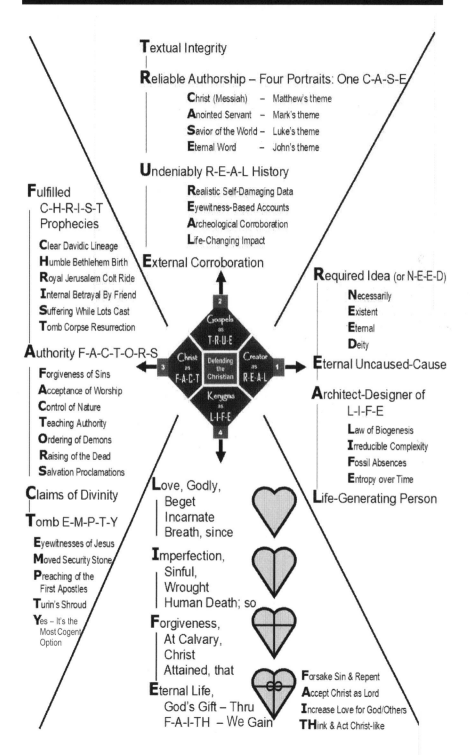

Textual Integrity

Reliable Authorship – Four Portraits: One C-A-S-E
- **C**hrist (Messiah) – Matthew's theme
- **A**nointed Servant – Mark's theme
- **S**avior of the World – Luke's theme
- **E**ternal Word – John's theme

Undeniably R-E-A-L History
- **R**ealistic Self-Damaging Data
- **E**yewitness-Based Accounts
- **A**rcheological Corroboration
- **L**ife-Changing Impact

External Corroboration

Fulfilled C-H-R-I-S-T Prophecies
- **C**lear Davidic Lineage
- **H**umble Bethlehem Birth
- **R**oyal Jerusalem Colt Ride
- **I**nternal Betrayal By Friend
- **S**uffering While Lots Cast
- **T**omb Corpse Resurrection

Authority F-A-C-T-O-R-S
- **F**orgiveness of Sins
- **A**cceptance of Worship
- **C**ontrol of Nature
- **T**eaching Authority
- **O**rdering of Demons
- **R**aising of the Dead
- **S**alvation Proclamations

Claims of Divinity

Tomb E-M-P-T-Y
- **E**yewitnesses of Jesus
- **M**oved Security Stone
- **P**reaching of the First Apostles
- **T**urin's Shroud
- **Y**es – It's the Most Cogent Option

Required Idea (or N-E-E-D)
- **N**ecessarily
- **E**xistent
- **E**ternal
- **D**eity

Eternal Uncaused-Cause

Architect-Designer of L-I-F-E
- **L**aw of Biogenesis
- **I**rreducible Complexity
- **F**ossil Absences
- **E**ntropy over Time

Life-Generating Person

Diamond center:
- 2 — Gospels as T-R-U-E
- 3 — Christ as F-A-C-T
- Defending the Christian
- 1 — Creator as R-E-A-L
- 4 — Kerygma as L-I-F-E

Love, Godly, Beget Incarnate Breath, since

Imperfection, Sinful, Wrought Human Death; so

Forgiveness, At Calvary, Christ Attained, that

Eternal Life, God's Gift – Thru F-A-I-TH – We Gain

- **F**orsake Sin & Repent
- **A**ccept Christ as Lord
- **I**ncrease Love for God/Others
- **TH**ink & Act Christ-like

"At this moment it seems as though science will never be able to raise the curtain on the mystery of creation. For the scientist who has lived by his faith in the power of reason, the story ends like a bad dream. He has scaled the mountains of ignorance; he is about to conquer the highest peak; as he pulls himself over the final rock, he is greeted by a band of theologians who have been sitting there for centuries."

—Robert Jastrow

Creator

1

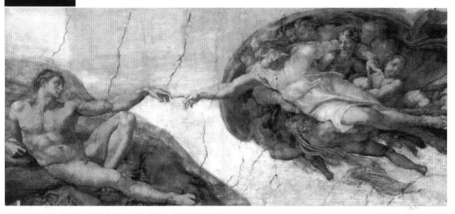

Pictured above is the renowned *Creation of Man* fresco painted by Italian artist Michaelangelo in 1437 on the ceiling of the iconic Sistine Chapel located adjacent to St. Peter's Basilica in Vatican City State.

Perhaps the most crucial question we can ever ask is: Does God exist? If such a being does exist, we would need to grasp all of reality, including our main purpose for existence, the way this cosmos has been created and our sense of moral obligation, with this being's presence always kept in mind. To cogently answer this question, this chapter has been divided into three main sections: #1 – Introduction: Understanding All the God Options, #2 – Constructing Sound Arguments: A Mini-lesson in Logic; and #3 – Theistic Apologetics: Examining Four Classic Categories. As we unpack these sections, we will observe, from the superfluity of available evidence, that the Christian concept of God as an eternal, personal Creator is absolutely undeniable, and that this Deity's existence is not only R-E-A-L but substantiated by unassailable findings of 21st-century science. Put simply, faith in a Creator God fits the facts.

"God does not play dice with the Universe."

—Albert Einstein, Time's Person of the 20th Century

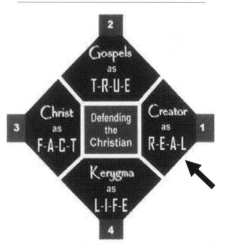

#1 – Introduction: Understanding All the "God" Options

Does God exist? If so, what type of God is he (or it)? Is the eternal, personal God of Christian theism the true Creator of this world, or should we be looking for another deity? After all, if a divine being is R-E-A-L we still have many "God" options from which to choose. In fact, outside of classical theism, *five theistic views* currently exist: (1) *Finite godism* purports that God is limited either in His power or goodness or both (e.g., consider the writings of Jewish rabbi, Harold Kushner); (2) *Pantheism* espouses that God and the world are one (e.g., consider the teachings of Zen Buddhism or the "force"

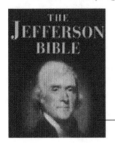

concept in Star Wars); (3) *Panentheism* claims the universe is God's "body" and that God's existence in the cosmos is as a mind is in a body (e.g., consider the philosophy of Alfred North Whitehead or Charles Hartshorne); (4) *Deism* contends that God crafted this cosmos, but then stepped back and let it unfold with no more miracles (e.g., consider the views of Thomas Jefferson who wrote the *Jefferson Bible* that "demythologized" the Bible by omitting the miracles); (5) *Polytheism* asserts there is more than one "god"(e.g., consider the ancient Greeks who believed in a pantheon of gods with Zeus as king).

The chart below sets forth all eight possible perspectives regarding how the term "God" may be viewed by humans. Although some belief-systems actually possess an amalgamation of two perspectives (e.g., consider Hinduism which is polytheistic and at the same time pantheistic in its Vedanta form), these are, logically speaking, the only available options:

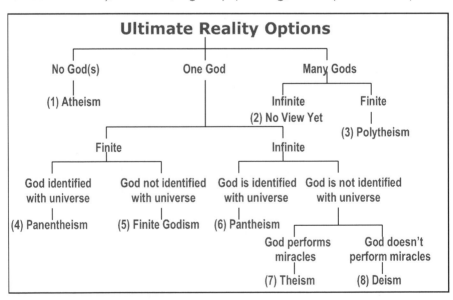

Ultimate Reality Options

Keeping these alternatives in mind, we should note that, if we want to engage in sound theistic apologetics, we must effectively do both "natural theology" (i.e., examine nature's data), by tackling the question of whether God exists in the first place, and "theology proper," by examining the scientific, historical and literary evidence which substantiates option (7) above. That is to say, we need to find solid and cogent reasons, if any, that exist for Christian theism.

ICON OF CREATOR CONCEPT

To accomplish this task, we will examine together 12 compelling arguments, not "absolute proofs," but sound, cogent arguments which, when cumulatively taken together, will show, in rationally convincing ways, that a necessarily existent, eternal, personal Designer indeed crafted this present universe, particularly for the purpose of providing a world in which humans could survive and prosper. We will organize these 12 arguments by utilizing the four classic categories of theistic arguments adapted by philosophers, namely, the ontological, cosmological, teleological, and anthropological categories. Our 12 arguments, put together, can be summarized by our first acrostic in the Diamond of Truth, namely, R-E-A-L. It unpacks as follows:

The Christian Creator is a(n):

DoT Acrostic #1

Required Idea (or N-E-E-D) — Three Ontological Arguments

Eternal Uncaused-Cause — Three Cosmological Arguments

Architect-Designer of L-I-F-E — Three Teleological Arguments

Life-Generating Person — Three Anthropological Arguments

At this point, before engaging in theistic apologetics, it is vital we briefly review a "mini-lesson" in logic. This mini-lesson, a reminder for the advanced reader, will benefit us considerably as we examine past, classical theistic arguments, and new versions for the 21st century.

#2 – Constructing Sound Arguments: A Mini-Lesson in Logic

LESSON #1: Since theistic apologists desire to construct cogent and sound arguments for God's existence, we need to first understand what we mean in logic by the idea of a <u>sound argument</u>. We already discussed what a cogent argument is, namely, one that is convincing by means of a clear and validated presentation. However, a sound argument is even more ironclad; sound reasoning is reasoning without logical defect. A sound argument in logic is one that (a) is completely unambiguous, (b) possesses all undeniably "true" premises and

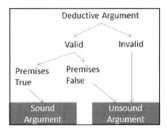

(c) is valid according to the rules of logic. To say an argument is sound, then, is to say that our conclusion is undeniable; it is the most powerful type of argument one can forge. Let us now look closer at these three prerequisites to get a sense of exactly what we need to do to construct a sound argument, one which undergirds any type of concluding truth-claim.

Prerequisite #1: First, to make a sound argument, we must have _clear terms_ which can be correctly understood by anyone who shares our linguistic code (e.g., English, Chinese, etc.). These terms should possess no ambiguity. Such clarity is often difficult to achieve, however, since (a) one term can possess different meanings (e.g., some dictionaries list up to 135 definitions for the word "run") and/or (b) a shift of meaning, or an equivocation, can occur with one of the words invoked in an argument and/or (c) even synonymous terms can possess differing connotations.

But this is not half the battle when it comes to generating clear terms in an argument. Clarity gets more difficult when we try to engage in language translation. Often, a certain language does not possess an equivalent word for one, or many, of the concepts found in another language. For example, in the Amerindian language Hopi, there exists only _one word_ for everything that flies except birds; this includes flying insects, airplanes, kites and even pilots. To bridge a linguistic gap, then, and

achieve clarity, often we must create _circumlocutions_ when translating ambiguous words, that is, we must put together many words — an equivalent phrase — from one language to get at the equivalent meaning of the second language's non-translatable term. When we use clever circumlocutions, we can, when translating, convey the correct meaning of any linguistic concept, and thus achieve clarity. Doing so can just take some effort. Yet achieving clarity is what we need to do every time we seek to construct a sound argument. We need to be as "clear" as possible to our target audience, for when we are not clear misunderstanding can follow. Interestingly, translation barriers have often caused humorous quandaries for American businesses as they have attempted to market their products internationally. For example, the Chevy Nova car did not sell too well in Latin American countries, since in Spanish "no va" means "it does not go."

Prerequisite #2: Secondly, to create a sound argument, we want to have statements proposed which are, in fact, <u>true premises</u>, with "true" meaning our best human grasp of absolute "Truth". That is to say, we want to be able to assert that the propositions found in our argument are most probably, and hopefully undeniably, correspondent to ultimate reality. Now, although readers familiar with contemporary epistemology could certainly argue here, as we saw earlier, that, outside of tautologies, we could never actually attain 100% certainty regarding any truth-claim, since our knowledge (i.e., our apprehension of Truth) is always to some degree person-relative and limited, I would argue (once again) however that the "truth" proposed in any argument does not have to be an absolute Truth (with a capital "T"), but only a human truth (with a small "t"), one which we have sound reasons to believe *aligns with* absolute Truth. Small "t" truths *can* be justified and we examined five tests for this on page 30. Since we can possess justified truth-claims, we can, in turn, forge undeniably true statements about reality. Although postmodernists raise a valid objection that we can never attain 100% certainty, this does not mean we have to doubt everything, For example, I undeniably know that I exist, even if I exist in a cyberspace reality. Raising a doubt about my existence would be irrational. This is why the philosopher Descartes called this type of belief a necessary truth; he famously said "cogito ergo sum" — or "I think, therefore, I am" — because he could not doubt the fact he was thinking and thus existing.

In sum, we can state certain human truth-claims and be supremely confident that these claims do, in fact, *line-up* with ultimate Truth. That is, all of the propositions that we justifiably *believe* to be true are most probably, *actually* True, even if we cannot *prove* this with 100% certainty. To produce a sound argument, then, what we need to produce are small "t" truths — human truths that are completely justified — to comprise each of the propositions we seek to propose in a formal argument.

Prerequisite #3: Finally, to construct a sound argument, we must combine premises to produce a "valid" <u>argument form</u>. To be valid in logic means that an argument is so constructed that, if the premises are jointly asserted, the conclusion *cannot* be denied without contradiction. Although dozens of valid argument forms exist in formal logic, let us consider here just *one* of the most popular, the Disjunctive Syllogism (DS). I cite this form because it is easy to construct and is the main form utilized in this chapter. DS arguments always takes the following form in logic:

The Disjunctive Syllogism	Premise 1: A or B or C	Ex: Jesus was a liar, a lunatic or Lord.
	Premise 2: Not A, Not B	He was not a liar and not a lunatic.
	Conclusion: Therefore, C	Ergo, he must have been the Lord.

The Disjunctive Syllogism is an example of a "valid" form because the truth of the conclusion is *guaranteed* if both propositions are "true" and if the argument is free from logical fallacy. Putting all three ideas together, we arrive at what is the classic formula for a SOUND ARGUMENT:

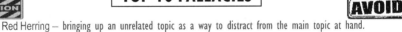

Clear Terms + True Premises + Valid Argument Form = A Sound Argument

This is how we should argue when engaging in apologetics or any discipline as this formula represents the essential rules of human reason. That said, these are not rules of a game we can change. They are rules of reality. Ergo, to disagree with an argument's conclusion, it must be shown that either (a) an ambiguous term and/or (b) a false premise and/or (c) a logical fallacy exists. Otherwise, to say "I disagree with the argument," even though it is sound, is to say: "You have proved your conclusion sound, but I will not accept this fact, for I am content to reside in a fake and false reality."

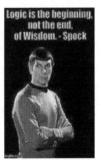

Logic is the beginning, not the end, of Wisdom. - Spock

LESSON #2: The second lesson apologists must inculcate regarding logic concerns <u>logical fallacies</u>. A fallacy is any type of erroneous reasoning which renders an argument unsound. That is, fallacies break our formula above in some way, either because (a) terms were not clear and/or (b) premises were not true and/or (c) the argument was not put into a valid form. Fallacies exemplify reasoning gone bad! One common fallacy we need to watch out for when using the DS form above is the fallacy of False Dilemma. We commit this fallacy each time we do not list *all* possible options. For example, if we argued that the behavior of identical twins is a product of either (a) genetics only or (b) environment only, we would be guilty of creating a false dilemma, since a third option exists, namely (c) the fact that both factors may be involved. Printed below is a listing of the top ten fallacies that I present to logic students when teaching them about the differences between cogent and sound reasoning verses fallacious and invalid reasoning.

TOP 10 FALLACIES   **AVOID**

# 1	Red Herring — bringing up an unrelated topic as a way to distract from the main topic at hand.
# 2	Ad Hominem — irrelevantly attacking an opponent's character rather than his or her argument.
# 3	Begging the Question — using as a premise some form of the very thesis at issue.
# 4	Appeal to Ignorance — arguing from the absence of proof that one's position is false to the contrary conclusion that it therefore must be correct (or vice-versa).
# 5	Hasty Conclusion — asserting an argument conclusion based upon relevant but insufficient evidence.
# 6	Equivocation — when a shift of meaning has occurred in one or more of the terms of an argument.
# 7	False Dilemma — not presenting all possible options in the first premise of a Disjunctive Syllogism.
# 8	Composition — assuming that a whole must have some particular property because all its part have it.
# 9	Post Hoc — arguing that, because something followed an event, it was surely caused by this event.
#10	Double Standard — judging the conduct of one group according to a different standard than another.

#3 – Theistic Apologetics: Probing Four Classic Categories

Let us now engage in theistic apologetics by examining the classic ontological, cosmological, teleological and anthropological argument categories, each of which developed at various periods in Christian history to demonstrate the R-E-A-L existence of the Christian God. As we unpack these categories, we will carefully analyze 12 theistic arguments in total, or three arguments for each category. The first two in each category will comprise the most well known arguments of the past constructed by experts. The third argument in each category will be my own version. As shown on page 39, we will use the acrostic R-E-A-L to serve as a concise summary of all the arguments we shall consider. With our first letter "R" we encounter the most analytic argument class, the ontological category, where God is always viewed as a "required" idea.

Required Idea (or N-E-E-D)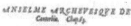
Three Ontological Arguments

All argument versions of the ontological category try to prove the existence of God by starting from the very idea of God as a perfect being. The word "ontology" refers to the branch of metaphysics that studies the nature of existence. The ontological argument is thus an *a priori* (independent-of-experience) argument for God which asserts that, as existence is a part of being perfect, and as God is conceived of as the most perfect being, it follows that God must exist. Two prominent versions of the ontological argument have become well known in history:

Ontological Version #1: ST. ANSELM

The first person credited with crafting the ontological argument was St. Anselm. Born in Piedmont in 1033, he became Archbishop of Canterbury, where he died in 1109. In his book, *Proslogian*, Anselm desired to create a single proof which could show *that* God is and *what* God is.[1] What he ended up creating is, perhaps, the most debated "proof" ever. Anselm's *a priori* argument focused on the term "greater" and can be condensed into three basic propositions:

(1) God is that which nothing greater can be thought.

(2) It is greater to exist in reality than in the mind alone.

(3) Ergo, God exists in reality as well as in the mind.

1584 Engraving of Anselm

Is Anselm's logic sound? No consensus exists. Some say yes; others say no. The perennial debate relates to the nature of the argument itself.

Contemporary critics of Anselm, such as Gaunilon, a Benedictine monk, argued that his argument was not a sound proof since we can think of "perfect" things that, in reality, do not exist, such as perfect islands. To this, Anselm replied that we can move from an idea to its existence in only one case, namely the case of that Being whose nonexistence cannot be thought. A conceptually perfect island does not *have* to exist, but God does. For Anselm, God is necessary.[1] God cannot not exist.

Ontological Version #2:   MALCOLM'S MODAL VERSION

Outside of Anselm, the most well-known ontological argument was created by philosopher Norman Malcolm who focused on Anselm's reply to Gaunilon in which Anselm clarified the concept of necessary existence. For Malcolm, Anselm's initial emphasis of existence as being a "great-making property" is fallacious, since existence is not really a property; Kant was the first to cite this point. But, for Malcolm, Anselm's response to Gaunilon, in which he posited the concept of necessary existence, was a different notion altogether; this type of existence is not a property, for it defines God as one who cannot fail to exist. Although some have objected that this definition of God tells us only what God would be like *if* he existed, and thus cannot establish the fact *that* he exists, Malcolm attempts to solve this by crafting a "modal" version of the ontological argument. For those not familiar with the term, *modality* in logic refers to the classification of propositions according to whether they are contingently true or false, possible or impossible, or necessary.

The gist of Malcolm's modal argument is as follows: God is by definition a being who does not merely happen to exist; he cannot simply pop in or out of existence; he is rather a being, if he exists, who must be *necessarily existent*. This means, by contrast, that, if he does not exist, then his existence is impossible. But either God exists or he does not, so God's existence is either (a) necessary or (b) impossible. Since it does not seem plausible to say God's existence is impossible, it follows his existence is necessary.[2] We can re-construct Malcolm's version with four basic points:

(1) God — the Greatest Conceivable Being (or GCB) — cannot be thought of as: (a) being necessarily nonexistent or (b) contingently existing, but only as (c) necessarily existing. — a being that cannot not exist.

(2) Logically, this means that the GCB concept is either (a) necessary or (b) impossible.

(3) But (b) is implausible to assert, since the GCB is a coherent concept.

(4) Therefore, the GCB (i.e., God) is necessary; this being must exist.

What are we to make of this version? Although it is logically valid in terms of form, is it sound? Yes. Malcolm's final "therefore" proposition is substantiated. But there is a catch here. The atheist *could* steadfastly maintain the impossibility of God's existence, and thus

SYMBOL FOR "THEREFORE" IN BOTH MATH AND LOGIC

reject premise (4) above. But this may be hard for the atheist to swallow. That is, even if we contend that this argument fails as a "proof" for God, it does force us to choose sides. Alvin Plantinga, a defender of a "possible worlds" version of the argument, believes that, even though the argument may be rejected as a proof, it does show the reasonableness of theism.[3] That is, re: the ontological *idea* of God's existence being possible (and thus necessary), although it may not rise to certainty, is a proposition which could be reasonably embraced by all rational human beings.

In other words, to deny this argument, an atheist would have to literally admit that either (a) the universe itself is the GCB (something we may be able to discredit via science) or (b) that the very concept of a necessarily existent being (i.e., a GCB that exists apart from the universe) is one that is incoherent, and thus impossible. Malcolm's modal argument, since it is valid, thus serves the purpose of "smoking out" the atheist, for anyone who wishes to deny the GCB's existence must claim that God's existence is impossible, and this may be something that the atheist does not wish to purport. In short, we *can* deny the argument, but we pay a heavy price in doing so, for to deny a proposition is logically equivalent to asserting another proposition. And in some cases, as in this particular case, the assertion required to reject this argument (namely, the statement that the GCB is impossible) may itself be quite troublesome for an atheist.

Carlson Version: GOD THE REQUIRED IDEA (or N-E-E-D)

Using the disjunctive syllogism, I have invented "practical versions" of each of the theistic argument categories presented in this chapter, including the above ontological category. This is so readers can use these arguments in dialogues. In my ontological version, I define the idea of God not as a GCB, but as a N-E-E-D, a memorable acrostic that says "God" is defined as a:

Necessarily
Existent
Eternal
Deity

How is this N-E-E-D concept defined precisely?

A Necessarily Existent Eternal Deity is a being that (1) cannot not exist and (2) possesses absolutely no beginning or ending as far as the concept of time is concerned. (i.e., NEED = God)

Shown below is my own ontological version constructed in the form of a disjunctive syllogism. One caveat: Explaining this argument is *not* easy, so the reader may want to avoid promulgating it in apologetics-based conversations, unless one's dialogue partner enjoys abstract philosophy.

This argument is sound, for to deny (A), we must assert (B), but modern astrophysics disproves (B), thus forcing pantheism to contend with atheism's same quandaries.➤

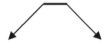
Pantheism is sexed-up atheism. Deism is watered-down theism.
— Richard Dawkins —

Draft Form

(1) Something must exist that cannot not exist, and we have only two options: Cosmos or N-E-E-D. The idea of a N-E-E-D (or Necessary Existent Eternal Deity), existing apart from the Cosmos, is either:

(A) Possible and thus necessary (or existent)
— OR —
(B) Impossible and thus nonexistent, making the Cosmos out to be necessarily existent.

(2) Yet option (B) cannot be true as the N-E-E-D idea is certainly plausible, i.e., it is not incoherent, and this point is fortified by (a) the fact that scientists now say the idea of the Cosmos as the N-E-E-D (pantheism) is not possible and (b) the absurdity of the idea the Cosmos can be non-necessary yet still be able to burst into being from nothingness.

(3) Therefore, (A) is our only cogent option – that is, the N-E-E-D idea is required, given the meaning of this concept; "God" is a REQUIRED IDEA.

Diagram Form

THE N-E-E-D
IDEA

(A) Possible & thus actual   **(B)** Impossible & thus incoherent

Not (B); Ergo, (A)

Note: Because this ontological argument version is very abstract, it is best used when a dialogue partner enjoys discussing abstract philosophy, since many have difficulty fully grasping the argument's potency.

Although this argument does raise the logical possibility that the cosmos itself could be the GCB), and thus lead to the cosmos), what we will cosmological versions is be eternal, given all the cannot be correspondent

Symbol of Pantheism

N-E-E-D (or Malcom's pantheism (where God = observe with subsequent that the cosmos cannot evidence, so pantheism to what is ultimate reality.

E Eternal Uncaused-Cause

Three Cosmological Arguments

Eternity

Cosmological arguments all attempt to infer the existence of a God from the existence of the cosmos. Most versions are categorized as first-cause arguments since they attempt to prove God must exist as the "first" (or ultimate) cause of the cosmos. Erudite philosophers, such as Plato, Aristotle, Aquinas, Dun Scotus, Samuel Clarke, Gottfried Leibniz, Richard Taylor and Richard Swinburne, have all offered various versions.

Cosmological Version #1: ST. THOMAS AQUINAS

The cosmological arguments of St. Thomas Aquinas are perhaps the most well-known in philosophy. Aquinas was a Dominican monk and quintessential theologian who is best known for his Summa Theologica, an erudite text written in 1272 which served as a sort of encyclopedic digest of the theological dogmas of the Roman Catholic Church; the work includes five brilliant theistic arguments, which Aquinas called the Five Ways. Of these five "proofs" for God, the first three are cosmological-type arguments. They are (1) the argument from change, (2) the argument from efficient causality and (3) the argument from time and contingency. In the interest of being concise and keeping our focus on basic apologetics, we will focus only on (2) above – i.e., the argument from efficient causality, since this argument encapsulates the essence of the other two.

Aquinas' argument from efficient causality is not difficult to grasp. It argues that, since everything in the cosmos is contingent and needs a cause to explain where it came from and/or how it continues to exist, there must exist something in the cosmos that needs no cause for its origination or continued existence, i.e., an Uncaused Cause that cannot not exist. For example, we humans could not exist right now without certain things on which we are dependent (e.g., hydration, the presence of oxygen, etc.). Ergo, an Uncaused Cause, i.e., a thing that possesses existence by its own eternal nature, must be the "something" on which all contingent things are dependent. This something Aquinas calls God.

But suppose a God does not exist. Could then *anything* be able to exist? No. A string of contingents going back ad infinitum is totally incoherent. Some eternal hand must have existed which set everything else in motion. In analyzing Aquinas' views, Boston College professors Peter Kreeft and Ronald Tacelli offer a creative analogy to explain why a God must necessarily exist as a non-contingent, "existence-giving" Uncaused Cause:

Existence is like a gift given from cause to effect. If there is no one who has the gift, the gift cannot be passed down from the chain of receivers, however long or short the chain may be. If everyone has to borrow a certain book, but no one actually *has it*, then no one will ever *get* it. If there is no God who has existence by his own eternal nature, then the gift of existence cannot be passed down the chain of creatures and we can never get it. But we do get it; we exist. Therefore, there must exist a God, an Uncaused Being who does not have to receive existence like us — and like every other link in the chain.[4]

How might we critique Aquinas' argument? Is it sound? This is hotly debated. Here is why. The argument does not force us to conclude that a non-material force is the eternal Uncaused Cause of the cosmos. Perhaps the cosmos itself is an Uncaused Cause that continually undergoes an

endless "big-bang-big-crunch" cycle. If so, then we should all validly be pantheists purporting that our "God" simply equals this "eternal" universe.

But is this view substantiated? Has the cosmos been exploding and crunching eternally? No. Something *apart* from the physical cosmos must exist as the Uncaused Cause since all the 21st-century data indicates the unseen force of "dark energy," which cosmologists believe comprises 68% of the cosmos, is *accelerating* the cosmos' expansion rate beyond a point where gravity could ever crunch it backwards. Given this data, most of the world's top scientists are concluding that the cosmos *is* indeed finite.

Cosmological Version #2: THE LOGIC OF KALĀM

Denying an infinite regress, kalam sa
metric time (MT) began, yet allows "Go
to still exist in beginningless, non-M

Outside of scientific findings, there is also a cogent philosophical reason which supports the notion that the cosmos, and even time itself, must be finite. This mind-blowing argument is called the Kalam Argument. The term "kalam" is Arabic and used to describe the view of Islamic philosophers that the world cannot be infinitely old. The kalam argument purports that an infinite temporal sequence of events is impossible and that any object which exists inside of spacetime, cannot be infinitely old, since infinity would always have to exist prior to any given point within metric time.

Consider here the progression of the kalam's undeniable logic: If the universe never began, then it always has been and is infinitely old. But if it is infinitely old, then an infinite amount of time would have had to have elapsed prior to (let's say) today, and thus an infinite number of days must have already been actualized, one day succeeding another, in order for this present day to arrive. Yet this is absurd. It is like trying to make a square circle—an impossible feat. Why is an infinitely old cosmos incoherent? It is because, if the present day has been reached, then an infinite sequence of history has *already* reached this present. But an infinite sequence could *never* logically reach today, or even any specific point *before* today. It must be the case rather that either (a) the present day has not been reached or (b) the process of reaching it was not infinite. These points suggest that even time itself had a beginning. Such a notion is not far-fetched when we study Einstein. See sidebar.

FASCINATING EINSTEIN FACTS: In 1905, Albert Einstein theorized that reality possesses no absolute time, only "time dilation" linked to an increase or decrease in an object's gravity and/or velocity in spacetime. Einstein's theory of spacetime is now seen as fact, even being built into all GPS satellites, a fact I learned while deployed as a U.S. Navy officer on a ship which used military GPS. Consider these stats. Since GPS satellites travel at faster rates relative to Earth objects, their rate of time runs more slowly due to Einsteinian time dilation. In fact, on average their GPS clocks lose 7 microseconds per day compared to Earth clocks. Yet, since GPS clocks are also farther away from Earth's gravity, time for them passes faster than Earth clocks, precisely 45 microseconds faster per day. Thus, for GPS satellites to provide accurate location data, their orbiting GPS clocks must account for a net daily time dilation gain of 38 microseconds. Time dilation gets more mind-blowing when applied to a hypothetical God, for this God's omnipresent spacetime vantage point - i.e., his divine "NOW" - must encompass all the googol of "nows" of every event and every point of reference everywhere in the cosmos. Such an ineffable potentiality re "divine time" is staggering, even hinting that all future "nows" related to human libertarian freedom (LF) must have countless open possibilities, limiting divine foreknowledge to only non-LF future events.

Given the substantiation for Kalam's contention that our cosmos, and its metric time (MT) ethos, cannot be infinitely old, shouldn't we still expect *something* non-MT-dependent to be eternal? Yes. This is valid. That said, fastidiously digest my cosmological version which presupposes eternality.

Carlson Version: GOD THE **E**TERNAL UNCAUSED-CAUSE

Draft Form

(1) Something must possess eternality. We have two options before us in this regard:

   (A) An Uncaused Cause (apart from the cosmos)
      —OR—
   (B) The Cosmos (alone or in a <u>panentheistic</u> sense)
     Note: see page 38 re: panentheism's claims.

(2) But the <u>Cosmos is not eternal</u> as evidenced by recent discoveries of modern science, and if we consider the kalam argument to be sound.

(3) Ergo, (A) exists apart from the Cosmos – that is, God = an ETERNAL UNCAUSED-CAUSE.

Diagram Form

Eternality

(A) Possessed by an Uncaused Cause, i.e., God (apart from the Cosmos)

(B) Possessed somehow by the Cosmos (solely or via panentheism)

Not (B); Ergo, (A)

Using the diagram form above, I have explained this cosmological argument with great success in countless conversations and debates. But is premise (2) above really true? Is the cosmos finite? Is it correct to assert that everything that makes up this universe is not and cannot be eternal? My argument stands or falls on the answer, yes or no. Strikingly, top 21st-century astronomers and  physicists are saying "yes" to these three questions. The cosmos is indeed finite; it is <u>not</u> eternal (see image). Why? The main argument has to do with *entropy*, or the "running-down" of the cosmos. Since the totality of physical matter/energy in the universe has a finite amount of order and is irreversibly moving from an ordered system to a disordered one, it follows that the universe cannot have existed forever. This fact of physics is difficult to overtrump as it takes both outside energy and a complex mechanism to overcome entropy.

Consider these three conclusions offered respectively by three widely published 21st-century scientists. Each man contends that, given all the scientific evidence, the cosmos is not eternal as pantheism contends:

Scientist #1:   S.A. Bludman, Physics professor at the University of Pennsylvania, writes the following regarding the necessity of a beginning for every conceivable cosmos scenario:

Whether closed or open, reversing or monotonically expanding, the severely irreversible phase transitions transpiring give the universe a definite beginning.[5]

Scientist #2:   In his 1994 book, *The Last Three Minutes*, Paul Davies, Ph.D, a world-renowned astrophysicist, writes these concluding remarks regarding the finiteness of the cosmos after surveying all of the current scientific data:

All the evidence points then, to a universe that has a limited lifespan. It came into existence at some finite time in the past, it is currently vibrant with activity, but it is inevitably degenerating toward a heat death at some stage in the future.[6]

ASTROPHYSICS SPOTLIGHT: The idea of the cosmos' *heat death* — aka the "Big Freeze" -- is a conjecture on the cosmos' ultimate fate which says the cosmos will evolve to a state of no thermodynamic free energy, meaning it will be unable to sustain entropy. Astrophysicists hypothesize the "Big Freeze" because they believe unseen dark energy is accelerating the cosmos' expansion rate beyond any possible gravitational reversal toward a "Big Crunch."

Scientist #3:   Dr. Walt Brown, a retired USAF colonel and mechanical engineering Ph.D. grad from M.I.T., has taught as a tenured professor at the U.S. Air Force Academy and served as Chief of Science & Technology at the Air War College. In the 2001 seventh edition of his mammoth book, *In the Beginning*, Brown puts to rest any notion that the cosmos could be infinitely old, given the laws of thermodynamics:

Heat always flows from a hot body to a cold body. If the universe were infinitely old, everything should have the same temperature. Because temperatures vary, the universe is not infinitely old. Therefore, the universe had a beginning. . . If the entire universe is an isolated system, then, according to the second law of thermodynamics, the energy in the universe available for useful work has always been decreasing. However, as one goes back in time, the energy available for useful work would eventually exceed the total energy in the universe that, according to the first law of thermodynamics, remains constant. This is an impossible condition, thus implying the universe had a beginning.[7]

In sum, all the current evidence proves the universe is *not* cyclical or eternal, that all matter/energy had a beginning. The second law of thermodynamics and astronomical findings irrefutably support this fact, which, in turn, validates the cosmological argument and totally negates atheism and pantheism. To counter the cosmological argument, one would have to claim, as *Hyperianism* purports, that the entire universe literally came into being from nothingness.

QUOTABLE:
"Nothing comes from nothing."
- Lucretius

Not only is this idea logically absurd, but all evidence backs up the logical notion that an Eternal Uncaused-Cause, *separate* from the cosmos, started the chain of cause and effect we now witness *inside* the cosmos.

Symbol of Hyperianism Cult created by founder, Morgue

Architect-Designer of L-I-F-E

Three Teleological Arguments

We now turn to the teleological category. Because the word "teleology" in philosophy refers to the study of the evidence of design or purpose in nature (deriving from the Greek root "telos" which refers to the inherent purpose of a thing), teleological arguments all begin by pointing to the presence of natural design in the cosmos and then try to show that such designs necessitate a divine Designer. The teleological argument is thus often called the Argument from Design. In a broad sense, a teleological argument is also a cosmological one since it too begins with cosmos' existence, but it differs in that it focuses on the character of the cosmos, particularly its orderly existence, rather than mere existence.

TELOS EX:

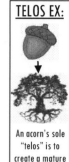

An acorn's sole "telos" is to create a mature oak tree.

The first recorded versions of a teleological-type argument appear in the writings of the philosopher Plato. The first extensive modern version appears in the writings of William Paley. Contemporary versions have been proposed by Richard Taylor. F.R. Tennan, Richard Swinburne and Michael Behe.[8] We will first examine William Paley's famous teleological reasoning and then consider Michael Behe's modern, refurbished version.

Teleological Version #1: WILLIAM PALEY (1743-1805)

William Paley (1743-1805), an English theologian and Archdeacon of Carlisle, indeed offered up the most well-known sustained treatment of the teleological argument. In his book, *Natural Theology*, Paley argues that, just as we correctly infer that an intricately designed watch must have been crafted by an intelligent designer, so likewise we can infer that our intricately designed world must have been designed by an intelligent Grand Designer. Often called the Watchmaker Argument, we can state Paley's teleological reasoning more formally as follows:

(1) Designs in Nature are analogous to manmade designs — like a watch.

(2) Manmade designs are always the result of intelligent design.

(3) Analogous effects will have analogous causes.

(4) Therefore, designs in Nature are the result of something analogous to intelligent design — that is, there must be an Intelligent Designer behind the origination of all of Nature's designs.[8]

How might we assess Paley's version? Is it sound? Yes. Yet many scholars, like David Hume (1711-1776), have argued vociferously against it.

In *Dialogues Concerning Natural Religion*, Hume contends that we can conceive of alternative explanations for why the cosmos is ordered the way it is. He argues that perhaps the order is somehow inherent in matter, or perhaps it is only *apparent* order, the result of mechanical processes.[9] Hume, an atheist, lived before Darwin, yet he seems to be intimating a Darwinian-type mechanical process in his rebuttals.

> The life of man is of no greater importance to the universe than that of an oyster. — David Hume

Can we forge a cogent reply to Hume's critique? Yes. Alternative explanations, other than God, would be ruled out if we could point to designs in the cosmos which *necessitate* an intelligent source to explain their origin, structure and/or purpose. Can this be done? Absolutely. In the 21st century, we have discovered certain natural designs which *necessitate* intelligence to explain their origin. These are called irreducibly complex designs. To grasp what "irreducible complexity" refers to precisely, let us probe its etymology and consider some key, potent, real-life examples.

Teleological Version #2: IRREDUCIBLE COMPLEXITY

The concept of "irreducible complexity" was first explained by Dr. Michael Behe, Professor of Biochemistry at Lehigh University, in his 1995 book *Darwin's Black Box*. This book ignited a firestorm of controversy in academia since it presented not only undeniable scientific data, but a conclusion which purported that super-intelligent design must, of necessity, be required to explain the irreducible complexity found in the microbiological "machines" we observe in nature.

Behe's argument refurbishes Paley's initial Watchmaker argument by placing teleological reasoning squarely within the realm of modern science. Dr. Robert Shapiro's commentary on *Darwin's Black Box* is worth noting here. Shapiro writes the following to describe the significance of Behe's work: "Michael Behe has done a top-notch job of explaining and illuminating one of the most vexing problems in biology: the origin of the complexity that permeates all of life on this planet. This book should be on the essential reading list of all those who are interested in the question of where we came from, as it presents the most thorough and clever presentation of the design argument that I have seen."[10] I concur.

But what is irreducible complexity (IC)? Is IC a significant concept for theistic apologetics? Absolutely. In fact, IC is now the most potent and important paradigm for explaining why an Architect-Designer *must* be behind nature's intricate complexity. So, it is vital that every 21st-century Christian apologist know how to talk about IC. To explain the definition and biological implications of irreducible complexity, Behe writes the following synopsis in *Darwin's Black Box*:

By *irreducibly complex* I mean a single system composed of several well-matched, interacting parts that contribute to the basic function, wherein the removal of any one of the parts causes the system to effectively cease functioning. And irreducibly complex system cannot be produced directly (that is, by continuously improving the initial function, which continues to work by the same mechanism) by slight, successive modifications of a precursor system, because any precursor to an irreducibly complex system that is missing a part is by definition nonfunctional. An irreducibly complex biological system, if there is such a thing, would be a powerful challenge to Darwinian evolution. Since natural selection can only choose systems that are already working, then if a biological system cannot be produced gradually it would have to arise as an integrated unit, in one fell swoop, for natural selection to have anything to act on.[11]

In his book, after explaining how a mousetrap is a rudimental human-made example of irreducible complexity, Behe discusses how he sought to find microbiological systems that exhibit this same type of complexity. What he found was mind-blowing. Behe discovered that biological designs such as the flagella of bacteria, and biochemical systems such as human blood clotting, are indeed irreducibly complex — that is, these designs absolutely could not have arisen via any type of progressive Darwinian fashion via mutations over time. Behe then argues, based on the scientific evidence, that biochemical irreducible complexity points undeniably to intelligent design over against all other cogitable scientific options, e.g., such as the Darwinian explanation that time plus chance plus natural selection could produce such designs.

Behe concludes that, in biology at least, a paradigm shift is now warranted, for macroevolution cannot yet explain, in a mechanistic way, the origin of even one example of biological irreducible complexity (IC), and hence, to quote Behe, macroevolution must either "publish or perish." That is, it must address IC or become extinct.

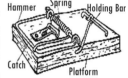

Invoking the best of 21st-century science, I have summarized below five incredibly powerful examples of irreducible complexity found in biological organisms and the cosmos at large. These illustrations include: (1) DNA, (2) the Bacterial Flagellum, (3) the Human Eye, (4) the Earth-Moon-Sun system and (5) the Cosmos' Anthropic Parameters. As we study each of these examples to demonstrate the veracity and cogency of 21st-century teleological reasoning, we shall observe that, indeed, the undeniable presence of natural irreducible complexity points decisively to an intelligent Architect-Designer behind nature's intricate engineering. The "time-plus-chance-plus-macroevolution" fantasy option simply cannot account for the irreducible complexity found in these natural designs.

Irreducibly Complex Design #1: DNA (Including Its Dire Implications for Macroevolution!)

We begin by carefully examining DNA. Nowadays, DNA is a universal abbreviation. We study its structure in high school biology. We hear about it in criminal trials. We see it being gathered and punctiliously tested on top-rated TV shows like Crime Scene Investigation (C.S.I). But what is so unique about DNA and why is it irreducibly complex — i.e., why is intelligence a necessary requisite to explain its origin and intricacy?

First, let us determine what DNA is. Formally deoxyribonucleicacid, DNA is contained in the nucleus of every living cell of every organism and, as such, it "programs" all characteristics of life, such as colors, size, gender, etc. The DNA molecule (see adjacent picture) is an extremely long chemical thread made up of two strands that are held as a pair forming a spiral or double helix. Each strand consists of a long chain of the sugar deoxyribose and phosphate residues. Two purines, adenine (A) and guanine (B), and two pyrimidines, thymine (T) and cytosine (C), are also found in DNA. In the DNA thread the purine and pyrimidine bases lie opposite one other making replication possible — a feat essential to all existent life on Earth.

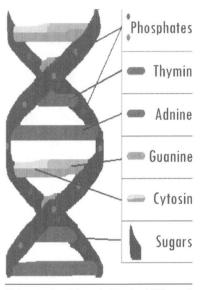

Phosphates

Thymin

Adnine

Guanine

Cytosin

Sugars

All human cell nuclei contain 23 pairs of DNA strands

What does DNA do exactly? In human beings, duplicate copies of DNA are coiled up in the nucleus of each of the human body's approximately 100 trillion cells and this coded information determines the arrangement of 10^{14} (100 thousand billion) cerebral electrical connections, 206 bones, 650 muscles, 10,000 auditory cells and 400 billion feet of blood vessels.[12] It is worth noting that DNA works exactly like a human language since it has four letters — A, B, T, C — and it conveys a genetic message. In fact, one could validly argue that the origin of DNA is actually the origin of information itself! DNA is estimated to contain instructions that, if typed out, would actually fill 1000 600-page books.[13]

Consider these three incredible illustrations which give us a better sense of the incredibly massive data-storage capacity of DNA:

Illustration #1: The DNA molecules of information needed to specify the design of all the species of organisms which have ever lived on planet Earth could be held in a tiny teaspoon and there would still be room left over to hold all the data in every book and magazine ever written![14] Could chance account for this?

One Tsp.

All Species

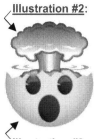

Illustration #2: If all the DNA in one cell were uncoiled, it would be seven feet long and so thin its details could not be seen under an electron microscope. Moreover, if all the DNA of one human body were placed end-to-end, it would stretch from Earth to the moon more than 500,000 times and Earth to the sun more than 800 times.

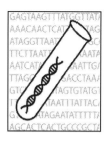

Illustration #3: If one cell's worth of DNA from every person who ever lived were placed in a collective DNA pile, it would weigh less than a single tablet of aspirin![15] That's >.38 g for 100B+ cells.

So, DNA is phenomenally efficient at storing data despite its tiny size. But is it irreducibly complex?—Yes. DNA does not just passively store data but intricately duplicates data amidst a plethora of essential, yet necessarily interdependent, molecular parts, all of which contribute to its function, which is to encode and replicate genetic information. If we take away any essential part, DNA ceases to function. That is, all its parts are needed all at once. We cannot progressively add parts. And it gets worse. DNA cannot function without at least 75 pre-existing proteins, and yet these are only produced by DNA, which means the DNA code and the external means of decoding it had to come into existence simultaneously.

Such a fact explains why Lous Pasteur's 1860 "Law of Biogenesis" is undeniable. It says life only comes from pre-existing life. Any type of DNA is vastly too complex to have originated by chance from non-living matter, meaning spontaneous generation is not possible given DNA's irreducible complexity. Indeed, DNA necessitates an intelligent source to explain its origin, order and complexity as it could not have arisen by chance or been advanced by natural selection in any type of Darwinian fashion.

Sadly, Charles Darwin (1809-1882), the very first scientist to propose natural selection as a mechanism for genetic change, did not know about DNA. He was unaware that natural selection simply cannot explain the *biochemical origin* of DNA. Let us briefly investigate Darwin's views and see what aspects of his theory of gradual evolution are still credible and which are not. In positing the notion of natural selection, Darwin claimed that subtle mutations that enable an organism to adapt

to environmental change and survive would ultimately be kept and passed on to offspring. If this kept up over time — e.g., over hundreds of millions of years — perhaps new and different species could evolve. This view of evolution is called macroevolution; it expresses the theory (one that we will see has NO merit) that increasing and inheritable complexity can perhaps, via natural selection, be gradually actualized over time.

That said, we must clearly distinguish between macroevolution, which I assert has never occurred, and microevolution, which is a fact of biology. Micro (not macro) evolution *has* been observed, but it does not involve increasing complexity, only changes *within* species in size, color, etc. Minor changes in species have been noticed well before Darwin. Consider dog variability. Over 200 varieties of dogs exist, yet all remain dogs. Macroevolution, on the hand, requires millions of "just right" mutations. As such, <u>macro</u>-evolution sees a *vertical* change in complexity, whereas <u>micro</u>-evolution is simply *horizontal* with a species.

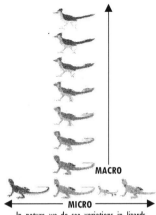

In nature, we do see variations in lizards (bottom) and birds (top), but in-between forms are never seen as fossils or species.

What Darwin rightfully observed on the Galapagos Islands during his 1831-1836 S.S. Beagle voyage around the world was, in fact, micro, not macroevolution. Darwin was correct to propose natural selection when observing finch beak variation, but he went too far in proposing macroevolution. If Darwin had known about DNA, he probably would not have made such an enormous leap of speculation.

Since natural selection cannot produce *new* genes within DNA, but only "select" among pre-existing genetic characteristics, natural selection can sometimes explain microevolution and the *survival* of the fittest, but it cannot explain the *origin* of the fittest, particularly given DNA's irreducible complexity, and the law of biogenesis, which states that all DNA originates from other DNA. In short, DNA could not have originated by chance, since it is a bio-machine system that depends on the integrated activity of essential, interactive components, no one of which can be removed without collapsing the entire system. The implications of this are "deadly" for macroevolution. DNA mutations would have to occur co-adaptively and simultaneously for any type of macroevolution to work. This fact explains why nearly *all* DNA mutations are lethal and why no known mutation has ever forged a life form with greater complexity than its ancestors.

Mendel's laws of genetics, which explain the variations we observe in species, proved the boundaries of DNA. He discovered that genes are merely reshuffled in successive generations. Different *combinations* form, but not new genes. The different composites can produce variations in a species, but there

Gregor Mendel

- Began experiments in 1857
- Austrian monk
- Studied genetics of peas
- Father of genetics
- Failed his math/science teacher exam

are innate *limits*. Breeding experiments have confirmed this, as has the fossil record. Indeed, we see "intermediates" to be 100% absent in the fossil record. But how is this possible? If macroevolution were true, billions of transitional mutated  forms should exist. Yet, remarkably, intransigent Darwinists cannot show one credible example. In fact, to date, re: the so-called ape-men paleo-anthropologist say they have found, e.g., such as Java Man discovered by Eugene Dubois in 1891), Piltdown Man (dug up by Charles Dawson in 1912), Nebraska Man (found by Harold Cook in England 1922) and Lucy (unearthed by Donald Johanson in Ethiopia in 1974), *all* have been shown *not* to be "missing links" at all. Not one credible example exists.

The story of Nebraska Man is worth noting here as an example. Nebraska Man was used by evolutionists in the famous Scopes Evolution Trial in Dayton, Tennessee in 1925 to "prove" that macroevolution was an acceptable theory to be taught in public schools. Williams Jennings Bryan, the lawyer for the creationist side, was in 1925 confronted with a battery of experts who stunned him with "facts" regarding Nebraska Man. Bryan had no retort except to say the evidence was too scanty. The "experts" scoffed. But what exactly was the proof for Nebraska Man? Did scientists have the "missing link?" No! They had ONE tooth. Yes. Fact: Harold Cook  found only one tooth in 1922. The top scientists of that day examined the tooth and appraised it as proof positive that a prehistoric race had existed in the Americas. However, years after the Scopes Trial, the entire skeleton from which the tooth came was found. And it turned out to belong to an extinct pig. The "experts" who initially ridiculed Mr. Bryan were certainly embarrassed. Yet no publicity ever revealed this monumental blunder. Even today some naïvely use the Scopes Trial to support evolution lessons when, in reality, intelligent design (ID) theory possesses much more *actual* evidence to support ID claims.

One "proof" often cited by macro-evolutionists is Archaeopteryx (meaning "old wing"), which was found in Germany in 1861. They claim birds evolved from reptiles and point to Archaeopteryx as a link between the two classes. Yet this cannot be true since modern bird fossils have been found in the same rock layers, meaning Archaeopteryx is not and could not be a bird forerunner. Plus,

The first Archaeopteryx imprint was found in 1861 in limestone deposits in Germany.

a recent find in China has put Archaeopteryx in its rightful taxonomical niche. In 2011, four Chinese scientists unearthed a fossil older than Archaeopteryx named Xiaothingia Zhengi. After comparing both fossils to birds and dinosaurs via computer analysis, the scientists concluded that neither creature could be directly related to modern birds at all.[16]

So where are the millions of half-scale-half-feather mutants showing that birds came from reptiles? Answer: They don't exist. But here is why. The most gargantuan problem (and death blow!) to reptile-to-bird evolution concerns their lungs. Reptile lungs have millions of tiny air sacs whereas birds have tubes, a design peculiar to birds enabling them to breath nonstop, since birds need high oxygen during flight. It is thus *impossible* for bird lung structure to have evolved from reptiles since any creature with a "middle" form between the two (half tubes/half sacs) would be *unable* to breathe.

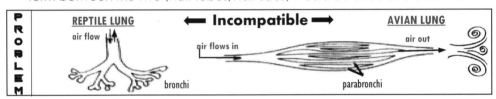

In addition, bird DNA simply could not have come from reptile DNA. The reason? DNA is information. And 21st century information theory has shown that mistakes cannot improve a code of information; mistakes can only reduce a code's ability to transmit meaningful information. So, for any DNA code to evolve upwards, e.g., from ameba to cow DNA, the DNA needs new, *meaningful* information. As DNA expert Bodie Hodge asserts, "for molecules-to-man evolution to happen, there needs to be a gain in *new* information within the organism's genetic material. For instance, for a single-celled organism, such as an ameba, to evolve into something like a cow, *new* information [not random base pairs, but complex and ordered 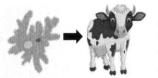 DNA] would need to develop over time that would code for ears, lungs, brains, legs, etc."[17] And there lies the problem. For macroevolution to be true, literally trillions of information-gaining mutations must have occurred in the past. Yet we always see the opposite.

Since new information results only from the focused expenditure of energy, and there is no micro-mechanism which promotes data-gaining DNA mutations, upward DNA change cannot happen. In fact, mutations arising from freak DNA changes are not only typically lethal (and at best harmful), they randomly occur once in about 10 million duplications of a DNA molecule.[18] Thus, mere random mutations cannot account for the literally trillions of information-gaining mutations that would have had to occur to produce (by chance) each of the billions of irreducibly complex designs found within the est. 8.7 million species which inhabit our planet, especially when we consider the incredible phenomenon of *convergence*.

Allow me to explain why *convergence* dismantles macroevolution. It refers to the fact that totally unrelated organisms still possess similar organs and structures. Yet these similar organisms, given their vast separation on the supposed evolutionary tree of life, must have, according to macro-evolutionists, each evolved their similar traits independently from different ancestral roots, each time starting from a completely dissimilar structural origin. Design adherents contend this is sheer fantasy. It is difficult enough to account for even one irreducibly complex structure — in fact it is likely impossible without intelligence — and yet macro-evolutionists ask people to believe that all examples of convergence can arise over time, by chance, from the presence of similar environmental demands. They ask us to believe the statistically insurmountable, that the sophisticated sonar systems of both bats and porpoises each evolved totally independently from one another, or that the irreducibly complex wing mechanisms found in insects, flying reptiles, birds, and bats (which are mammals), evolved totally independently *four* separate times. This is statistical

nonsense. No fossil transitions exist that show the ability to fly evolved independently 4x. If this were not enough to convince, there also exist mind-blowing examples of *double convergence* in nature, such as the independently rolling eyes and coiled tails of both sea horses and chameleons. Dr. Scott M. Huse, author of *The Collapse of Evolution*, accurately addresses convergence as follows:

The evolutionary development of numerous highly intricate structures, habits, and physiologies that are identical, despite the fact that they arose from widely different anatomical origins, is completely inconceivable, an absolute impossibility. Cases of double convergence reveal the preposterous nature of such an unfounded concept. Clearly, evolutionary convergence must be rejected as a complete absurdity.[19]

Yet the deathblow to macro-evolution is that we indeed see the total absence of transitional forms in the fossil record. Millions should exist, yet we cannot find even *one* credible example of a true transition. It is quite interesting that the view of species proposed in Genesis 1 better explains the fossil data. Genesis 1 claims 10x that each living thing was made "according to its own kind." Indeed, scientists may observe varieties within species possessing a common ancestry due to microevolution, but we have *never once* seen speciation occurring.

WANTED: TRANSITIONAL FORMS

FISHIBIAN   AMPHITILE   REPBIRD

REWARD !

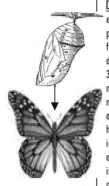

CREATURE SPOTLIGHT: Is there enough shown in nature so that humanity has no excuse? Yes. Consider how the BUTTERFLY is an unequivocal example of intelligent design (ID), particularly when we ponder how it (a) dissolves its caterpillar body and organs inside its chrysalis, a feat gradualism cannot explain, (b) how it changes from having a mouth to a feeding tube, 16 legs down to six, and 12 eyes down to two, and how it (c) rearranges its cells to forge engineering built for 360° flight, an insanely complex feat. While airplanes harness forces of thrust and lift, butterflies use much more sophisticated methods, including wave capture, wing edge vortices, and "clap-and-fling" mechanisms, all of which combine to form an irreducibly complex (IC) flight system. In fact, all flight ability necessitates some type of IC-based apparatus. Yet, for macroevolution to be true, flight would have had to originate from "mutated" IC structures, by pure chance, four independent times, namely, in insects, bats, birds and pterosaurs. But ID geneticists now understand that such a freak assemblage of IC-based systems is not even feasible ONE time given the nature of mutations, which happen once in every 10 million duplications of a DNA molecule, and which are always degradative, meaning that mutations never add new *utile* data to pre-existent DNA coding. In short, butterflies had a Designer.

To sum up, if Charles Darwin would have been exposed to modern biochemistry, particularly the irreducible complexity of DNA, he would have likely abandoned his own theory (cf. Darwin's quote on page 63). Unfortunately, in the 20th century, macroevolution turned itself into a rigid ideology, not allowing its views to be falsified. Renowned law professor, Philip Johnson, points this out well in his 1991 classic work, *Darwin on Trial*, arguing that macroevolution as a scientific theory "rests squarely on ... philosophical beliefs that are not subject to scientific test and refutation."[21] In other words, macroevolution is based on faith (not fact), a faith in philosophical naturalism. Microevolution is based on science, to be sure, but macroevolution is not. Ergo, given all the 21st-century data, I undeniably assert now that macroevolution is a dead theory. That said, I have listed in the BOX BELOW all the direct scientific evidence which can be used to *prove* undeniably that the theory of macroevolution is an established "truth" of science as some scientists still audaciously assert:

??

Bottom Line: Not a smidgen of evidence exists for macroevolution, not one scintilla. When we consider human intelligence, which has been

able to create irreducibly complex supercomputers and spaceships, the intellect required to artificially create a machine (like CDR Data from Star Trek) that can store data in the same manner as DNA, and even replicate itself like DNA, would far exceed human limits. So how is DNA here? By chance? Not a chance! A divine Architect-Designer must have purposely created DNA.

To help intelligent design advocates use scientific facts to defend this conclusion and aptly address the creation/evolution debate in the 21st century, I have drafted on page 61 a very useful essay on how one can talk scientifically about the origin of L-I-F-E with a macroevolutionist.

How to Scientifically Discuss the Origin of L-I-F-E

Life on Earth originated from an intelligent designer. There is no question about it if one honestly examines the current scientific data. But how can a proponent of intelligent design theory talk sensibly and scientifically about the origins of life with a diehard macro-evolutionist? One method I have found helpful is to simply use the acrostic L-I-F-E. Each of these four letters can be used to represent one well-established fact of science. Indeed, whenever a creationist talks with an evolutionist, science and science alone must be invoked. So listed here are <u>four scientific facts</u> that one could confidently disseminate when discussing the origin of L-I-F-E:

L — Law of Biogenesis	——	A Fact from Biology
I — Irreducible Complexity	——	A Fact from Biochemistry
F — Fossil Absences	——	A Fact from Paleontology
E — Entropy over Time	——	A Fact from Physics

L — If no intelligent designer (i.e., a necessarily existent life-force) exists to explain the origins of contingent life on Earth, then we must accept by faith — yes faith — that the impossible occurred, namely, that the first living organism originated by "spontaneous generation" from non-living matter, despite the undeniable fact that the <u>Law of Biogenesis</u> (proved by Louis Pasteur in 1860) states such a notion is impossible, that new life arises only from pre-existing life. Macro-evolutionists should always be reminded of this key fact of biology.

I — We have already discussed one illustration of biological "irreducible complexity" — viz., DNA. The irreducible complexity of nature's microbiological "machines" (like DNA) needs to be effectively explained to macro-evolutionists. <u>Irreducible complexity</u> (IC) has forever put macroevolution in the grave, but many macro-evolutionists do not yet fully grasp why. Therefore, proponents of intelligent design (ID) must be able to cogently demonstrate exactly why designs in nature which exhibit irreducible complexity must have originated from an intelligent source. This remarkable IC-based insight of 21st-century science needs to be proactively promulgated so that the now "unfit-to-survive" theory of macroevolution can be labeled as officially extinct.

F — We already looked at two examples from the fossil record — Nebraska Man and Archaeopteryx — which macro-evolutionists have, in the past, used to "prove" their so-called "scientific" theory. But the fact is that no credible "missing link" between species has ever been found! <u>Fossil absences</u> instead are what abound in the fossil record! That is, instead of finding the literally billions of "transitional forms" that should exist in the fossil record (if macroevolution were true), we have yet to find one "undisputed" example. As Dr. Duane Gish, Ph.D notes, "the fossil record shows the sudden appearance, fully formed, of all the complex invertebrates (snails, clams, jellyfish, sponges, worms, sea urchins, brachiopods, and trilobites) without a trace of ancestors."[20] Creationists need to gently remind macro-evolutionists of this fact of paleontology (cf. p. 59 "WANTED" poster).

E — Finally, ID adherents need to raise the topic of entropy. <u>Entropy over time</u>, no matter how one tries to "spin" this fact of physics, is a serious quandary for macroevolution. Why? It is because entropy says that everything in the cosmos is degenerating. Yet macroevolution says the <u>exact opposite</u>, claiming that living things have supposedly evolved from chaos to greater complexity — all by chance over time. This is untenable given that it takes both "energy expenditure" and a "complex mechanism" to overcome the law of entropy.

All in all, as the ID debate rages on in the 21st century, it is going to become increasingly important for ID adherents to show — with compelling arguments — that their views are based on science and science alone. Citing the four scientific facts above regarding L-I-F-E on Earth is surely a **sound and potent place to begin.**

Irreducibly Complex Design #2: A BACTERIAL FLAGELLUM

Like DNA, bacteria may be small, but they are definitely not simple! The flagellum of some bacteria, or the device that enables bacteria to swim, is a wonderful example of something that is irreducibly complex. Why? Just look at the adjacent diagram. From this image, we see that the flagellum is made up of many perfectly-matched parts all of which are *essential* to its

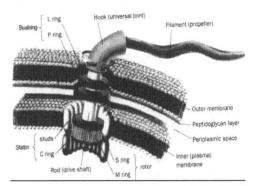

The Biochemical Complexity of a Bacterial Flagellum[22]

function. That is, if all the parts are not present simultaneously, in perfect position, this device is useless. So, a flagellum is so complex it never could have gradually "evolved" unless (a) all the parts of it were available all at once and (b) each of these parts was perfectly assembled in perfect sequence and position to achieve the bio-machine's main function. Fascinatingly, biochemists discovered in 1973 that the flagellum mirrors the complexity of a man-made boat propeller, since both possess three components: a rotor, a drive shaft and a propeller.[23] Each machine is irreducibly complex, to be sure, but, ounce for ounce, the flagellum is much faster. It must have been intelligently engineered.

Irreducibly Complex Design #3: THE HUMAN EYE

Human vision is also irreducibly complex as all parts of the eye are essential to its function. In other words, the eye would be utterly useless unless it was fully formed all at once. Since the eye only functions as an integrated whole, there is zero chance that this masterpiece of engineering could have originated by a gradual, step-by-step, trial-and-error, evolutionary process. No wonder my ophthalmologist once opined that "study of the eye is a definite cure for atheism." The eye is a miracle. Furnished with automatic focusing and auto-aperture adjustment, the eye can function from near complete darkness to bright sunlight, see the diameter of a fine hair, and make over 100,000 motions per day, providing a continuous display of color

Optometry Symbol

A Worthy Sidebar: Before its link to the Greek deity of healing, Asciepius, the *caduceus* (staff + snake) actually originated from the "brass snake" healing story of Num. 21:5-9, one Jesus turns into a *simile* about his cross in John 3:14: "As Moses lifted up the snake..., so the Son of Man must be lifted up." In citing the healing power of a cursed Christ on the cross in Gal. 3:13 & 2 Cor. 5:21, Paul too, like Jesus, saw Num. 21 as a *foreshadowing* of the cross.

stereoscopic pictures. In fact, we now know our eyes do their own internal maintenance as we sleep.[24] Given all this data, eyes *had* to be engineered.

Historical Highlight: Digest the above sidebar to see how the staff/snake-laden symbol of optometry is directly connected to the cross of Christianity.

Darwin himself (1809-1882), the first scientist to posit natural selection (or the mechanism allowing for biological evolution wherein subtle mutations that promote organism adaptation and survival are passed on to offspring), questioned the validity of the "macro" part of his theory when contemplating the incomprehensible complexity of the human eye. Darwin, who at low tide was a committed agnostic, and at high tide a devout theist, writes the following words concerning the possibility that the human eye could have ever originated over time via his proposed evolutionary mechanism of natural selection:

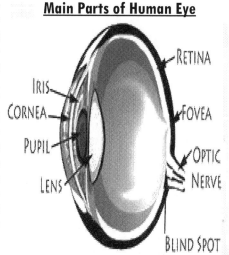

Main Parts of Human Eye

RETINA
IRIS
CORNEA
FOVEA
PUPIL
OPTIC
LENS
NERVE
BLIND SPOT

To suppose that the eye, with all its contrivances for adjusting the focus to different distances, for admitting different amounts of light, and for the correction of spherical and chromatic aberration, could have been formed by natural selection, seems I freely confess, absurd in the highest possible degree. The belief that an organ as perfect as the eye could have formed by natural selection is more than enough to stagger anyone.[25]

You see, Darwin knew well that his theory of gradual evolution by means of natural selection carried with it an incredible burden and massive Achilles heel. For something like the eye to have progressively evolved, part by part, was unfathomable. Recognizing this reality, Darwin wrote the following honest assessment of the vulnerability of his theory:

If it could be demonstrated that any complex organ existed which could not possibly have been formed by numerous, successive, slight modifications, my theory would absolutely breakdown.[26]

THE HUMAN EYE NEEDS ABOUT 40 SUBSYSTEMS ALL WORKING TOGETHER AND IN HARMONY WITH EACH OTHER...

LOGICALLY... THEY ALL HAD TO APPEAR INSTANTLY TOGETHER - OR WE WOULD ALL BE BLIND.

Since we have demonstrated the impossibility of gradual, successive modifications happening in just three of nature's irreducibly complex (IC) designs, namely, DNA, the bacterial flagellum, and the human eye (which, as per the adjacent infographic, has at least 40 interdependent IC subsystems), we see that a total meltdown for Darwinism has already occurred. In fact, as 21st-century scientists begin to grasp the fact that all of life's IC designs are a product of mind-blowing engineering, many are also coming to realize that the words of Psalm 139:14 ring true now more than at any other time in history, for it appears that humans (and all living creatures) are indeed "fearfully and wonderfully made."

Irreducibly Complex Design #4: THE EARTH–MOON–SUN SYSTEM

Having examined some of the recent discoveries of biochemistry, let us now turn to some findings of 21st-century physics and astronomy, for we observe irreducible complexity not just in biological organisms, but in the very Earth-Moon-Sun system that enables all organisms to survive. Carefully consider these five features of the Earth-Moon-Sun system, which not only exemplify irreducible complexity, but also appear to be specifically designed for the purpose of sustaining living creatures:

Earth Image from NASA's Apollo 17 Mission

Feature #1: The earth is positioned approximately 93 million miles from the sun, just the right distance from the sun so that we receive exactly the right amount of heat to support life. The other planets are either too cold or too hot to sustain life.

Feature #2: The earth has a perfect rotation rate. Any tiny change in the rate of rotation of the earth would make life impossible. For example, if the earth were to rotate at 10% its present rate, all plant life would be burned to a crisp.[27]

Feature #3: The earth also has a perfect axis tilt, which is 23½ degrees from the perpendicular to the plane of its orbit. This tilting in conjunct with the earth's sun revolutions enables our seasons to occur, which is essential for food growth.

Feature #4: The moon is also perfectly positioned to support life. The moon revolves around the earth at a distance of about 240,000 miles causing harmless tides. If the moon, however, were located only 20% further away, our seven continents would be completely submerged twice a day![28]

Feature #5: The earth also has a perfect atmosphere. Its two primary elements, nitrogen (78%) and oxygen (20%), create a critical ratio essential to all life forms.

These are clearly astounding facts. Yet the Earth-Moon-Sun system is just one example of the fine-tuned complexity of the universe. Scientists have now identified over two dozen parameters that must be carefully fixed in value for any kind of conceivable life to exist at any time in the history of the universe. One example, at the atomic level, is the strong nuclear force constant. If this constant were any larger, the nuclei essential for life would be unstable. If this constant were any smaller, no atom other than hydrogen would exist.

Hydrogen Atom
PROTON
ELECTRON

Because of these narrow life-sustaining parameters, which seem to have been built into the fabric of the universe, both on the cosmic and atomic levels, 21st-century astronomers have postulated a principle they call the *Anthropic Principle*, which states that the cosmos as a whole, not just the "Goldilocks Zone" parameters of the Earth-Moon-Sun system, seems to possess all of the "just right" qualities for humans to survive and flourish.

This final illustration of irreducible complexity, namely the cosmos' fine-tuned, perfectly-set-for-life parameters, will fortify further our teleological case for God and reveal that the universe's Architect-Designer is not only a supremely *intelligent* being, but an extremely *caring* being.

Irreducibly Complex Design #5: THE COSMOS' PARAMETERS

In Psalm 19:1, we read that the "heavens declare the glory of God." Amazingly, in the 21st century, the Anthropic Principle and the scientific data surrounding it, is incredibly substantiating this famous statement of the psalmist. The cosmos, as if it was meant to be a divine masterpiece, seems to have been perfectly "fine-tuned" for humans to flourish. In fact, the fine-tunedness of the cosmos is often so precise that many of nature's numbers must be kept precisely fixed for any kind of life to even possibly exist. And

even when the numbers are allowed a bit of leeway, the give permitted is infinitesimally small. For example, if the strong nuclear force constant were even 0.3 percent stronger or two percent weaker, no life could exist.[29] Such remarkable data reveals that the cosmos is incredibly fine-tuned at many different levels. It seems to have been specifically tailor-made for life to exist and prosper.

Dr. Hugh Ross, a world-renowned astronomer, points out the "just-right-for-life" exactitude of the universe's numbers in his erudite work, *The Cosmos and the Creator*, an anthology of essays by top scientists who offer undeniable evidence of a supreme Creator intellect at work. Ross writes:

It seems as though somebody has fined tuned nature's numbers to make the universe. More than two dozen parameters for the universe must have values falling within narrowly defined ranges for life of any kind to even possibly exist.[30]

Consider the fine-tuning-of-the-cosmos chart below as It describes just a few of the universe's narrow parameters. This chart has been condensed from its original version crafted by Dr. Ross in which he lists 25 examples. I selected five of the most easy-to-grasp examples:

Five Fine-Tuned Cosmos Parameters

1. The gravitational force constant
   If larger: stars would be too hot and would burn up quickly and unevenly
   If smaller: stars would remain so cool that nuclear fusion would never ignite

2. The entropy level of the universe
   If larger: no star condensation would occur within the protogalaxies
   If smaller: no protogalaxies would form

3. The velocity of light
   If larger: all stars would be too luminous for life to exist
   If smaller: all stars would not be luminous enough

4. The electromagnetic force constant
   If larger: elements more massive than boron would be too unstable for fission
   If smaller: would create a universe of insufficient chemical bonding

5. The polarity of the water molecule
   If greater: heat of fusion and vaporization would be too great for life to exist
   If smaller: liquid water would become too inferior a solvent for life
   chemistry to proceed; ice would not float, leading to a runaway freeze-up [31]

In evaluating this data, we must ask a fundamental question. Do these narrow parameters point to (a) the work of an intelligent Architect or (b) does the data show that there is only "apparent" design in the cosmos, and that such design features are merely coincidental, the product of chance over time? We must decide. In referencing the Anthropic Principle, cosmologist Bernard J. Carr frames this point exceedingly well in an article entitled, "On the Origin, Evolution and Purpose of the Physical Universe." Carr writes the following about our choices regarding the design features of the cosmos:

One would have to conclude that the features of the universe invoked in support of the Anthropic Principle are only coincidences or that [it] was indeed tailor-made for life. I will leave it to the theologians to ascertain the identity of the tailor. [32]

So, Carr also offers us two options: Chance or Tailor? Of the two, in my judgment, we must choose the Tailor. For me, it takes far way more faith to believe in chance origins than a Creator God, given all the data, particularly since each of the cosmos' design parameters operates in an intertwined matrix of irreducible complexity. This is what is mind-blowing. If any of the "fixed" parameters breaks down, life as we know it will immediately cease. Fascinatingly, a multitude of secular astronomers in the 21st-century are beginning to come to this same conclusion. As Ross points out, "the discovery of design in the universe is having a profound theological impact on astronomers."[33] Dr. Paul Davies, a world-renowned physicist, is a case in point. He offers a personal admission regarding the power of the Anthropic Principle over his thoughts:

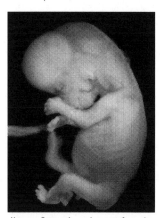

There is for me powerful evidence that there is something going on behind it all . . . It seems as though somebody has fine-tuned nature's numbers to make the Universe. The impression of design is overwhelming.[34]

Indeed, we have seen, as Paley first argued, that design implies a Designer and that irreducibly complex designs necessitate a supremely intelligent one. And now we see that the Anthropic Principle points not just to an intelligent Designer, but a caring Designer, since this divine being, it appears, has precisely "tailor-made" everything for life.

To summarize this section on "irreducible complexity" (IC), then, we can soundly conclude that, in the 21st century, the teleological argument for God's existence has never been stronger. In explaining this IC concept, we have indeed significantly refurbished Paley's Watchmaker argument. We investigated five examples of irreducible complexity which *necessitate* an intelligent source, including the Anthropic Principle, the fact that the universe itself seems to be incredibly intricate and delicate, possessing a vast array of interconnected fine-tunedness that only a supremely intelligent architect could have precisely engineered. These 21st century ideas, natural irreducible complexity and the Anthropic Principle, demand a verdict! So, I ask: Chance or Designer? What option is *ultimately* responsible for the origin of the mind-blowing, irreducibly complex, yet incredibly fragile, life-design illustrated by the adjacent image? I will let the reader decide.

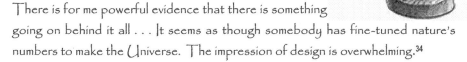

Human Fetus: 6 cm long at 8 weeks

Below is my own practical version of the teleological argument. It is easy to construct, and it is sound. Memorize the diagram form as it is effective for engaging in dialogical theistic apologetics with others who desire to discuss the evidence for theism and intelligent design (ID). I predict ID theory will only become more potent as time marches on.

Carlson Version: GOD THE **A**RCHITECT-DESIGNER

Draft Form

(1) Irreducibly complex designs exist in many parts of the natural world. And there exist only two ways that any type of design can possibly come about:

    (A) By intelligent design

    — OR —

    (B) By chance over time

(2) Option (B) is absolutely impossible since irreducibly complex designs <u>necessitate</u> an intelligent source to explain their origin.

(3) Therefore, (A) is the only credible option to explain the origin of natural irreducibly complexity. A supremely-intelligent being, an ARCHITECT-DESIGNER must exist.

Diagram Form

Natural Irreducible Complexity

(A) Originated as a result of Intelligent Design

(B) Originated as a result of Time + Chance

Not (B); Ergo, (A)

I have used this argument countless times and, more often than not, convinced my dialogue partner that theism is true. This is because the notion of natural irreducible complexity, if fully grasped, leads to only one conclusion, namely, that an Architect-Designer must exist.

Interestingly, Paul used his own form of teleological reasoning in the book of Romans. In Romans 1:20, he describes why we humans have no excuse for disbelieving in the eternal, invisible Architect-Designer of the visible world:

For since the creation of the world God's invisible qualities — his eternal power and divine nature — have been clearly understood from what has been made, so that men are without excuse.

Dubbed the Pillars of Creation, this iconic image, found in the Eagle Nebula, was taken by the Hubble Telescope in 1995, revealing incredible, monolithic trunk structures of dust & gas.

Although Paul's word choice here might seem hyperbolic to some, what he purports is fully accurate. We as humans are indeed without excuse, particularly in this generation as we now see that 21st-century science is substantiating what Paul and the author of Psalm 19:1 already knew, that the "the heavens declare the glory of God." We now turn to our last argument category, the anthropological form, which will round out our case for theism and reveal that the Creator of this cosmos is not only intelligent and eternal, but *personal.*

Life-Generating Person

Three Anthropological Arguments

All anthropological arguments begin by citing human attributes and then conclude that a personal being can be the only explanation for the origin of such traits. Here are two compelling historical examples:

Anthropological Version #1: C.S. LEWIS

In *Mere Christianity*, C.S. Lewis offers a classic, anthropological-type argument by pointing to the concept of human desire, which he argues can inductively lead us to consider the truth of the proposition that some type of *other-world* reality exists. Consider his simple logic:

Creatures are not born with desires unless satisfaction for these desires exists: A baby feels hunger; well, there is such a thing as food. A duckling wants to swim; well, there is such a thing as water. Men feel sexual desire; well, there is such a thing as sex. If I find in myself a desire which no experience in this world can satisfy, the most probable explanation is that I was made for another world.[35]

How should we assess this argument? Is it sound? Since it asserts a probable explanation, soundness does not apply. But the argument is cogent. That is, it makes rational sense to assert the premise that every innate human desire corresponds to some real object in the world which can satisfy that desire. If there indeed exists in us intrinsic desires which nothing on earth can satisfy, it is credible to state that there must exist something, outside of this world, which can satisfy these innate (but unfulfilled) desires. To be sure, there appears to be an almost universal phenomenon where humans crave for ultimate meaning and purpose.

Such an observation inspired Pascal to craft a now-popular quote of Christian pastors. He wrote: "Within the heart of every man is a God-shaped vacuum, and until that vacuum is filled, man is restless and insecure." Pascal is reinforcing Lewis' point, namely that humans crave for things that the natural world cannot deliver. One of the 20th century's most famous atheists, Jean-Paul Sarte (1905-1980), admitted that "there comes a time when one asks, even of Shakespeare, even of Beethoven, 'Is that all there is?'" It seems clear that part of us does crave for another world. Yet this argument is really only the tip of the iceberg.

Anthropological Version #2:   GREGORY A. BOYD

In *Letters from a Skeptic*, Dr. Gregory A. Boyd crafts a different type of anthropological argument than Lewis by saying that the attributes of human personhood, e.g., consciousness, rationality, love and morality, simply could not have originated from an impersonal reality. According to Boyd, to explain the origination of personal qualities, we must rather conclude that ultimate reality itself must also be *personal*. Boyd's argument is one of the most persuasive I have ever read, so I have cited Boyd's most compelling points at length since his extremely powerful version of the anthropological argument deserves a careful consideration. Boyd begins his argument by defining what personhood specifically entails:

Consciousness, rationality, love, morality, and meaning: these, I maintain, constitute the essence of what it is to be a person in the full sense of the term. Now the dilemma we face is this: either we exist in an environment (viz. the cosmos) which is compatible with these attributes, or we do not. My contention is that unless our environment is ultimately itself personal, unless the ultimate context in which we live is self-aware, rational, loving, moral, and purposeful, then our cosmic environment does not at all answer to our personhood. In other words, unless there is a personal God who is the ultimate reality within which we exist, then we humans can only be viewed as absurd, tortured, freaks of nature; for everything that is essential to us is utterly out of place in the universe. This, on the other hand, renders human nature completely unexplainable. How could brute nature evolve something so out of sync with itself? . . . If the ultimate canvas against which the cosmos is painted is not personal like we are, then we are very much like fish out of water. We desperately cry out for water, but there never was such a thing as water! . . . My point, then, is that the characteristics of personhood, and the longings which arise from personhood, require that the ultimate cause and context of personhood is personal.[36]

How should we assess this argument? Is it sound? Absolutely. Think about it. How could impersonal reality end up creating all the "intangibles" of a human, a being who can exhibit at least 10 personal capacities that animals do not possess, namely, self-reflection, abstract reasoning, codified language, moral conscience, creative artistry, purposeful inventing, altruistic capacity, worship desire, a thirst for meaning, and a longing for eternity. If an impersonal reality, outside of us, is all that exists, then such a reality could care less about us. We could validly say, as the atheist Jean-Paul Sartre often did, that "life is ultimately pointless." Such a sad proposition rings eerily true if no God exists.

That God does not exist, I cannot deny. That my whole being cries out for God I cannot forget.

JEAN-PAUL SARTRE

In fact, if the cosmos is really all there is, and it is completely impersonal, then it could be soundly argued that humans are amazing freaks of nature. We are, as Boyd phrases it, truly "fish out of water." Nature is impersonal, and yet we possess personal qualities which cry out for ultimate meaning and purpose. We

ask: Why are we here? What is the purpose of existence? Yet nature cannot and will never provide us with an answer, for we are locked in a cold, heartless, impersonal reality. Our time is finite and, in the end, our lives are utterly pointless. But what a dismal way to view existence.

Isn't it more credible to assert that a personal God exists, a God who can answer our deepest longings, a God who can explain the existence and meaning of our incredible personal capacities? If God exists, then all of life takes on new significance, for we not only can live our lives with a sense of God's steadfast presence, but we can hope that, once we pass from this earthly realm, our life journey is not over.

All in all, I believe Boyd's logic is unparalleled in its potency. Since his argument is the most accessible of the 11 we have studied, I recommend it be the first one presented when doing theistic dialogical apologetics. I have crafted below my own version of Boyd's argument, a version which I have found works well in conversations with others who question God's existence, but who earnestly desire to know the Truth.

Carlson Version: GOD AS A Life-GENERATING PERSON

Draft Form

(1) Humans possess *personal* capacities, such as the ability to love, to be self-aware, to use reason, to judge morality, to invoke language, to create art, etc., and these capacities, which no animal possesses, must have been forged by one of two options: (A) A Personal Source
— OR —
(B) Impersonal Chance

(2) Option (B) cannot at all account for (1) above.

(3) Ergo, a Life-Generating Personal Source exists.

Diagram Form

Personal Capacities

(A) Generated from a Personal Source

(B) Generated from pure Impersonal Chance

Not (B); Ergo, (A)

To my delight, I have used this argument in dozens of dialogues and found it to be potent in persuading others that theism is sound given humankind's innate personal capacities, things no animal possesses. Try using the argument with a diehard atheist. Its cogency is difficult to deny.

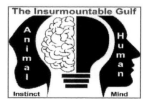

A Brief Summary

To sum up, after examining the 12 theistic arguments above taken from the ontological, cosmological, teleological and anthropological categories, it is clear that we have produced a sound basis for theism. Like one rope strand, each argument is strong. But when juxtaposed together, like intertwined strands of a rope, these arguments establish an overall case for God that is extremely compelling. Hence, the words of Psalm 14:1 and Psalm 53:1 should not surprise us. Here the psalmist says:

The fool says in his heart, "There is no God."

Indeed, our theistic case has shown that atheism is totally untenable. One could argue, in fact, that it is impossible to be an atheist when we see that atheism purports an absolutist claim. Dr. Ron Carlson notes this paradox in his book, *Fast Facts on False Teachings*. Carlson writes: "It is philosophically impossible to be an atheist, since to be an atheist you must have infinite knowledge in order to know absolutely there is no God. But to have infinite knowledge, you would have to be God yourself. It's hard to be God yourself and an atheist at the same time!"[37]

All in all, theism seems undeniably credible! As we saw, to deny God would be to deny the idea of a *Necessarily Existent Eternal Deity*, a being who is the *Uncaused Cause* of the cosmos, the *Architect-Designer* of nature's irreducible complexity and the *Life-Generating Person* behind the personal attributes that humans possess. It is interesting to note that the "God" toward which our theistic arguments point is beginning to look like the God of Christianity, for the Christian God is indeed (a) necessarily existent in regards to the cosmos, (b) initiative in regards to causality, (c) intelligent in regards to creation and (d) personal in regards to character.

Before moving on, we must note that Hebrews 1:2 claims that God "made the universe" through Christ. So, although theism is cogent, we must still investigate Christ. To do this, we turn now to where Christianity finds its foundational roots, the pages of the four biblical Gospels, for it is in these documents that we see emerge the possible historicity and true identity of Christ. If the Gospels are true, then Christianity possesses a solid foundation; if they are false, then Christianity collapses.

Note: For those curious about the specific "God" viewpoints of the most widely-practiced world religions outside of Christianity, namely, Judaism, Islam, Hinduism and Buddhism, I have added a useful chart on page 73.

Views on "God" from Four World Religions

JUDAISM

The Star of David

Judaism began about 4000 years ago when Abraham, the father of the Jewish faith, was living in the land of Canaan. Jews believe that God, who is eternal and personal, chose them to be his special people and made a covenant (contract) with Abraham wherein God promised to care for the Jewish nation and give them a "Promised Land" if they, in turn, would follow his laws and obey him. The Jewish Bible — or Tenakh — which possesses the exact same writings as the Christian Old Testament, teaches that God is a "jealous God" and that he detests disobedience to his laws as well as idolatry (the worship of false gods). As recorded in the Tenakh, early on in Jewish history, there arose the prophetic hope of a leader called the "Messiah" who would be sent by God to re-establish a Jewish kingdom and a permanent age of prosperity, peace and justice. Jesus ≠ God or Messiah.

ISLAM

The Crescent and Star

Founded in the early 600"s A.D. by the prophet Muhammad, Islam is — to date — practiced by about one billion Muslims. Muslims believe first and foremost that "there is no God but Allah, and Muhammad is His prophet." This declaration is called the Shahadah. Islam teaches that Allah is "eternal" and "absolute," meaning that He is not dependent on any person or thing, but all is dependent on Him. Thus, the basic "God" message of Islam is that Allah and His Creation are distinctively different entities. The most concise definition of God in Islam is given in the four verses of Sura Iklas (Chapter 112) of the Qur'an (the Holy Book of Muslims). Here it says: "He is Allah, the One and Only. Allah, the Eternal, Absolute. He begets not, nor is He begotten. And there is none like unto Him." Muslims thus firmly reject the Christian concepts of the divine Trinity and Incarnation. Jesus is a prophet.

HINDUISM

The Sound-Symbol "Om"

Founded in India in c. 1750 B.C., Hindus believe in Braham, an absolute, unchanging reality, a reality that exists beyond the tangible world of appearances. Some Hindus see Braham as God, and as such — even though Hinduism is polytheistic and purports thousands of gods — these Hindus believe that all of the "gods" expressed in Hinduism are simply representations or aspects of the one reality, the one supreme God, which is often referred to in the Hindu Scriptures (or Vedas) as "It." This "It" — or Braham — in its natural state, is both formless and attributeless, both transcendental and intermixed with everything; it is the Supreme reality. Thus, the ultimate goal of a Hindu is to achieve a perfect state of moksha, a state where a person is released from the cycle of death and rebirth (samsara) and free to become "one" with this invisible reality. Moksha is nearly identical to the Buddhist concept of nirvana. Of 1B+ Hindus, 79% live in India.

BUDDHISM

The Eight-Spoked Wheel

Buddhism actually grew out of Hinduism and is based upon the teachings of a Hindu prince named Siddartha Gautama who lived from 563 — 483 B.C. and was (supposedly) the first human being ever to become "enlightened" — to understand the meaning of all things. Hence, the title "Buddha" (which means enlightened one) was attributed to Gautama. Buddha believed that we must rid ourselves of desire in order to free ourselves from suffering, and when we do this perfectly, we can achieve — as Buddha did — the state of nirvana, or a state of being in which we are freed from the cycle of rebirth. For Buddha, the need to address the problem of suffering was too urgent to waste time in empty speculation about the question of whether God exists. Though Buddha did not answer the "God" question, most Buddhists today, in general, are pantheistic in their approach, believing that God is an impersonal force which is made up of all living things.

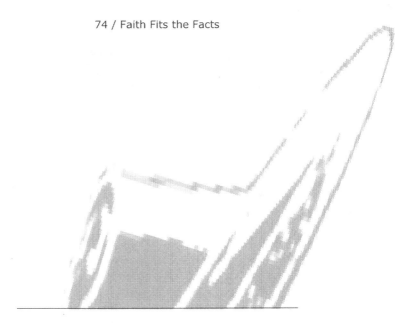

"Evidences from the first and second centuries reveal that eyewitness testimony about Jesus emerged rapidly and circulated reliably. The New Testament texts relied on testimonies from apostolic eyewitnesses, and all of these texts were completed while the eyewitnesses were still alive."

– Timothy Paul Jones

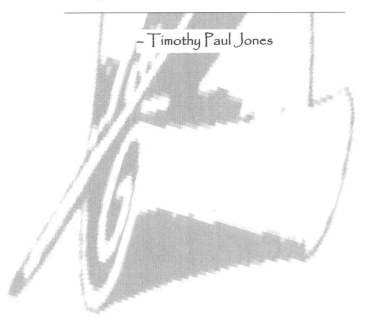

Gospels

2

> "I have read in Greek and Latin, scores of myth, but I did not find the slightest flavour of myth here. There is no hysteria, no careful working for effect, and no attempt at collusion."

— Scholar J. B. Philipps
describing his first meticulous analysis
of the four biblical Gospels

Pictured above is a fragment of the *Dead Sea Scrolls*, first-century writings of the Jewish Essenes, discovered at Qumran, Israel in 1947. This photograph offers an excellent depiction of how the original Gospel papyri manuscripts of Matthew, Mark, Luke, John would have appeared to readers.

The four Gospels are without a doubt the most important books for Christianity, for in the Gospels we come face to face with the historic Jesus. Through the Gospel texts, we learn most of what we know about Jesus' life. Although we have fragments of Jesus' words and acts from the New Testament epistles, this in no way compares to the details found in the four Gospels. So, if we want to cogently defend the Christian worldview, we must first defend the works that tell us about its founder, and these works are the four biblical Gospel accounts of Matthew, Mark, Luke and John.

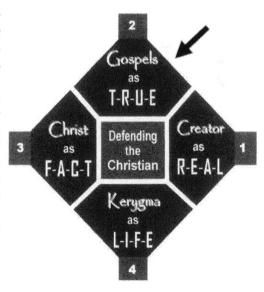

Fast Fact: Collectively, the 4 Gospels present 3,779 separate verses written in Koine Greek.

To begin, let us examine AT-A-GLANCE the basic outline divisions and themes of each Gospel to get a sense of how these books are organized.

#1: Viewing AT-A-GLANCE the Gospels' Themes & Divisions

MATTHEW AT-A-GLANCE

THEME	Offer of the Messiah			Rejection of the Messiah			
REFERENCE	1:1	4:12	8:1	11:2	16:13	20:29	28:1 28:20
DIVISION	Presentation of Messiah	Proclamation of Messiah	Power of Messiah	Rejection of Messiah	Preparation of Disciples	Presentation & Rejection	Proof of Power

MARK AT-A-GLANCE

THEME	He Came Humbly to Serve			He Came to Sacrifice		
REFERENCE	1:1	2:13	8:27	11:1	16:1	16:20
DIVISION	Presentation of the Servant	Opposition to the Servant	Instruction by the Servant	Rejection of the Servant	Resurrection of the Servant	

LUKE AT-A-GLANCE

THEME	Advent	Activities	Admonition	Authentication
REFERENCE	1:1 4:14	9:51	19:28	24:53
DIVISION	Early Life of the Savior	Ministry of the Savior	Rejection of the Savior	Crucifixion & Resurrection of the Savior

JOHN AT-A-GLANCE

THEME	Incarnation	Revelation	Rejection	Instruction	Salvation
REFERENCE	1:1	1:19	5:1	13:1	18:1 21:25
DIVISION	Incarnation of Son of God	Presentation of Son of God	Opposition of Son of God	Preparation of the Disciples	Death/Resurrection of Son of God

As we examine the outlines of these works, we can see that each book indeed provides us with vital data about Christ. Consider the limited bio-facts that can be gleaned from NT sources apart from the Gospels:

New Testament Data on Jesus Apart from the Gospels

1. He was a descendant of David (Rom. 1:3)
2. He was raised as a Jew under the law (Gal 4:4)
3. He was truly a man (1 John 4:1-3)
4. He was poor as a child (2 Cor. 8:9)
5. He was gentle and meek (2 Cor. 10:1)
6. He was a righteous man (1 Pet. 3:18)
7. He was perfectly sinless (2 Cor. 5:21; 1 Pet. 2:22)
8. He was a humble man (Phil 2:6)
9. He was truly tempted (Heb. 2:18; 4:15)
10. He said love neighbors as oneself (Rom. 13:9)
11. He presided over a Lord's Supper (1 Cor. 11:23)
12. He experienced a Transfiguration (2 Pet. 1:17)
13. He experienced hostility (Heb. 12:3; Rom. 15:3)
14. He was betrayed (1 Cor. 11:23)
15. He was crucified under Jews (1 Thess 2:14)
16. He suffered without resisting (1 Pet. 2:21)
17. He rose from the dead (1 Cor 15:3)
18. He ascended into heaven (Eph. 4:8)
19. He said to love our enemies (Rom. 12:14)
20. He said the Holy Spirit would come (Acts1:8)[1]

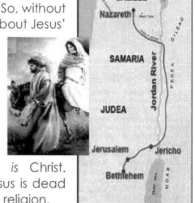

These verses offer some detail about Jesus' life and teachings, but they are fragmentary. So, without the Gospels, we would lack most details about Jesus' life. For example, we would never know Mary and Joseph had to walk about 90 miles in order for Jesus to born in Bethlehem (a prophecy of Micah 5:2; see map) So, it is thus vital we defend the reliability of the Gospels if we are to cogently establish the reality of Jesus' divinity, as well as the veracity of Christianity itself, for Christianity really *is* Christ. Indeed, if the Gospels are false, then Jesus is dead and Christianity is a fake and meaningless religion.

#2 – Seeing the Gospels as "Portraits" – Not Biographies

Before engaging in Gospel apologetics, we must first understand that these books are technically not biographies in the ordinary sense, but evangelistic portraits. Although they are often referred to as biographies, they do not really fit that literary genre. Their accounts of Jesus' life are too incomplete, and topics are often arranged topically, not chronologically. Also, they contain no physical description and little is said of Jesus' youth. Matthew 2 recounts his birth, visit of Magi, and escape to Egypt, while Luke 2 recounts his birth, day-eight circumcision, and Jerusalem Passover visit (age 12). And nothing is said about Jesus' Nazareth years except Matt. 2:23 indicates that he grew up in that tiny Galilean village. ➡

Jesus' Hometown: He Grew Up Poor

In John 1:46, Nathanael comments about Jesus, "Can anything good come from Nazareth?" Why? Because it was known to be a desolate and poverty-stricken town. Archeologists now claim it had no more than 150 residents.

However, if we understand first-century literary techniques, we see why the Gospel authors wrote what one might expect, for each Gospels was written in Koine Greek (see alphabet below). As one who minored in biblical Greek in college, I learned Greek literary conventions permeated

most Jewish literature. What did these say? In a nutshell, first-century writers had complete freedom to rearrange their source material. So, it should not surprise us that Matthew and Mark have many events in Jesus' life placed in different order. The Gospels were not meant to be chronological biographies in a technical sense. Many Gospel critics miss this key point.

The lack of insight regarding the Gospels' literary conventions has often caused well-meaning interpreters to posit absurd theories to explain the presence of Gospel details that conflict with their view that the Gospels must be chronologically arranged. As a result, Jesus is claimed to have performed the same miracle more than once, to have been twice crowned with thorns or denied by Peter six or more times, and so on.[2] When we understand, however, that the Gospel materials were frequently arranged for topical rather than chronological reasons, such fallacious reasoning can be avoided. In his *IVP Bible Background Commentary*, Dr. Craig S. Keener reinforces that chronology was not of primary importance to first-century Greek writers, including the Gospel writers. Keener writes:

Although Jesus, like other Jewish teachers, surely repeated the same sayings on separate occasions, some of his sayings probably occur in different places in the Gospels simply because the writers were exercising the freedom ancient biographers had to rearrange their material.[3]

This Greek-based freedom enabled each Gospel writer to preach about Jesus as well as to report about him, to craft unique theological perspectives about Christ in addition to recalling his words and deeds. As Dr. Greg Boyd puts it, "the Gospels do what no *snapshot-tape-recording* account of Jesus could ever do; they bring out the theological and personal significance of His life and teachings for readers. They can only be faulted for doing this if they were themselves trying to adhere to a 21st-century *snapshot-recording* criteria of literary accuracy."[4]

The Gospels were not meant to be bio-data recordings of Jesus life.

What each Gospel writer drafted then was not a detailed story of Jesus' entire life, but a *vivid portrait* of his person and ministry, a distinct image designed to create faith among non-believers and to fortify faith among believers. Although all four Gospels portray Jesus as one who (a) was uniquely sent by God, (b) performed great miracles, (c) associated with societal outcasts, (d) taught a virtuous ethic, (e) lived out a sinless life,

(f) experienced hatred from top Jewish leaders and (g) was by God's design crucified and raised from the dead, each Gospel is also very unique. That is, in the Gospels we encounter the person of Jesus Christ through the eyes of four unique writers, each of whom sought to portray Jesus in purposeful and distinctive ways in order to meet the particular needs of the people for whom they were writing:

4 GOALS

Matthew: for the *Jews*, to demonstrate that Jesus of Nazareth was the promised Christ (or Messiah) of Israel, the fulfillment of OT messianic prophecies;

Mark: for the *Romans*, to present Jesus as the Anointed Servant of the Lord in all his conquering and miraculous power;

Luke: for the *Greeks*, to portray Jesus as the perfect human Savior of humankind;

John: for the *Church*, to reveal Jesus as the Eternal Word made flesh, the incarnate God-man who had secured eternal life for all who believe.

From the very beginning, it appears the church desired each of these four perspectives. It is an impressive fact that from an early date, well before the end of the second century A.D., the four Gospels (and none other) were accepted and recognized by the universal Christian church as part of the authentic Christian Scriptures. In fact, other so-called "gospels," such as the Gospel of Thomas, were firmly rejected. So were attempts to turn the four Gospels into one composite volume.[5] The Church was clear that all four records were needed; each added valuable insights to the total picture of Christ, his mission, teachings and miracles.

In sum, the Gospels, when placed together, provided for the early Church a multi-faceted, fourfold portrait of the risen Jesus, a portrait which was sufficient to convince others of Jesus' true identity. Each Gospel thus forms part of a whole; if we keep the whole portrait in mind as we seek to do Gospel apologetics, we shall come to see the whole Christ.

#3 – Gospel Apologetics: Showing that the Gospels are T-R-U-E

But do the Gospels measure up to rigorous scrutiny? Are they each historically accurate, reliable and true? This is really the bottom line: truth! The Gospels must be true for Christianity to be true. If the Gospels are false, the world's two billion Christians might as well close down every Christian church and find a new religion, for Christ would still be dead.

Let us now investigate then the best of Gospel apologetics and see if we can build a cogent case which demonstrates that the Gospels *are*, in fact, T-R-U-E accounts of Jesus' life, words, ministry, death and resurrection. We shall build a cumulative case here by carefully examining four attributes of the Gospels which relate to both internal and external evidence categories. Our case can be summarized by the second main acrostic in our Diamond of Truth, i.e., T-R-U-E., which unpacks as follows:

DoT Acrosic #2

The Christian Gospels possess:

Textual Integrity — Passing Three Bibliographic Tests

Reliable Authorship — Four Portraits: One C-A-S-E

Undeniably R-E-A-L History — Internal & External Evidence

External Corroboration — Works of Josephus, Tacitus & Pliny

These four arguments will provide cogent answers to the following four respective questions, each of which must be effectively addressed if we are to produce a compelling Gospel apology:

T – (1) Is the text that we now see in the Gospels what was originally written?

R – (2) Is what was written compiled by reliable, trustworthy and credible authors?

U – (3) Is what these Gospel authors wrote completely accurate and historical?

E – (4) Can the Gospels be corroborated in any way by unbiased external sources?

If we can show that "yes" is an appropriate answer to all of these questions, then the Gospels can be relied upon to give us an accurate and T-R-U-E portrayal of Jesus, something that is vitally important if we are to ultimately construct a cogent case for Christ. So, let us now turn to addressing question (1) above: Is what we now have in the Gospels actually what the Gospel writers originally wrote? This question addresses the crucial bibliographic issue of the Gospels' textual integrity.

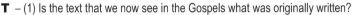

Textual Integrity

Passing Three Bibliographic Tests

The testing of ancient documents for authenticity is actually a common practice among literary scholars. Such testing falls under the well-established principles of historiography, or the academic discipline concerned with establishing proper techniques and methods for historical research and scholarship. So, we need not reinvent the wheel here. To determine the *authenticity* of ancient works, historiographers always use what is called the Bibliographic Test. This test addresses a critical issue. It

attempts to carefully examine ancient documents and determine the accuracy of textual transmission over the centuries, e.g., to see if any tampering has occurred. As applied to the Gospels, the issue before us is whether our current copies are accurate reproductions of the original Greek manuscripts first produced.

The Bibliographic Test is not just one test, but three separate tests. That is, it attempts to answer three distinct questions regarding the textual transmission of any ancient document that we desire to evaluate:

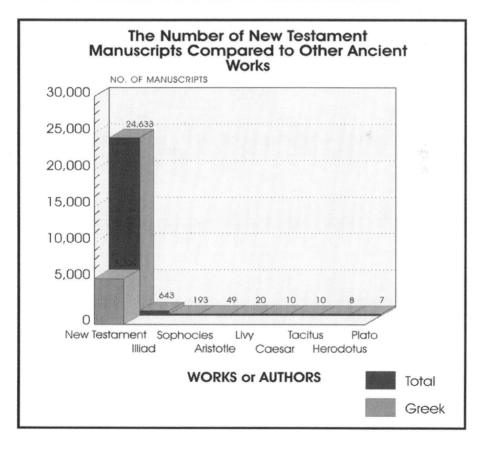

Bibliographic Test #1 — How many manuscripts exist of the ancient document(s)?
Bibliographic Test #2 — How early are the manuscripts that we possess?
Bibliographic Test #3 — How accurately were the manuscripts copied over time?

We must now apply each of these tests to the Gospels, and to the New Testament as a whole, if we are to be truly confident of the textual integrity of these bibilical sources. Let us begin.

Bibliographic Test #1: HOW MANY MANUSCRIPTS EXIST?

Answer: More than 24,000 handwritten copies of the New Testament currently exist, far more than any other ancient document.[6] Consider the 3-D graph I have created below which compares the amount of New Testament documents vis-à-vis other well known ancient works:

The Number of New Testament Manuscripts Compared to Other Ancient Works

NO. OF MANUSCRIPTS

30,000

25,000 — 24,633

20,000

15,000

10,000

5,000

0

New Testament   Sophocies   Livy   Tacitus   Plato
        Illiad   Aristotle   Caesar   Herodotus

643   193   49   20   10   10   8   7

WORKS or AUTHORS

■ Total
■ Greek

Bibliographic Test #2: HOW EARLY ARE THE MANUSCRIPTS?

Answer: The Bodmer and Chester Beatty papyri (c. A.D. 175-250) consist of major copies of the New Testament which were written approximately 100-150 years from the originals, earlier than any other ancient work! The 3-D graph below shows specifically how early these documents are vis-à-vis the best and earliest examples of secular ancient literature:

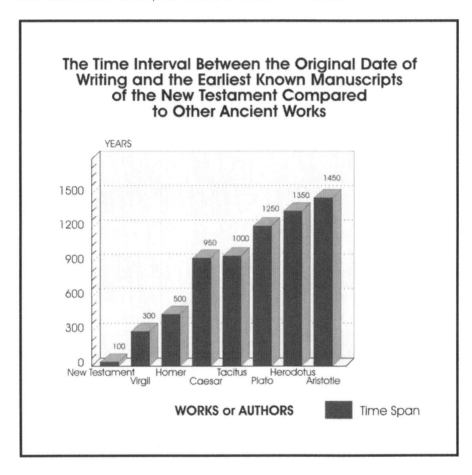

As we can see from the above data, no other ancient literary work even comes close to the Gospels when it comes to the topic of time interval between the original source and its later copies. Consider the words of Bible scholar, Dr. Bruce Metzger, on this point:

The works of several ancient authors are preserved to us by the thinnest possible thread of transmission. In contrast, the textual critic of the New Testament is embarrassed by the wealth of his material.[7]

Bibliographic Test #3: HOW ACCURATE ARE THE COPIES?

Answer: The data for the New Testament is incredible vis-à-vis other ancient documents. Only 40 lines — or 1/5 of 1% — are distorted.[8] This is 25x more accurately copied than the best of ancient literature. Again, consider the graphic depiction of this amazing fact:

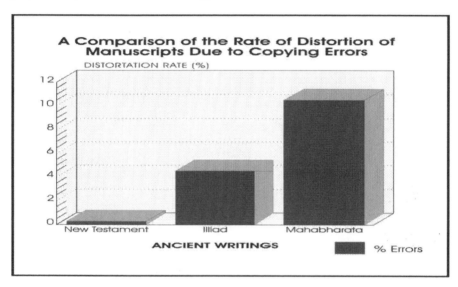

A Comparison of the Rate of Distortion of Manuscripts Due to Copying Errors

Given this remarkable data, which satisfies our three tests above, it is no surprise that Dr. F.F. Bruce, a world-renowned expert in the field of historiography, has determined the New Testament to be superior vis-à-vis all other ancient manuscripts. His erudite findings provide an excellent summary of what we can confidently conclude regarding the three-parts of the Bibliographic Test. Bruce is probably quoted in apologetics books more than any other scholar. As such, I have consolidated his most famous quotes in an all-in-one format here for easy reference:

F.F. BRUCE QUOTATIONS

Re: Test #1:   There is no body of ancient literature in the world which enjoys such a wealth of good textual attestation as the New Testament.[9]

Re: Test #2:   No other ancient book has anything like such early and plentiful testimony to its text [as the NT], and no unbiased scholar would deny that the text that has come down to us is substantially sound.[10]

Re: Test #3:   The variant readings about which any doubt remains among textual critics of the New Testament affect no material question of historic fact or of Christian faith.[11]

It is difficult to formulate conclusions which are more erudite than those of Dr. Bruce. So, I will not try. I will just say that, if the reader desires to investigate these historiography issues further, in a detailed manner, Bruce's works are some of the most extensive in the world (see Endnotes).

R Reliable Authorship
Four Portraits: One C-A-S-E

We have demonstrated that the Gospels pass bibliographic tests. But how can we know that what the first-century writers wrote is actually true? Can we *trust* the writers? Maybe Mark liked fairy tales or John was a pathological liar. Just because we have an authentic record, does not mean that we possess T-R-U-E history. So far, we have only showed that, in comparison to other works of antiquity, Christianity possesses (a) more manuscripts, (b) earlier manuscripts and (c) more accurately copied manuscripts. But how can we know that the portrait of Christ which was painted by the Gospel is really the portrait of the real historical Jesus? We were not present to see Jesus' life and deeds, so how can we be confident that what the Gospels *say* happened really *did* happen?

Consider this real-life anecdote. My firstborn son, Joshua David Carlson, whom I so named in honor of Jesus' Aramaic name *Jeshua*, once proudly told me he had "ridden a bike" to the store. I was stunned since he, being age four, did not know how to ride a bike. Later, I found out that Joshua did not specify what had actually occurred. His nanny had supported him while he rode. I add this anecdote to illustrate that, whenever we encounter a truth-claim, even one made by an innocent child, we cannot "assume" such a claim is accurate. This is especially true if we are investigating the historical truth-claims of ancient authors. To be

fair apologists, we must always distinguish indisputable fact from innocently told (or intentionally concocted) fiction, for all historical truth-claims, including the Gospel miracles, need to be meticulously scrutinized. Indeed, we must always be open to all possibilities, and *never* blindly "assume" any proposed truth-claim to be true.

At this point, we have only established one undeniable truth, that the Gospel authors painted a unified collage of Jesus. That is to say, they all agreed that Jesus was truly sent by God. Although each man showed this fact in distinct ways in accordance with the needs of his audience, when we fuse the Gospels together, we do see a single C-A-S-E emerge regarding the identity of Jesus, a case which points to a divine being who fulfilled God's plan for salvation as prophesied by the OT. Consider here the overall C-A-S-E that the Gospels make for Jesus' divine origins:

Four Gospel Portraits: One C-A-S-E

Christ (Messiah) : Matthew's Judaistic theme: "...*of whom was born Jesus, who is called Christ*" (1:16)

Anointed Servant : Mark's Roman theme: "*You are my Son whom I love; with you I am well pleased.*" (1:11)

Savior of World : Luke's Greek theme: "*The Son of Man came to seek and to save what was lost.*" (19:10)

Eternal Word : John's Church theme: "*In the beginning was the Word ...and the Word was God*" (1:1)

This C-A-S-E is nice to point out to a dialogue partner. But is it a *sound case?* Was each individual Gospel writer really a reliable source of data concerning this person named Jesus? Just because each Gospel author *said* Jesus was truly from God does not mean he actually *was.* This leads us to a pivotal issue: Reliable Authorship. Were the Gospel authors reliable sources of history? If the Gospel authors were not wholly credible (e.g., they did not base their accounts on eyewitness sources and/or had clear motives for formulating falsehoods), then we simply cannot trust what they purport, even if all four Gospel writers happen to agree (coincidentally?), as pointed out above, that Jesus was truly from God.

To establish their credibility as honest historians then, we must carefully investigate the identity and reliability of each Gospel author separately — Matthew, Mark, Luke, and John — particularly each author's eyewitness-based connection(s) to Jesus as well as the approximate time period at which each man crafted his specific portrait of Christ.

Author #1: JOHN MARK (Amanuensis of Peter the Disciple)

Nearly all scholars concur that Mark was the first Gospel written since (1) John was written last and (2) the literary similarities and differences between the three Synoptic Gospels, Matthew, Mark and Luke, reveal that

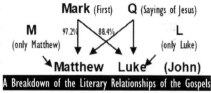

A Breakdown of the Literary Relationships of the Gospels

Matthew and Luke definitely (a) used Mark as a primary source (since 97.2% & 88.4% of Mark is paralleled in Matthew and Luke, respectively) and (b) Matthew and Luke used a source called "Q" (a collection of Jesus' sayings common only to their books), in addition to their own writing. These literary relationships are illustrated by the above diagram.

But who exactly authored Mark, the first Gospel written? There exists compelling evidence that John Mark was the author of Mark and that he set down Jesus' story as he heard it directly from the apostle Peter, who was a direct eyewitness of Jesus' ministry. The early second-century church father, Papias of Hierapolis, only one generation removed from the apostles, corroborates this fact. Papias tells us that, indeed, John Mark was the amanuensis of Peter and that he recorded Peter's words.[12]

Such usage of an "amanuensis" (or secretary) was common in the first century and would certainly explain why the Gospel of Mark is so

remarkably vivid; Mark indeed has the feel and substance of an eyewitness account. Consider these examples: (1) Whoever told Mark about the Mount of Transfiguration described Jesus' dress as being "dazzling white, whiter than anyone could bleach them" (see Mark 9:3); (2) And only Mark tells us Peter sat among the Jewish guards during Jesus' beating "warming himself" by the fire (see Mark 14:67). These are vivid, eyewitness-dependent details.

A companion to both Peter and Paul, John Mark's name occurs often in the Book of Acts and in Paul's epistles; "John" was the Jewish name and "Mark" the Latin name. In Acts 12:12, we see Mark's mother had a house in Jerusalem where the early church met. He was said to be a comfort to Paul in prison (see Colossians 4) and, as Peter's close travel companion, John Mark was loved by Peter as if he was Peter's own son (see I Peter 5:13). And so, it appears, based on the internal evidence from the NT as well as the external testimony of Papias of Hierapolis, that Peter himself, through John Mark as a secretary, gave us what is now called the Gospel of Mark. As such, this Gospel stems from a direct eyewitness of Jesus,

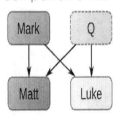

Rome's Colosseum was completed by Titus in A.D. 80.

one who himself became a martyr for Christ in Rome. Peter's martyrdom under Emperor Nero also corroborates the point that Peter, from Rome, was the source of Mark's Gospel, since John Mark wrote with a Roman constituency in mind, particularly given his use of Latin words and the pains he takes to explain Jewish customs to his Roman audience.

Author #2: LUKE THE PHYSICIAN (Companion of Paul)

In contrast to Mark's fast-moving pace, Luke offers the fullest life-story of Jesus. The biblical evidence and earliest church traditions from the first and second centuries point to the fact that Luke the physician, Paul's companion on his missionary journeys, was the author of the Gospel which

bears his name. We also know, from the way Luke changes from "they" to "we" in the Book of Acts (see Acts 16:10; 20:25; 27:1), that he was present at many of the early church events he describes. So, Luke is a reliable source regarding what eyewitnesses were saying about Jesus. As an early Christian and Paul's aide, Luke is, curiously, the only non-Jewish NT writer.

It appears Luke based much of his work on Mark's prior account and "Q" (mentioned earlier), in addition to his own material. This is significant since Luke's Book of Acts ends with Paul's detention in a Roman prison in A.D. 60-62. Since Luke does not record Paul's death (c. A.D. 67) nor

Jerusalem's destruction which took place in A.D. 70 and was prophesied by Jesus himself (see page 108), we can justifiably assume that Luke wrote both his Gospel and Acts before A.D. 62, which, in turn, means that Mark circulated his Gospel even earlier. In other words, we have before us two biblical Gospels which were clearly written during the time that eyewitnesses of Jesus were still alive, just three decades (or less) after Jesus' reported resurrection. This is a remarkable literary fact that bolsters the case that both of the texts of Mark and Luke were authentic historical accounts of the life of Jesus. In fact, as compared to any other ancient world document, the early drafting and dissemination of the Gospel manuscripts is unique. In fact, the pre-70 A.D. dating of Mark and Luke speaks volumes  about the trustworthiness of these authors' accounts. Any contemporary who lived at this time could have read their accounts and said: "Liar. That's not what happened!" But we see no ancient contemporary doubted the historicity of what these Gospel writers asserted.

Luke's Gospel is part one of a two-part history of Christian origins: (1) the Gospel of Luke and (2) the Book of Acts. Both of the documents are dedicated to the same person, Theophilus, called "most excellent" by Luke (see Luke 1:3 and Acts 1:1). Scholars are not exactly sure who Theophilus was. But there are some interesting theories. Since Theophilus can be translated "loved of God," some scholars have suggested that Theophilus is actually a *title* referring to a general audience and not a proper name. But this is unlikely. In the first century, the adjective "most excellent" designated an individual, particularly one of high rank. Most scholars believe Theophilus was an important Roman citizen (either a new believer or one curious about Christ), since Luke spends considerable effort trying to  offer Theophilus true facts about Christianity and early church history, particularly facts which could counteract the distorted rumors flying about at that time.[13] It appears that Luke wants to set the record straight for Theophilus regarding the verity of Christian belief.

Regardless of the identity of Luke's audience, Luke/Acts claims to be based on a thorough historical investigation and seeks to produce an "orderly account." Consider Luke's own words from Luke 1:1-4:

Many have undertaken to draw up an account of the things that have been fulfilled among us, just as they were handed down to us by those who from the first were eyewitnesses and servants of the word. Therefore, since I myself have carefully investigated everything from the beginning, it seemed good also to me to write an orderly account for you, most excellent Theophilus, so that you may know the certainty of the things you have been taught.

We know that Luke was a consummate historian because his accounts square perfectly with other respected secular historians of that era, such as the Jewish historian Flavius Josephus. Consider the following five historic references wherein Luke and Josephus find full agreement:

◆ Luke's account of the sudden death of Agrippa I in A.D. 44 (see Acts 12:20-33) is confirmed in detail by Josephus (12:20-23; cf. *Jewish Antiquities* 19:344-49).

Ananias
—High priest
(AD 47-58)
—Bribes, thief
—Murdered by
Zealots in 66

◆ Luke's report of a major Roman famine "in the days of Claudius" (see Acts 11:28) is also confirmed by Josephus (cf. *Jewish Antiquities* 220:101).

◆ Luke's report of the naming of Ananias as high priest in A.D. 47 (see Acts 23:2) is also recorded by Josephus (cf. *Jewish Antiquities* 20:103). See textbox for Josephus' data.

◆ Luke's reference to Felix as Roman procurator along with his Jewish wife Drusilla (see Acts 24:24) is corroborated by Josephus (cf. *Jewish History* 5:9) and also the Roman historian, Cornelius Tacitus (cf. *Annals* 12:54).

◆ Luke's mentioning of Agrippa II and Bernice, elder sister of Drusilla and widow of Herod (see Acts 25:13), is also cited by Josephus (cf. *Jewish Antiquities* 10:145).

Such perfect corroboration bolsters the case that what Luke wrote was entirely historically accurate. Outside of Josephus, two other external sources perfectly corroborate Luke's account of first-century history:

◆ Luke's identification of Gallio as the proconsul of Achaia in A.D. 51 (see Acts 18:12) has been confirmed by an inscription discovered at Delphi.

◆ Luke's report of Claudius' expulsion of the Jews from Rome in A.D. 49 (see Acts 18:2) is mentioned also by the historian Suetonius.

Luke's geographic accuracy was also impeccable. He cites 32 countries, 54 cities and nine islands in Luke/Acts without a single mistake. In sum, Luke was a quintessential historian. He did not want to fabricate fables. Instead, he says he "carefully investigated everything from the beginning" and constructed an "orderly account" (Luke 1:3) of Jesus' life the history of the early church. Consider the conclusions of three world-renowned experts regarding Luke's status and credibility as a historian:

Luke's symbol is the winged ox as his Gospel is about Jesus' sacrifice and the ox represents sacrifice. It has wings to show that Christ was a heavenly propitiation.

Expert #1: F.F. Bruce says: "Luke's record entitles him to be regarded as a writer of habitual accuracy."[24]

Expert #2: E.M. Blaidock, professor of classics at Aukland University, concludes: "Luke is a consummate historian, to be ranked in his own right with great writers."[25]

Expert #3: Sir William Ramsay, one of the world's greatest geographers, concluded, after 30 years of examining the external evidence for Luke's accounts, that "Luke is a historian of the first rank . . . one of the greatest."[26]

Author #3: MATTHEW THE DISCIPLE

But Luke was not the only meticulous historian to construct a Gospel portrait. The Gospel of Matthew was also carefully crafted so as to be linked to real history. Matthew, for example, records Jesus' Jewish family lineage (see Matt. 1), the visit of the Magi from the East and King Herod's decree to slaughter babies, aged two and below, in Bethlehem (see Matt. 2), the beheading of John the Baptist by Herod Tetrach (see Matt. 14), and the names of leaders, such as Caiaphas the high priest and Pontius Pilate, procurator of Judea (see Matt. 27).

But who wrote Matthew? The Gospel does not name its author but from earliest times it was attributed to Matthew, Jesus' disciple who served as a Jewish tax collector before joining the twelve. Like Luke, a majority of Matthew is identical with Mark, so Matthew used Mark as one of his sources in addition to his own memory as an eyewitness.[14]

Most biblical scholars date Matthew in the 60's A.D. It is unique among the other Gospels in one sense: it was written by a Jew for Jews. The Gospel contends that, in Jesus of Nazareth, the entire OT reached its appointed goal. Jesus was Israel's promised Messiah. As such, Jesus is identified with such Jewish titles as the "Son of David" (see Matt. 1:1), "God with us" (see Matt. 1:23), the "Son of Man" title (a divine title from Daniel 7) and the "Suffering Servant" (from Isaiah 53). So, Matthew's eyewitness position and Jewish heritage make him a credible source.

Author #4: JOHN THE "BELOVED" DISCIPLE

We now come to the Gospel of John. The author calls himself "the disciple whom Jesus loved" (John 21:20). By process of elimination, given that all other disciples are mentioned, scholars unanimously agree that the author must be the disciple John, son of Zebedee, brother of James. The early church believed it too. An ancient church tradition corroborated by Irenaeus, Tertullian and Clement, all second-century church fathers, says that an aged John dictated his Gospel from Ephesus in present-day Turkey. The John Rylands Fragment, found in Egypt, is the earliest known second-century copy of John and is dated at c. A.D. 117, proving undeniably that the Gospel had a first-century origin. His perspective is significant in that he, along with Peter and James, was allowed by to see Jesus' transfiguration (see Mark 9:2), he was the one to whom Jesus, from the cross, told to care for his mother (see John 19: 26-27), and was one who not only ran to the empty tomb, but saw the risen Jesus. So John was an extremely close source to Christ.

But we do not have to end with John. Look what happens when we examine the epistles of Paul, which were drafted even earlier than the Gospels. Paul, a former persecutor of Christians who knew the disciples personally (see Gal. 1:17), wrote at least 10 (likely 13) letters between A.D. 50 and 60 which capture essential events of Jesus' life. In fact, very early, within three decades of Jesus' death (since Paul died under Nero in A.D. 67), Paul taught that (a) Jesus was the virgin born (Gal. 4:4) and (b) pre-existent Creator of the cosmos (Col. 1:15-16) who had (c) existed as "God" and "man" (Phil. 2:5,8), (d) was a descendant of David (Rom. 9:5), (e) was betrayed the night he instituted a memorial Supper (1 Cor. 11:23), (f) was crucified by Rome (1 Cor. 1:23), and (g) rose from the dead after three days, having been seen by 500+ eyewitnesses (1 Cor. 15:4).

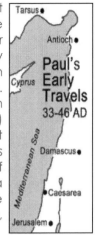

Paul's Early Travels 33-46 AD

To summarize this section on reliable authorship then, when we include Paul's early writings, we possess five reliable biographical sources for the life of Christ. The Gospel of Mark was written by John Mark, the secretary (or amanuensis) of Peter, a disciple who was an eyewitness of Christ and the primary source behind Mark's work. Given the synoptic data, it is clear Mark wrote his Gospel first and, hence, his portrait must be dated

prior to A.D. 62, since Luke used Mark as a source, and Luke's work includes historical events known to have occurred prior to and up to A.D. 62. The Gospel of Luke was written second-hand by Luke, yes, but he was nonetheless a close companion to Paul and a consummate historian who attempted to write an "orderly account." The Gospel of Matthew was written by the disciple Matthew and the Gospel of John by "the disciple whom Jesus loved" (John 21:20), namely John, son of Zebedee. Both these men, as members of Jesus' chosen 12, were direct eyewitnesses to his ministry. All in all, this data suggests that we can be extremely confident the Gospels originated from authentic, firsthand information regarding the life of Christ as the Gospel authors were each in perfect positions to write accurate portraits of Jesus' life and ministry.

U Undeniably R-E-A-L History

Internal & External Evidence

Having credible authors is important, to be sure. But the ultimate test, if we are judging the credibility of an ancient author, is also whether the author's claims can be substantiated both internally and externally.

To determine whether or not our Gospel writers, who seem to be credible, indeed constructed undeniably R-E-A-L history, we must apply internal and external tests used worldwide by historiographers. Internal tests establish criteria which apply "inside" historical documents while external tests apply "outside". Internal and external evidence for the Gospels as reliable historical documents is immense and can be concisely encapsulated by the acrostic R-E-A-L, which shows that the Gospel portraits present to us these four essential internal/external attributes:

R – Realistic Self-Damaging Data
E – Eyewitness-Based Accounts
A – Archeological Corroboration
L – Life-Changing Impact

The Romanesque tympanum found on the Church of St. Trophime in Arles, France depicts four winged creatures surrounding Christ, each of which symbolizes one the four Gospel evangelists.

 Realistic Self-Damaging Data

First off, we must realize that, if an ancient document is brutally honest, incorporating realistic "self-damaging" material which could possibly cast a negative image on a story's hero, this is a good "internal" indication that the author had truth as a central motive for writing. And the Gospels are full of realistic self-damaging data. For example, each of the disciples, for example, are consistently portrayed in a bad light. Jesus is always asking them, "Where is your faith?" For example, Simon Peter, the "rock," is shown to have thrice denied Jesus (see Matt. 26:75; Mark 14:72; Luke 22:61 and John 18:27) and Thomas, well he is now forever referred to as the "doubter." Moreover, aspects of Jesus' life are included which, if the story were being fabricated to fully convince others of Jesus' Messiahship, would certainly have been left out. Consider how two Gospels record that, while Jesus was suffering on the cross, he cried out: "My God, my God, why have you forsaken me?" There was no motive to add this other than the fact it actually took place.

Seven Last Words of Christ

1 — Father, forgive them; for they do not know what they are doing (Luke 23:34) – a prayer for the Jewish people and the Roman soldiers.

2 — Today, I tell you the truth, you will be with me in paradise (Luke 23:43) – his word to the repentant thief who was crucified beside him.

3 — Woman, here is your son! Here is your mother! (John 19:26-27) – commending his mother to the care of John, the "beloved" disciple.

4 — Eloi Eloi, lama sabachthani – which means, My God, my God, why have you forsaken me? (Matthew 27:46; Mark 15:34) – expressing the words of Psalm 22:1 as he felt abandonment.

5 — I am thirsty! (John 19:28) – a human reaction.

6 — It is finished! (John 19:30) – aware of his mission.

7 — Father, into your hands I commit my spirit (Luke 23:46) – revealing his steadfast faithfulness.

Citing these difficult-to-explain words does not help the Gospel writers' case. If their driving purpose was to portray Christ as the Messiah, this was *last* thing they would want to include. The only motive Matthew and Mark could have had to include Jesus' brutal question — *Eloi, Eloi Lama Sabachthani?* — is because Jesus actually stated these Aramaic words. They simply recorded what transpired, which we now know was the human nature of Jesus experiencing complete abandonment as he "who knew no sin became sin" (2 Cor. 5:21) on the cross. It is interesting to note here that the inclusion of the Aramaic text of Jesus' cry adds credence to the case that the sayings of Jesus, as stated in the Gospels, were derived from the historical Aramaic-speaking Jesus, not from the "imagination" of the Gospel writers. This is a key fact since it points to an early dating of the Gospels. Although Jesus and his disciples spoke in Aramaic, we know that in A.D. 50,

the early church began to speak mostly in Greek. Yet it appears many of the Gospel sayings of Jesus (recorded in Greek) were translated from Aramaic. Consider Dr. Greg Boyd's solid commentary on this point:

A very compelling case can be made . . . that many (if not all) of the sayings of Jesus in the Gospels are translations from an Aramaic original. For example, Jesus' statement that the Pharisees "strain out a gnat but swallow a camel" (Matt. 23:24) makes much more sense as an Aramaic pun, for in Aramaic gnat (galma) and camel (glama) sound nearly identical.[15]

E — Eyewitness-Based Accounts

As shown above, the Gospels' inclusion of realistic, self-damaging material, particularly material that quotes original Aramaic phrases, confirms that which we have already shown via our "Reliable Authorship" argument, namely, that the Gospels were based on eyewitness accounts. But do we have any other evidence to corroborate this claim? Yes. Consider this second "internal" argument. Eyewitness accounts are typically full of material, especially vivid details, which are not essential to a story. Fabricated accounts, by contrast, tend to be extraordinarily generalized. Do the Gospels then contain the types of vivid detail, and especially irrelevant detail, that typically accompanies eyewitness accounts? Definitely! Allow me to offer here one outstanding example of this fact which serves as an accurate characterization of the vivid writing style present in all the Gospels. Carefully read the John 20:1-8 resurrection-related passage below. Interwoven with John's text, I have underlined and italicized my own comments and questions. These underlined commentaries "flag" the presence of "irrelevant" and eyewitness-dependent details each time they surface in John's account, details which substantiate that John was indeed writing as an eyewitness.

In John 20:1-8, John, who labels himself Jesus' "beloved disciple" (see John 21:20), writes the following resurrection narrative:

Early on the first day of the week, while it was still dark (*who cares if it was dark*), Mary Magdalene went to the tomb and saw that the stone had been removed from the entrance. So she came running to Simon Peter and the other disciple, the one Jesus loved (*this is John's modest way of referring to himself*) and said, "They have taken the Lord out of the tomb, and we don't know where they have put him." So Peter and the other disciple started for the tomb. They were running, but the other disciple outran Peter and reached the tomb first (*John again is referring to himself; but who cares about who got their first?*) He bent over (*the tomb entrance appears to have been low — a specific detail consistent with archeological finds re: first-century tombs*) and looked in at the strips of linen lying there but did not go in (*why not?, irrelevant*). Then Simon Peter, who was behind him (*again John is reminding us of the fact that he was first to the tomb, not Peter!*), arrived and went into the tomb. He saw the strips of linen lying there, as well as the burial cloth that had been around Jesus' head (*irrelevant but interesting detail to ponder*). The cloth was folded up by itself, separate from the linen (*irrelevant but also fascinating: Jesus seems to have folded his shroud before he left*). Finally, the other disciple, who reached the tomb first (*again John points this fact out to us for a third time*), also went inside (*another irrelevant detail*).

I think the point has been made. There is absolutely no reason for John to throw in these types of *irrelevant details*, except for the fact that it is just a part of what transpired. John offers these details simply because, as he is writing, he is mentally recalling the events that he had experienced. He also shows a bit of human pride in the sense that he makes certain that we know — three times — that *he* got to the tomb first. The passage is undeniably eyewitness-dependent. A myth maker, trying to fabricate a story, simply would not write an account of this nature. And, interestingly, each of the Gospels are full of eyewitness-based accounts like this one.

So, we have looked at two "internal" features above pertaining to what eyewitness accounts typically include, namely self-damaging material and irrelevant detail, and we have demonstrated that the Gospels aptly pass these internal tests of authenticity. But what about "external" factors such as corroboration from archeology and/or secular history? How do the Gospels fare? Let us investigate these areas.

A ⚒ Archeological Corroboration

As one who enjoys archeology, I can find no archeological finding which refutes anything in the Gospels. But I do know of archeological evidence that undeniably corroborates these books. As famed archeologist Millar Burrows of Yale once noted: "On the whole, archaeological work has unquestionably strengthened confidence in the reliability of the scriptural record."[16] Consider these three examples of archeological corroboration which significantly substantiate the reliability of the Gospel records:

These three archeological finds relate to three major governmental figures — viz., Pontius Pilate, Caesar Augustus and Herod the Great — who presided over Palestine, the Roman Empire and Judea, respectively, during Jesus' day. These examples confirm, beyond any reasonable doubt, that the Gospel writers related their portraits of Jesus to the authentic history of the Roman-dominated society in which they lived.

Example #1: PILATE'S POST

Uncovered in 1961 at Caesarea Maritima, Israel, this inscription reads: "Pontius Pilate, the Prefect of Judea, has dedicated to the people of Caesarea a temple." The inscription provided the first archeological confirmation of Pilate's existence as well as his post in Rome's empire. All of the Gospel authors claim that this was indeed Pilate's job (cf. Matt. 27:11, Mark 15:1, Luke 3:1, and John 18:35-38.

Example #2: CAESAR'S CENSUS

We now know that the Roman empire, beginning with Augustus, held a census every 14 years.[17] The stone inscription above, citing Augustus Caesar, confirms that he ruled during the same period as the Luke 2 census, which forced Mary and Joseph to travel to Bethlehem, Joseph's ancestral town. The Luke 2:1-4 account is thus indisputably accurate, showing Luke tied his gospel to real history and locations.

Example #3: HEROD THE GREAT AND HIS HERODIUM PALACE

This photo portrays the remnants of a palace built by Herod the Great (72–4 BC) who ruled as King of Judea from 37 BC 'til his death. This palace / fortress, referred to as the Herodium, was built on a mound located three miles southeast of Bethlehem. It is here where Herod was buried. Many ancient sources corroborate the Matthew 2:17  theme that Herod was a violent ruler. Matthew records how Herod, in an attempt to kill the baby Jesus (whom the Magi called a king), ordered the massacre of all of the males in Bethlehem aged two-years-old and below.

And more examples of biblical archeological accuracy can be cited. Liberal scholars, for instance, used to argue that a town named Nazareth, Jesus' supposed hometown, did not exist during Jesus' day. But in recent decades archeologists have uncovered several references to this small, insignificant village. Similarly, John's long-doubted reference to the "pool of Bethesda" (see John 5:2) has also now been confirmed.

L — Life-Changing Impact

So, archeology undeniably bolsters our cumulative case. But one final "external" factor must be considered as we assess Gospel history. We must realize that Christianity was born in a very hostile environment. There were contemporaries of Jesus who, if they could, would have certainly refuted the Gospel portraits, particularly the resurrection claim. Dr. Greg Boyd aptly addresses this point in *Letters from a Skeptic*. He writes:

The leaders of Judaism in the first century tended to view Christianity as a pernicious cult and would have loved to see it stamped out. And this would have been easy to do — if the "cult" had been based on fabrications. Why, just bringing forth the body of the slain Jesus would have been sufficient to extinguish Christianity once and for all.[18]

Yet Christian believers exploded in the first century. Christians by the thousands, many of whom were monotheistic Jews, were even willing to undergo brutal deaths as martyrs. Peter is a prime example. Origen and Eusebius, second-century church fathers, both say Peter was "crucified upside down" because he did not consider himself worthy to be crucified in the same manner as his Lord.[19] Yet who would die in this way for a *known* lie? No sane person.

Vatican Sculpture of the Crucifixion of Peter

Were early Christians then *duped* into believing falsehoods? Not a chance. The evangelistic message that was preserved by the Gospel writers and proclaimed by the early apostles, such as Peter and Paul, was true, and, as such, it brought with it a LIFE-CHANGING IMPACT. In fact, we know conclusively that monotheistic Jews, who would detest worshipping a man, were, as early as A.D. 64, worshipping the God-man Jesus as Lord (see Pliny's epitome on page 99). What is to explain this incredible phenomenon other than the fact that the accounts concerning Jesus were based on real history? Indeed, opponents of Christ simply had no rebuttal that could stop the colossal tidal wave of Christian conversion.

Perhaps the most important fact to consider here is the *empty tomb* of Jesus. It is interesting to note that no person in the first century doubted that Jesus' tomb was empty; there was disagreement as to what happened to the Jesus' body. But no one doubted the tomb's *emptiness*.

Jewish leaders made up the story that the disciples "stole the body" (see Matthew 28:11-15). But how could the disciples have maintained such an elaborate hoax for even one minute without somebody exposing their lie? It is more credible to conclude that the disciples' passion about the resurrection stemmed from the fact that this event had actually occurred.

Consider the conclusion of scholar Robert Grant in his *Historical Introduction to the New Testament* as he comments on the fact that the eyewitnesses of Jesus possessed ironclad testimony. Dr. Grant writes:

At the time they [the synoptic gospels] were written or may be supposed to have been written, there were eyewitnesses and their testimony was not completely disregarded . . . This means that the gospels must be regarded as largely reliable witnesses to the life, death and resurrection of Jesus.[20]

In sum, the life-changing impacts manifested in the lives of people as a result of the Gospel stories took place very early on in the history of the church, within the period of the eyewitnesses, and this, in turn, attests to their complete authenticity. No honest person can dismiss this key fact.

External Corroboration

Works of Josephus, Tacitus & Pliny

Finally, in constructing a cogent defense of the Gospels, we need to be knowledgeable about the presence of external corroborating sources. Although when it comes to Christian sources, the corroboration is enormous, since the writings of early church fathers, such as Polycarp (see image below), Eusebius, Ignatius, and Origin, all significantly corroborate the Gospels' historicity, we must be careful, since one might contend that these early Christian historians had a pre-commitment to Christ, and hence a motive to assume Gospel authenticity. So, as we probe this area of Gospel apologetics, it is essential we find direct external corroboration from non-Christian, first-century historians. Three relevant ones exist: (1) Flavius Josephus, (2) Cornelius Tacitus and (3) Pliny the Younger. These three sources are secular, yes, but this is good because these men had no direct ties to Christianity; they were non-believers and thus had no motive to

POLYCARP

Most Famous Quote

"Eighty and six years have I served Him, and He has done me no wrong. How can I blaspheme my King who saved me?

"prove" Christ. Yet, remarkably, each man provides solid corroboration of many of the details found in the Gospels and the Book of Acts. So, let us examine all of these authors' works to see how the Gospels and Acts possess congruence with secular history.

Secular Historian #1: JOSEPHUS

The Jewish historian, Flavius Josephus, was born in A.D. 37, the year Gaius acceded to the throne of the Roman Empire, and he died in A.D. 100. He was the son of a priestly family and became a Pharisee at age 19. In A.D. 66 he was commander of the Jewish forces in Galilee. After being captured by the Romans, he was attached to the Roman headquarters where he did most of his writing and became a Roman citizen.[21] A contemporary of Christ, Josephus wrote of "the brother of Jesus, the so-called Christ, whose name was James" (*Jewish Antiquities* XX 9:1) and, most importantly, he wrote a brief epitome about Jesus himself.

Historical Portrait of Josephus Purchased in Jerusalem Market

Consider this remarkable, albeit contested, passage about Jesus taken directly from Josephus' *Jewish Antiquities* (XVIII, 63-64):

At this time there lived Jesus, a wise man, if indeed one ought to call him a man. For he was one who wrought surprising feats and was a teacher of such people as accept the truth gladly. He won over many Jews and many Greeks. He was the Messiah. When Pilate, upon hearing him accused by men of the highest standing amongst us, had condemned him to crucified, those who had in the first place come to love him did not give up their affection for him. On the third day he appeared to them restored to life, for the prophets of God had prophesied these and countless other marvelous things about him. The tribe of Christians, so called after him, has to this day not disappeared.

In this epitome, we see Josephus is the first secular historian to mention crucifixion, which he later wrote was "the most wretched of deaths." Referred to as Josephus' Testimonium, the epitome appears to be our most astounding reference by a non-Christian source to Jesus being the Jewish Messiah. Yet this is contested. Some scholars have thought it unthinkable that a Jewish historian would make such a claim.

Therefore, some have surmised that Josephus' passage must have been altered at a later stage to include the distinctive Christian elements. But, in my opinion, it is unlikely that the Testimonium is a late fabrication, since the text is quoted as authentic by the fourth-century historian Eusebius, a man who thoroughly researched all his sources.[22] It is then left for some unknown Christian scribe in the time before Eusebius to have supposedly altered the Testimonium to include more details about Christ.

But this assumes that such a scribe was willing to engage in an obvious fraud, contrary to the moral axioms of their faith. Moreover, the early church simply did not depend on secular historians such as Josephus for proof of Christ, so it is difficult to fathom that a Christian scribe doctored the original text of the Testimonium. I believe it is authentic.

When I was a seminary student, I became aware of the contested nature of Josephus' Testimonium after studying the passage in depth. At that time, I dismissed Josephus as a source. Perhaps all of his writings were in dispute. But in March of 1994, after touring the nation of Israel with my father, Rev. Dr. James H. Carlson, I learned from our tour guide, an expert on Josephus, that Josephus was actually an historian of the first rank.[23] Josephus corroborates not just the death and reported resurrection of Jesus, but a vast number of the events recorded in Acts (cf. page 88).

Secular Historian #2: CORNELIUS TACITUS

We now turn to our second historian. Like Josephus, Cornelius Tacitus (A.D. 55 -117) wrote during the reign of the Roman Emperor, Nero, who some conjecture went mad soon after his ascension to the throne. During Nero's reign, on the night of June 18 A.D. 64, a great fire broke out in Rome which lasted for six days and seven nights and then flared up sporadically for three more days. Ten of Rome's fourteen sectors were completely destroyed and Rome's citizens demanded justice. Some claimed that Nero himself had set the blaze.[27] A Roman citizen, Tacitus lived through this catastrophe and wrote much about Nero's life and his tortures.

This Roman coin from pre-A.D. 64 bears the image of Emperor Nero, a brutal ruler who executed thousands of early Christians.

In the epitome below, Tacitus explains how Emperor Nero wanted to find a scapegoat for the burning of Rome and that he picked the "Christians" to be his target. That is why Paul, for example, died under Nero in A.D. 67. Consider Tacitus' words from his *Annals* XV.44:

Hence to suppress the rumor [that Nero had burned the city of Rome], he [Nero] falsely charged with the guilt, and punished with the most exquisite tortures, the persons commonly called Christians, who were hated for their enormities. Christus, the founder of the name, was put to death by Pontius Pilate, procurator of Judea in the reign of Tiberius: but the pernicious superstition, repressed for a time, broke out again, not only through Judea, where the mischief originated, but through the city of Rome also.

This is an important fragment as it is not disputed. Although we see in Acts that "the disciples were first called Christians at Antioch" (see Acts 11:26), Tacitus is first secular historian to cite the label Christian to describe the *people of the Way*, which was the initial epithet used by Romans to describe believers in Jesus (see Acts 9:2, 19:9, 19:23, 22:4, 24:14 & 24:22). That is, Tacitus corroborates with Luke (and Josephus) that believers were called Christians as early as A.D. 64, the year of Rome's great fire under Nero. In referring to Christians, Tacitus also cites a brief but important fact concerning Jesus, namely, that his death was ordered by Pontius Pilate, procurator of Judea. All four Gospels, in Matthew 27, Mark 15, Luke 23 and John 18, corroborate that, indeed, this was Pilate's Roman post.

Secular Historian #3: **PLINY THE YOUNGER**

A final corroborating historian to consider is Pliny the Younger, a man who wrote his historical accounts in c. A.D. 111, the year that he was

appointed by Roman Emperor Trajan to be the governor of Bithynia. We know much about Pliny from his own writings. Whenever somebody sent the new governor a list of Christians' names, Pliny rounded them up and vigorously questioned them, for he knew that the new religion was illegal in Rome.

When confronting Christians, Pliny required that they (a) pray to the Roman gods, (b) burn incense to Emperor Trajan and (c) curse Christ, something he had heard Christians would never do.

Statue of Pliny in Como, Italy

If anyone refused, he had them executed, not so much for being Christian, as for their obstinacy. If they were a Roman citizen, he sent them to Rome to be imprisoned.[28] In a letter to Trajan, Pliny recites his achievements as the Bithynian governor, including his execution of many Christians. Pliny wrote he had tried to "make them curse Christ, which a genuine Christian cannot be induced to do" (Epistles X.96). In this same letter to Trajan, Pliny describes the practices of second-century believers:

They were in the habit of meeting on a certain fixed day before it was light, when they sang a hymn to Christ as to a god, and bound themselves to a solemn oath, not to do any wicked deeds, and never to deny a truth when they should be called upon to deliver it.

When we consider Pliny's words in connection with the writings of Tacitus and Josephus, the following five-part, secular perspective regarding Christ and early Christianity emerges:

(1) Jesus was crucified under Pontius Pilate.

(2) Some individuals, such as Jesus' disciples, sincerely believed Jesus had risen from the dead.

(3) The sect of Christianity, whose followers were called Christians, could not be contained, but spread like wildfire even to Rome.

(4) Nero and other Roman authorities persecuted and martyred many early Christians, especially if they did not curse Christ.

(5) Yet these early Christians persevered in worshipping Christ and leading dedicated lives in accordance with his teachings.

In summary, the secular portrait painted by these non-Christian historians, contemporaries of Jesus, is congruent with the historical data presented by the Gospels. Therefore, we can be fully confident that the  Gospel authors, when they crafted their portraits, were careful to deliberately tie their accounts to real history, despite the known fact that, in accordance with first-century literary conventions, each author (as we saw) used his freedom to rearrange material topically in order to present Christ with relevance to a given audience. Although each Gospel writer indeed tried to convince others of the truth of Christ, each man did so by drafting accounts consistent with factual T-R-U-E history. Their accounts are thus *undeniably reliable*. That said, it is not surprising that the Encyclopedia Britannica uses over 20,000 words, more than for any other figure, to describe the life of Jesus. Regarding all independent secular accounts of Jesus, like the three above, the article concludes: "These independent accounts prove that in ancient times even the opponents of Christianity never doubted the historicity of Jesus."

A Brief Summary

We have come to the end of our apology of the Gospel accounts. Let us now summarize, in five distinct points, what we have learned:

(1)   We saw that the Gospels should be viewed as portraits of Christ, not as biographies in the technical sense. In accordance with common Greek literary conventions, each Gospel author portrayed Jesus in distinctive evangelistic ways in order to meet the particular needs of the audience for whom they were writing.

(2)   Upon applying bibliographic tests used by historiographers, we saw that the Gospels possess incredible textual integrity and that, from the original papyrus copies to our modern-day versions, we can be extremely confident that the Gospels were passed down to us substantially sound. Specifically, in comparison to all other extant works of antiquity, the New Testament possesses (a) more manuscripts, (b) earlier manuscripts and (c) more accurately copied manuscripts than any other ancient work — no trivial feat.

(3)   When we include writings of Paul, we saw that a solid C-A-S-E can be made that we possess in our Bibles five reliable sources regarding Jesus' life. Each author composed their Jesus accounts from either a direct eyewitness perspective, such as Mark (through Peter), Matthew and John did, or wrote based on a thorough researching of firsthand accounts, such as Luke claims to have done. In sum, we saw that each of the Gospel authors were, undeniably, in credible, eyewitness-related positions to write an *accurate portrait* of the life, death and resurrection of Christ.

(4)   Based upon the fact that the Gospel records possess (a) realistic self-damaging material, (b) eyewitness-based accounts, (c) archaeological corroboration (such as that pertaining to first-century rulers like Pilate, Augustus and Herod the Great) and the fact that (d) the Gospels made a Life-changing impact on so many, we can conclude that the Gospel writers indeed presented R-E-A-L history based on solid truths, not fabrications or legends.

(5)   Finally, we saw that many of the historical events and teachings recorded in the Gospels are corroborated by external historians such as Josephus, Tacitus and Pliny. Josephus corroborates the Messiah claim of Jesus, his trial under Pontius Pilate and the resurrection claim; Tacitus corroborates the Gospels' account of Pilate's post; and Pliny confirms the undeniable fact that early Christians worshipped Christ as if he were God, a potent chronicle.

In short, the four biblical Gospels can be relied upon to provide us with an accurate historical collage of who Jesus was, what he said, and what he did. Dr. Clark Pinnock has written a sound conclusion about the trustworthiness of the Gospels in his 1968 publication, *Set Forth Your Case*. It is a conclusion that I believe is worth citing as a closing exclamation point (!) to this chapter on the biblical Gospels. Pinnock writes:

There exists no document from the ancient world witnessed by so excellent a set of textual and historical testimonies, and offering so superb an array of historical data on which an intelligent decision may be made. [We] cannot dismiss a source of this kind.[29]

Having established the accuracy and reliability of the Gospel records, i.e., the four unique "portraits" of Jesus offered by Matthew, Mark, Luke and John, we now turn to the third base in our Diamond of Truth, namely, defending Christ as F-A-C-T, for the divine nature of Christ must indeed be a fact if ecumenical Christianity is to be deemed undeniably true.

"You may accept the lofty claims of Jesus. ...
Or else you must reject Him as a miserable, deluded enthusiast.
There is really no middle ground. Jesus refuses to be pressed
into the mold of a mere religious teacher."

— J. Gresham Machen

Christ

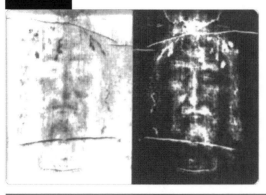

Pictured left is a real photo negative juxtaposed with the actual facial portion of the effigy present on the Shroud of Turin, a piece of linen kept in the Cathedral of St. John the Baptist located in Turin, Italy. Many Christians, including this author (cf. page 132), believe this shroud to be the authentic burial cloth of Jesus, one wrapped around his body after the crucifixion. There are no paints or dyes on the shroud and the imagery appears to have been caused by a heat or light scorch. The image's three-dimensionality has not yet been able to be reproduced or scientifically explained.

" Jesus is the son of God, you know." — The Archbishop of Canterbury

"Maybe he is for you, but he's not for me." — Response by Ms. Jane Fonda

"Well, either he is or he isn't." — Reply by the Archbishop

Conversation on the Dick Cavett Show, 1971

If we ask – What is Christianity? – the most accurate answer is Christianity is Christ. As soon as we open our Bibles we are confronted with prophecies and narratives concerning the person of Jesus Christ. Before investigating Christ, it is vital to note from the outset that if we examine the name *Jesus*, and the title, *Christ*, we see that both these terms affirm Jesus' true identity. The name Jesus was derived from the Greek form of the name *Jeshua* or *Joshua* which means "Jehovah-Savior"

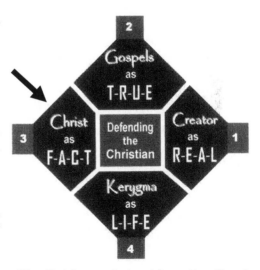

or the "God who saves"while the title Christ was derived from the Greek word for "Messiah" (or the Hebrew Mashiach; cf. Daniel 9:26) and means "the anointed one." So Jesus' name and title perfectly suit him if he was the God-man. But who was the real historical Jesus? Was Jesus really "divine" as claimed ecumenically by all Christian denominations? Or was Jesus a delusional rabbi who remains buried and dead? We all must decide.

To cogently answer this pivotal question, it is essential that we meticulously examine four miraculous aspects of Jesus' life as portrayed in the Gospels (which we have already seen to be reliable): (1) Jesus' fulfillments of prophecy, (2) his authority as the God-man, (3) his claims of divinity and (4) his resurrection. These four areas can be summarized by the third main acrostic fond in our Diamond of Truth: F-A-C-T. As we unpack this acrostic, one that can be potently used in person-centered dialogues, we shall see that Jesus, was in point of F-A-C-T, the promised Messiah, a God-man who not only fulfilled all Old Testament messianic prophecies and performed miraculous wonders, but a person who clearly claimed to be divine and substantiated this claim by accomplishing the greatest miracle of all, rising from the dead. Such an apologetic is vital to construct since many pseudo-Christian "cults" deny the divinity/eternality of Jesus. The F-A-C-T acrostic unpacks as follows:

Found in Syria & dated to 325, this is the oldest known Jesus' depiction.

The Christian Christ had:

DoT Acrostic #3

Fulfilled C-H-R-I-S-T Prophecies — Six Messianic Facts

Authority F-A-C-T-O-R-S — Seven God-man Powers

Claims of Divinity — The Trilemma: Liar, Lunatic or Lord

Tomb Made E-M-P-T-Y — Five Resurrection Evidences

F Fulfilled C-H-R-I-S-T Prophecies

Six Messianic Facts

To substantiate the assertion that Jesus was the promised Messiah, NT authors appealed to the fact that Jesus fulfilled OT prophecies. Luke summarizes this theme of prophetic fulfillment in Acts 3:18 (Amplified):

Thus has God fulfilled what He foretold by the mouth of all the prophets, that His Christ (the Messiah) should undergo ill treatment and be afflicted and suffer.

But did Jesus actually fulfill all, or even one, of the OT's prophetic utterances? Yes. When we examine the Gospels, we see Jesus perfectly fulfilled over 60 major messianic prophecies.[1] The chances of that taking place by coincidence has been accurately measured to be 1 in 10 to the power of 157, or the number 10 followed by157 zeros.[2]

What these odds mean is that either (1) this impossible feat did in fact occur, or (2) the Gospel writers deliberately manufactured Jesus' life to appear like it was prophetic, or (3) Jesus' fulfillments of prophecy were truly authentic. These are, logically speaking, our only options. Thus, we need to build a case which substantiates option (3) above if we want to validly add the subject area of prophecy to our defense of Christ's deity. To begin, consider the following list, with OT and NT references included, of just 20 major prophecies taken from the 60 supposedly fulfilled by Jesus throughout his life:

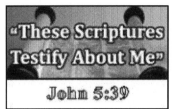

#1 — Born of a Virgin	Isaiah 7:14	Matthew 1:18-25
#2 — Of the Tribe of Judah	Genesis 49:10	Luke 3:23, 33
#3 — Descended from Jesse	Isaiah 11:	Luke 3:32
#4 — Of the house of David	Jeremiah 23:5	Matthew 1:17
#5 — Born in Bethlehem	Micah 5:2	Matthew 2:1
#6 — Preceded by a Messenger	Isaiah 40:3	Matthew 3:1-2
#7 — Carried by a Colt	Zechariah 9:9	Luke 19:35-37
#8 — Betrayed by a Friend	Psalm 41:	Matthew 26:48
#9 — Betrayed for 30 Coins	Zechariah 11:12	Matthew 26:15
#10 — Silent before His Accusers	Isaiah 53:7	Matthew 27:12
#11 — Pierced in His Hands/Feet	Psalm 22:16	Luke 23:33
#12 — Crucified with Thieves	Isaiah 53:12	Matthew 27:38
#13 — Able to Pray under Duress	Isaiah 53:12	Luke 23:34
#14 — Stripped of His Garments	Psalm 22:18	John 19:23
#15 — An Observer of Lots Cast	Psalm 22:18	John 19:24
#16 — Offered Gall and Vinegar	Psalm 69:21	Matthew 27:34
#17 — Free from Broken Bones	Psalm 34:20	John 19:33
#18 — Pierced in His Side	Zechariah 12:10	John 19:34
#19 — Buried with the Rich	Isaiah 53:9	Matthew 27:57
#20 — Raised from the Dead	Psalm 16:10	Acts 2:31

Cultural Fact: Genealogies were vital to the Jews as these showed the birthright to Abrahamic blessings & if one could serve as a Levite priest. Luke 3 tells us that the lineage of Jesus' mother, Mary, traced back to King David, whose descendant was prophesied to be the Jewish Messiah.

Jesus' Genealogy

Abraham

Jesse

David
Solomon — Nathan
Jeconiah — Heli
Joseph — Mary

If we examine only six uncontrollable messianic prophecies (out of these 20) which Jesus supposedly fulfilled, this will be sufficient to establish an undeniable case. I have concisely summarized these six prophecies by creating the below chart which utilizes the title C-H-R-I-S-T as an acrostic:

The Chi Rho Christogram: This widely-used ancient symbol is a monogram of the first 2 Greek letters found in the title Christ.

Prophecy Event	OT Reference	NT Reference(s)
Clear Davidic Lineage	Jeremiah 23:5	Matthew 1:17; Luke 3:31
Humble Bethlehem Birth	Micah 5:2	Matthew 2:1-2; Luke 2:4
Royal Jerusalem Colt Ride	Zechariah 9:9	Luke 19:35-37
Internal Betrayal By Friend	Psalm 41:9	Matthew 26:48-50
Suffering While Lots Cast	Psalm 22:16, 18	Mark 15:24; Luke 23:34
Tomb Corpse Resurrection	Psalm 16:10	Acts 2:31

Now let us examine the references of each of these six C-H-R-I-S-T prophecies to show how each represents a valid messianic prophecy uniquely fulfilled by Christ. If Jesus were a mere mortal, he simply would not have been able to orchestrate any one of these prophecies.

A
C
L
O
S
E
R
L
O
O
K

Prophecy C: CLEAR DAVIDIC LINEAGE

Prophecy: Jeremiah 23:5

Fulfillment: Matthew 1:17   The Star of David

"The days are coming," declares the Lord, "when I will raise up to David a righteous Branch, a King who will reign wisely and do what is just .

Thus there were fourteen generations in all from Abraham to David, fourteen from from David to the exile in Babylon and fourteen from the exile to the Christ

Prophecy H: HUMBLE BETHLEHEM BIRTH

Prophecy: Micah 5:2

Fulfillment: Matthew 2:1-2

But you, Bethlehem Ephrathah, though you are small among the clans of Judah, out of you will come for me one who will be ruler over Israel, whose origins are from old, from days of eternity.

After Jesus was born in Bethlehem in Judea, during the time of King Herod, Magi from the East came to Jerusalem and asked, "Where is the one who has been born king of the Jews? We have seen his star in th e east..."

Prophecy R: ROYAL JERUSALEM COLT RIDE

Prophecy: Zechariah 9:9

Fulfillment: Luke 19:35-37

Rejoice greatly, O Daughter of Zion! Shout, Daughter of Jerusalem! See, your king comes to you righteous and having salvation, gentle and riding on a donkey, on a colt, the foal of a donkey.

They brought it [the colt] to Jesus, threw their cloaks on the colt and put Jesus on it. As he went along, people spread their cloaks on the road. . .The whole crowd began joyfully to praise God in loud voices.

Commentary: The legend of the Jerusalem Donkey is a fascinating one. Nubian donkeys all possess crosses on their backs. Why? It is said that this donkey breed carried Jesus to Jerusalem on Palm Sunday and that, in reward for the humble love of the donkey for Jesus, the Lord caused the shadow of the cross to fall across its back so that the Jerusalem donkey could, in perpetuity, carry this symbol of the love of God for all to behold. I had the privilege of being able to ride the donkey species in Jerusalem in 1994 and indeed they wear a perfect cross adorned upon their back spine.

Prophecy I: INTERNAL BETRAYAL BY FRIEND

Prophecy: Psalm 41:9

Even my close friend, whom I trusted, he who shared my bread, has lifted up his heel against me.

JUDAS: THE BETRAYER

Fulfillment: Matt. 26:48

Now the betrayer had arranged a signal with them: "The one I kiss ... arrest him." Going at once to Jesus, Judas said, "Greetings, Rabbi!" and kissed him.

Prophecy S: SUFFERING WHILE LOTS CAST

FAST FACT:
Many believed God's will was discernable via "cleromancy," or the casting of lots.

Prophecy: Psalm 22:16, 18

A band of evil men has encircled me, they have pierced my hands and my feet. They divide my garments among them and cast lots for my clothing.

Fulfillment: Mark 15:24

And they crucified [Jesus]. Dividing up his clothes, they cast lots [dice] to see what each would get.

Prophecy T: TOMB CORPSE RESURRECTION

Prophecy: Psalm 16:10

You will not abandon me to the grave, nor will you let your Holy One see decay.

Fulfillment: Acts 2:31

Seeing what was ahead, he [David] spoke of the resurrection of the Christ, that he was not abandoned to the grave.

These C-H-R-I-S-T prophecy fulfillments form a potent case, to be sure. That said, Jesus' own prophetic predictions also came true. Consider these TWO Gospel-based examples, one regarding Jesus' prophecy of his own resurrection and one regarding the prophecy of the Jerusalem temple's future destruction:

#1: Jesus' Prophecy of a "Three-Day" Burial

Many have questioned the accuracy of Jesus' resurrection prophecy in Matthew 12:40 when he claims that just "as Jonah was three days and three nights in the belly of a huge fish, so the Son of Man will be three days and three nights in the heart of the earth." Skeptics ask: How could Jesus have remained buried for three days and nights since he was crucified on Friday and rose on Sunday? Although it is a perplexing question, the answer has to do with the conventional Jewish method of reckoning time. Different cultures talk about time in different ways. And the Jews were no exception to this.

For Palestine Jews in the first-century, any part of a day was reckoned as a full day, as evidenced by the *Babylonian Talmud* (Jewish commentaries) which states that, "The portion of a day is as the whole of it" and the *Jerusalem Talmud* which says, "We have a teaching, 'A day and a night are an Onah and the portion of an Onah is as the whole of it.'"[4] An Onah simply means a period of time. Scholars call this practice "inclusive reckoning" re the days, months, years, and events cited in the Old and New Testaments. Now we are ready to apply this "inclusive reckoning" concept to Jesus' resurrection story.

Since Jesus was in the tomb for at least a portion of three days, it is not at all culturally contradictory for Jesus to use the three-day analogy of Jonah to foretell his resurrection. When Jesus made this prophetic statement, it was idiomatic. Jesus' main point was that, after spending three "Onahs" in the grave, he would rise again on the third day. And he did. That said, it is worth noting that, although a few scholars cogently argue that Jesus was crucified on a Thursday, given that in 30 AD two Sabbaths were celebrated, these Thursday proponents still must use "inclusive reckoning" to account for that first day.

#2: Jesus' Prophecy of the Temple's Destruction

In Jesus' day, the Jewish temple located in Jerusalem was called the Second Temple. The first one – built by Solomon – was destroyed by the Babylonians in 586 B.C. In 520 B.C., the temple was rebuilt on a smaller scale under Zerubbabel. In 20 B.C., King Herod – not content with Zerubbabel's building – decided that he would build a lasting tribute to himself by doubling the area of the Temple Mount to what today would be the size of 20 soccer fields.[5] In doing this, Herod created the largest man-made platform in the ancient world. In Mark 13:1-2, as Jesus and his disciples were departing the temple, Jesus put forth an amazing prophecy regarding the "future" of this elaborate and enormous structure:

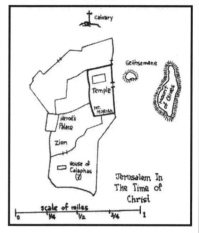

As he [Jesus] was leaving the temple, one of his disciples said to him, "Look, Teacher! What massive stones! What magnificent buildings! "Do you see all these great buildings?" replied Jesus. Not one stone here will be left on another; every one will be thrown down."

Jesus' prophecy of the obliteration of the Second Temple came to fruition ca. 40 years later when the 12th and 15th Legions of the Roman army — led by Titus, the son of Emperor Vespasian — destroyed Jerusalem (to put down a Jewish revolt) and burned the temple on ca. 28 August A.D. 70. Although the temple's immense retaining wall has endured the test of time and still dominates the vista of Jerusalem, only rubble remains of the original building.

BEFORE A.D. 70

This replica of the Second Temple (built to a 1:50 scale) can be seen at the Holyland Hotel in Jerusalem. During Jesus' day, this temple was admired as one of the most magnificent structures in the ancient world.

AFTER A.D. 70

As prophesied by Jesus in Mark 13:2, the temple walls were indeed "thrown down" by the Roman army in A.D. 70. Stone ruins excavated from the temple can still be seen lying adjacent to the western retaining wall.

Authority F-A-C-T-O-R-S

Seven God-man Powers

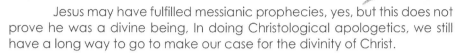

Jesus may have fulfilled messianic prophecies, yes, but this does not prove he was a divine being, In doing Christological apologetics, we still have a long way to go to make our case for the divinity of Christ.

For example, some heresies enunciated in church history, such as the Arianism of Arius, have argued that Jesus was indeed sent by God, but that he was still a finite and created being. As Arius used to say (and even sing), "There was a time when the Son was not!" But is such a proposition true? Was Jesus only a finite being, albeit a God-sent one? Or did Jesus' words and deeds substantiate that his true identity was divine? The bottom-line question is this: Did Jesus, in fact, have the divine AUTHORITY to do and say things only a God-man could do? Amazingly, in Matthew 28:18, Jesus himself boldly asserted the claim that he possessed ultimate divine authority when he made this remarkable statement:

> All authority in heaven and on earth has been given to me.

But how can we verify this claim? Fortunately, the four Gospels tell us much about Jesus' divine authority, namely, his authority over natural law (e.g., his ability to heal, to create food, to control weather, etc.), his authority to accept worship and forgive sin, and his authority over death and demonic forces. As we engage in Christological apologetics in order to substantiate the ecumenical Christian claim that Jesus was God with a human face, let us examine seven specific authority F-A-C-T-O-R-S which demonstrate undeniably and unambiguously that Jesus, as an alleged God-man, indeed possessed at least seven unique God-man powers, ones that could only be effectuated if Jesus were truly a divine being:

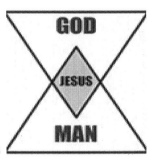

Divine Power	Gospel Text(s)
Forgiveness of Sins	Luke 5:18-25
Acceptance of Worship	Matthew 14:25-43
Control of Nature	Mark 4:35-41
Teaching Authority	Luke 4:31-32; John 7:14-18
Ordering of Demons	Luke 4:33-36
Raising of the Dead	John 11:17-18, 38-45
Salvation Proclamations	John 3:13-17; 14:6-7

As we examine these Gospel texts, we see they combine to make an overall case for the deity of Christ that is credible and undeniable. Carefully digest each passage and memorize the F-A-C-T-O-R-S.

The acrostic is useful for dialoguing with others, such as Muslims and Mormons, who claim Jesus was sent by God, but who, nonetheless, deny his divinity.

HEAVEN'S KEYS SYMBOL

Power F: FORGIVENESS OF SINS

Luke 5:20-25

[20]When Jesus saw their faith, he said, "Friend, your sins are forgiven." The Pharisees and the teachers of the law began thinking to themselves, "Who is this fellow who speaks blasphemy? Who can forgive sins but God alone?" Jesus knew what they were thinking and asked, "Why are you thinking these things in your hearts? Which is easier: to say, 'Your sins are forgiven,' or to say, 'Get up and walk'? But I want you to know that the Son of Man has authority on earth to forgive sins." So he said to the paralyzed man, "I tell you, get up, take your mat and go home." Immediately he stood up in front of them, took what he had been lying on and went home praising God.

Commentary

Fascinatingly, Jesus here took care of the most important thing first, that the paralized man be forgiven. But he also knew that the Pharisees were watching. He was, in essence, baiting them because he knew all about their dark hearts. That said, the Pharissees were still right in their assumption that only God can forgive sins. But the Pharisees were wrong in thinking that Jesus was being blasphemous. To the contrary, what Jesus was demonstrating to all present was that he was actually God. Anyone can say sins are forgiven, but only a God-man can make a man of palsy become perfectly whole.

Power A: ACCEPTANCE OF WORSHIP

Matthew 14:29-33

Then Peter got out of the boat, walked on the water and came toward Jesus. But when he saw the wind, he was afraid and, beginning to sink, cried out, "Lord, save me!" Immediately Jesus reached out his hand and caught him. "You of little faith," he said, "why did you doubt?" And when they climbed in the boast the wind died down. Then those who were in the boat worshipped him saying, "Truly you are the son of God."

More Gospel Examples: See Matt. 2:11, Matt, 28:9, Mark 16:1 and John 20:28.

Commentary

Here we encounter the miracle story of Jesus walking on water, and then Peter stepping out by faith to walk on the water too, toward Jesus. After seeing this incredible miracle, it is stated that the disciples in the boat worshipped Jesus. But who is worthy of worship? Only God. So, Jesus was either delusional or totally evil to embrace such worship, or he knew his divine identity and was thus able to accept their heartfelt worship.

Power **C**:  CONTROL OF NATURE

Mark 4:35-41

That ay when evening came, he said to his disciples, "Let us go over to the other side." Leaving the crowd behind, they took him along, just as he was, in the boat. There were also other boats with him. A furious squall came up, and the waves broke over the boat, so it was nearly swamped. Jesus was in the stern, sleeping on a cushion. The disciples woke him and said to him, "Teacher, don't you care if we drown?" He got up, rebuked the wind and said to the waves, "Quiet! Be still!" Then the wind died down and was completely calm. He said to his disciples, "Why are you so afraid? Do you still have no faith?" They were terrified and asked each other, "Who is this? Even the wind and waves obey him!"

Commentary

The cry of the disciples during the sudden storm which arose on the lake was obviously one of great fear and doubt. In fact, the squall got so bad that they thought they were going to die. After waking up, Jesus gives a double command, one of silence and stillness. And, to no surprise, since he was the Creator of every atom in the wind and the waves roaring at that time, physical nature instantly obeyed his rebuke. Many demythologists have tried to explain away the story. But we cannot viably interpret the passage in any other way than to concede Jesus indisputably effectuated this miraculous feat over nature because he was the one true Designer of nature.

SEA OF GALILEE

This photo of the Sea of Galilee, which I took in 1994, shows a possible location where Jesus miraculously calmed the violent storm (mentioned in Matthew 8:23-27, Mark 4:35-41 and Luke 8:22-25) as well as the place where Jesus was seen "walking on the lake" (see Matthew 14). The Lake of Galilee is the world's lowest fresh-water lake (680 feet below sea level) and covers an area of about 90 square miles. Violent storms can indeed strike this lake suddenly (as mentioned in the text above). Much of Jesus' ministry took place on and around this beautiful body of water. The panorama above was taken from the vantage point of the Tiberias fishing harbor (John 6:23).

Power T:━➤ TEACHING AUTHORITY

The New [Testament] is in the Old concealed. The Old is in the New revealed. — St. Augustine of Hippo

FAMOUS QUOTE

Luke 4:31 / John 7:14-18

Commentary

Then he went down to Capernaum ... and on the Sabbath began to teach the people. They were amazed at his teaching because his message had authority. / Not until halfway through the Feast did Jesus go up to the temple courts and begin to teach. The Jews were amazed and asked, "How did this man get such learning without having studied?" Jesus answered, "My teaching is not my own. It comes from him who sent me. If anyone chooses to do God's will, he will find out whether my teaching comes from God.

In the first text shown, Luke tells us something that all gospel writers said — viz. that people were always amazed at Jesus' teaching because he taught as one with great authority. In the second text, we see that Jesus makes it clear to his Jewish listeners that his teaching comes *directly* from God. Many times when Jesus taught, he would say things like, "You have heard it said, but I tell you that ....", and then he'd offer his God-man insight, just like when he re-defined *adultery* as being not just an act, but also being linked to the heart's lust. Clearly, Jesus' teaching carried divine wisdom.

Power O:━➤ ORDERING OF DEMONS

Satanic Symbols of Evil

Luke 4:33-36

Commentary

In the synagogue, there was a man possessed by a demon, an evil spirit. He cried out at the top of his voice, "Ha! What do you want with us Jesus of Nazareth? Have you come to destroy us? I know who you are — the Holy One of God!" "Be quiet!" Jesus said sternly. "Come out of him!" Then the demon threw the man down before them all and came out without injuring him. All the people were amazed and said to each other, "What is this teaching? With authority and power he gives orders to evil spirits and they come out!"

In this text, we see an incredible supernatural encounter where a demon had invaded a man's persona. Knowing that God's Son would come in the flesh to save humanity, this demon recognizes Jesus as the "Holy One" and asks if Jesus had come to destroy him and his fellow fallen angels. The demon's knowledge of Jesus' identity is congruent with a great truism promulgated by James 2:19, where James says: "You believe that there is one God. Good! Even the demons believe that — and shudder." So, we see why this fallen angel was afraid of Jesus. He knew Jesus' identity.

Power R: ➤ RAISING OF THE DEAD

John 11:35-45

Jesus wept. Then the Jews said, "See how he loved him!" But some of them said, "Could not he who opened the eyes of the blind man have kept this man from dying?" Jesus, once more deeply moved, came to the tomb. It was a cave with a stone laid across the entrance." Take away the stone," he said. "But Lord," said Martha, the sister of the dead man, "by this time there is a bad odor, for he has been there for four days." Then Jesus said, "Did I not tell you that if you believed, you would see the glory of God?" So they took away the stone. Then Jesus looked up and said, "Father, I thank you that you have heard me. I knew that you always hear me, but I said this for the benefit of the people standing here, that they may believe that you sent me." When he had said this, Jesus called in a loud voice, "Lazarus, come out!" The dead man came out, his hands and feet wrapped with strips of linen, and a cloth around his face. Jesus said to them, "Take off the grave clothes and let him go." Therefore, many of the Jews who had come to visit Mary, and had seen what Jesus did, put their faith in him.

Commentary

Perhaps no other passage substantiates Christ's divinity more than John 11, for here we see a power at work that ONLY the author of life could perform, namely, the power to resurrect Lazarus from the dead, even after Lazarus, the brother of Mary and Martha, had been in the grave for four days. Customarily, a corpse was laid on a sheet of linen, wide enough to fully envelop the body and more than twice the length of the corpse. The body was placed on the sheet, and then the sheet was drawn over the head and back down to the feet. The feet were bound at the ankles, and the arms were tied to the body with linen strips, while the face was bound with a cloth. A person so bound could likely hop but not walk. So, when Jesus told Lazarus to come forth, and when Lazarus did, it is understandable that Jesus gave the practical order to remove Lazarus' grave clothes.

WHY DON'T THE SYNOPTIC GOSPELS MENTION LAZARUS? The above John 11 story of the raising of Lazarus from the dead is well-known. Yet, for some reason, Matthew, Mark, and Luke don't mention Lazarus. This head-scratching absence has raised a lot of questions. The story seems too significant to just leave out. Skeptics thus think John made it up. But could there be a good reason that the earlier Gospels left out the narrative? Yes. The answer has to do with anonymity. After all, John 12:10-11 notes that "the chief priests made plans to put Lazarus to death as well, because on account of him many of the Jews were going away and believing in Jesus." That is to say, Lazarus was a thorn in the side of the Jewish leaders because he was convincing Jews to follow Jesus by simply walking around. Because Jewish leaders continued to persecute the early church for decades, the early Synoptic Gospel writers likely had to leave Lazarus out of their narratives for his own safety and protection from assassins.

Power S ➤ SALVATION PROCLAMATIONS

John 3:13-17 & 14:6

"No one has ever gone into heaven except the one who came from heaven—the Son of Man. Just as Moses lifted up the snake in the desert, so the Son of Man must be lifted up, that everyone who believes in him may have eternal life. For Go so loved the world that he gave his one and only Son, that whoever believes in him shall not perish but have eternal life. For God did not send his Son into the world to condemn the world, but to save the world through him." / Jesus answered, "I am the way and the truth and the life. No one comes to the Father except through me."

Commentary

No sane person would say the things that Jesus is alleged to have said in these verses of the Gospel of John, unless they knew definitively that they were actually divine. Jesus did know exactly who he was, God-in-human-flesh, and so he indeed proclaimed that he had come down from heaven, that he had the power to save the world, and that no human would ever be able to come to the Father except through him. What bold exclusivity. If Jesus was not the real Lord, then we must call him either an evil liar or mad lunatic (see pp. 117-21 re this trilemma).

These F-A-C-T-O-R-S are certainly compelling. Jesus said and did things one would expect only a God-man could say and do. But the case for deity gets stronger if we look at the claims Jesus made about himself, and those made about him, in the Gospels. For example, Matt. 28:20 claims Jesus is omnipresent and John 5:27 indicates that all humanity will face him at the final judgment. Astonishing.

The NT epistles also add sound credence to the case that Jesus was fully divine. He is said to be *eternal* in Hebrews 1:12 and *omnipotent* in Hebrews 1:3. He is said to be the Creator of all things in both Colossians 1:16 and Hebrews 1:12, and he is even said to be the One who holds all things in the universe together in both Hebrews 1:3 and Colossians 1:15-17. Consider the below potent words of the latter passage, and then examine the practical map on page 115 where Jesus' unambiguous divine miracles were observed by thousands of people in the region of Palestine:

He [Christ] is the visible image of the invisible God. He is supreme over all creation, because in connection with him were created all things — in heaven and on earth, visible and invisible, whether thrones, lordships, rulers or authorities — they have all been created through and for him. He existed before all things, and he holds everything together." — Colossians 1:15-17 (CJB)

A Map of Jesus' Ministry & Miracles

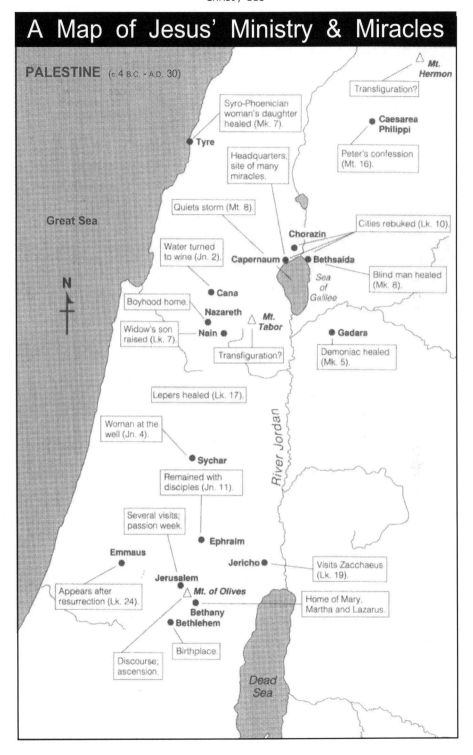

PALESTINE (c 4 B.C. - A.D. 30)

Mt. Hermon

Transfiguration?

Syro-Phoenician woman's daughter healed (Mk. 7).

Caesarea Philippi

Tyre

Headquarters, site of many miracles.

Peter's confession (Mt. 16).

Great Sea

Quiets storm (Mt. 8).

Chorazin

Cities rebuked (Lk. 10).

Water turned to wine (Jn. 2).

Capernaum

Bethsaida

Sea of Galilee

Blind man healed (Mk. 8).

N

Cana

Boyhood home.

Nazareth

Mt. Tabor

Widow's son raised (Lk. 7).

Nain

Gadara

Transfiguration?

Demoniac healed (Mk. 5).

Lepers healed (Lk. 17).

Woman at the well (Jn. 4).

River Jordan

Sychar

Remained with disciples (Jn. 11).

Several visits; passion week.

Ephraim

Emmaus

Jericho

Visits Zacchaeus (Lk. 19).

Jerusalem

Appears after resurrection (Lk. 24).

Mt. of Olives

Home of Mary, Martha and Lazarus.

Bethany

Bethlehem

Birthplace.

Discourse; ascension.

Dead Sea

Claims of Divinity

The Trilemma: Liar, Lunatic or Lord

A third category of evidence to consider in our defense of Christ is Jesus' own claims. If Jesus claimed to be a divine being, or God with a human face, and this claim was meant to be taken literally (i.e., not mystically as a guru would mean in citing pantheism), then we logically only have three options. That is, if Jesus truly claimed to be divine (i.e., his alleged statements were not legends), he was either: (1) a LIAR, (2) a LUNATIC or (3) the LORD. These are the only logical alternatives available.

Apologist Josh McDowell, in *Evidence Demands a Verdict*, first termed this quandary the trilemma.[6] In constructing the trilemma, are we setting up a false dilemma, that is, are we guilty of not listing all the options? No! In making clear claims to deity, Jesus forced us to choose between these three options and these alone; he did not allow us the alternative of viewing him as simply a great moral teacher, rabbi or sage; one cannot call Jesus this and, at the same time, deny his bold assertions of divinity.

C.S. Lewis, once an agnostic, makes this point well in his classic, *Mere Christianity*, by convincingly showing that we have a limited number of options regarding how we can view Jesus' identity, given his claims. Lewis writes:

I am trying here to prevent anyone saying the really foolish thing that people often say about Him. "I'm ready to accept Jesus as a great moral teacher, but I don't accept His claim to be God." That is one thing we must not say. A man who was merely a man and said the sort of things Jesus said would not be a great moral teacher. He would either be a lunatic — on a level with the man who says he is a poached egg — or else he would be the Devil of Hell. You must make your choice. Either this man was, and is, the Son of God: or else a madman or something worse. You can shut him up for a fool, you can spit at Him and kill Him as a demon; or you can fall at His feet and call Him Lord and God. But let us not come up with any patronizing nonsense about His being a great human teacher. He has not left that open to us. He did not intend to.[7]

On the next page is a useful chart which outlines the trilemma regarding Jesus' identity in light of his recorded claims of divinity. The chart presents us with a valid and powerful disjunctive syllogism (see page 41), for it forces us to choose one of the three logical options available to us.

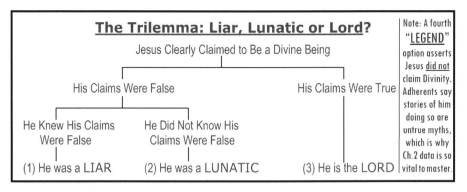

The Trilemma: Liar, Lunatic or Lord?

Jesus Clearly Claimed to Be a Divine Being

His Claims Were False — His Claims Were True

He Knew His Claims Were False — He Did Not Know His Claims Were False

(1) He was a LIAR — (2) He was a LUNATIC — (3) He is the LORD

Note: A fourth "LEGEND" option asserts Jesus _did not_ claim Divinity. Adherents say stories of him doing so are untrue myths, which is why Ch.2 data is so vital to master.

So, we have three options. But this does not end our need for Christological apologetics, for the trilemma is only valid _if_ Jesus actually claimed to be divine in a literal (i.e., non-mystical) manner. If Jesus did not claim a "literal" divinity, then the Liar-Lunatic-Lord argument is useless.

Did Jesus in fact do this then? Did he ever make an unequivocal claim that he was a divine being? Yes. Undeniably. We do observe in the Gospel accounts (documents we have already determined to be reliable and credible) that Jesus absolutely made four distinct claims to divinity. Consider these four claims and corresponding biblical references:

#1 — Claim to be the **MESSIAH**   John 4:25-27
#2 — Claim to be the **SON OF GOD**   Mark 14:60-64
#3 — Claim to be the divine **I AM**   John 8: 53-59
#4 — Claim to be one with the **FATHER**   John 10:24-33

Let us now dive into each of these Gospel passages to determine the precise significance of each of Jesus' audacious claims about himself.

Divinity Claim #1:   THE MESSIAH   Messiah

John 4:25-27   Commentary

The woman said "I know that Messiah (called Christ) is coming. When he comes he will explain everything to us." Then Jesus declared, "I who speak to you am he." Just then his disciples returned and were surprised to find him talking with a [Samaritan] woman.

Note: See "commentary" to grasp why Jesus' disciples were so surprised and read all of John 4 to gain contextualization.

Both Jews/Samaritans longed to see the prophesied "Christ" and, in John 4, Jesus is the quintessential egalitarian, for the _first_ soul to whom he revealed _he_ was the Messiah was the _last_ we'd ever expect, since she was a female (to whom a rabbi would _never_ speak in public), a Samaritan (enemy of the Jews), and a 5x-divorcee to boot. Yet Jesus treated this woman with loving, unbiased equality/dignity, smashing that era's normal Jewish conventions re gender, ethnicity and opprobrium.

Divinity Claim #2:   THE SON OF GOD

ΙΧΘΥΣ

JESUS CHRIST GOD'S SON SAVIOR

Mark 14:60-64

Then the high priest stood up before them and asked Jesus, "Are you not going to answer? What is this testimony that these men are bringing against you?" But Jesus remained silent and gave no answer. Again the high priest asked him, "Are you the Christ, the Son of the Blessed One?" "I am," said Jesus. "And you will see the Son of Man sitting at the right hand of   the Mighty One and coming on the clouds of heaven." The high priest tore his clothes. "Why do we need any more witnesses? You have heard the blasphemy. What do you think?" They all condemned him as being worthy of death.

Commentary

The tearing of one's clothes was understood to be a sign of great grief in Jewish culture.[4] In the case of the high priest in this passage, it meant that he'd been exposed to a major blasphemous statement.   Jesus, a mere man, was claiming to be the Son of God in front of the entire Sanhedrin, which was the supreme official, judicial counsel of Judaism comprised of 71 members and headquartered in Jerusalem. After Jesus' statement, we see the entire Sanhedrin condemned Jesus as worthy of death. So, Jesus claim of divinity was very clear to all present; his claim also appears to have been incredibly inflammatory. Normally in the Sanhedrin, in capital cases, a guilty verdict had to be postponed by at least one day; but in Jesus' case, they didn't want to wait at all.

Before we move on, we must address Jesus' use of the title "Son of Man," since some misinterpret what the phrase means. It does not mean "of human origin" as some have mistakenly suggested.   Consider William Craig's explanation regarding Jesus' use of this title:

"Son of Man" is often thought to indicate the humanity of Jesus. In fact, just the opposite is true. The Son of Man was a divine figure in the Old Testament book of Daniel who would come at the end of the world to judge mankind and rule forever. Thus, the claim to be the Son of Man would be in effect a claim to divinity.[8]

Craig is speaking of Daniel 7:13-14 where Daniel sees a vision of the future and writes the following summarization: "In my vision at night I looked, and there before me was one like a son of man, coming with the clouds of heaven. He approached the Ancient of Days and was led into his presence. He was given authority, glory and sovereign power; all

This iconic symbol of Christ's deity is circled by the Latin prayer: "Lord Jesus Christ, Son of God, have mercy on me." In Daniel 7, the "Son of Man" is also a divine appellation which sees Jesus as the final judge and ruler over all humankind.

nations and peoples of every language worshiped him. His dominion is an everlasting dominion and is kingdom ... will never be destroyed."

Divinity Claim #3: THE DIVINE "I AM"

John 8:53-59   Commentary

Are you greater than our father Abraham? He died, and so did the prophets. Who do you think you are? Jesus replied, "If I glorify myself, my glory means nothing. My Father, whom you claim as your God, is the one who glorifies me. Though you do not know him, I know him. If I said I did not, I would be a liar like you, but I do know him and keep his word. Your father Abraham rejoiced at the thought of seeing my day; he saw and was glad." "You are not yet 50 years old," the Jews said to him, "and you have seen Abraham!" "I tell you the truth," Jesus said, "before Abraham was born, I AM!" At this, they picked up stones to stone him., but Jesus hid himself, slipping away.

Here, Jesus is claiming two aspects of deity for himself: (a) the eternality of God and (b) the name of God, as he was harkening back to Exodus 3:14 where God tells Moses that His name is "I AM" (see KJV verse below). Jesus' Jewish audience would have clearly grasped his deity claim, which is why they picked up stones to kill him. He infuriated these monotheists who said God was only & utterly transcendent.

GOD SAID TO MOSES,_____

"I AM WHO I AM."
AND HE SAID, **SAY THIS TO THE PEOPLE OF ISRAEL, 'I AM HAS SENT ME TO YOU.'**
EXODUS 3:14

Fascinatingly, in John's Gospel, we see that this sacred "I AM" phrase from Exodus 3:14 was not only invoked by Jesus to dauntlessly express the aforementioned divinity claim, but it was elucidated by him another 23x to address various life issues. In seven of these instances, Jesus joined the "I AM" phrase with seven powerful metaphors, each of which was pointedly designed to express his salvific relationship to the world. Consider this useful chart which lists each of these seven potent metaphors along with each one's correspondent verse(s):

The Seven "I AM" Metaphors of Christ

Metaphor	John's Reference
"I AM the Bread of life"	6:35, 41, 48, 51
"I AM the Light of the world"	8:12
"I AM the Door of the sheep"	10:7, 9
"I AM the Good Shepherd"	10:11,
"I AM the Resurrection and the Life"	11:25
"I AM the Way, the Truth and the Life"	14:6
"I AM the true Vine"	15:1,

Divinity Claim #4:   ONE WITH THE FATHER

אַבָּא

Hebrew "Abba" = Father

John 10:24-33

The Jews gathered around him, saying, "How long will you keep us in suspense? If you are the Christ, tell us plainly." Jesus answered, "I did tell you, but you do not believe. The miracles I do in my Father's name speak for me, but you do not believe because you are not my sheep. My sheep listen to my voice; I know them, and they follow me. I give them eternal life, and they shall never perish; no one can snatch them out of my hand. My father, who has given them to me, is greater than all; no one can snatch them out of my Father's hand. I and the Father are one." Again the Jews picked up stones to stone him, but Jesus said to them, "I have shown you many great miracles from the Father. For which of these do you stone me?" "We are not stoning you for any of these," replied the Jews, "but for blasphemy, because you, a mere man, claim to be God.

Commentary

Some sects, such as the Jehovah's Witnesses, purport that Jesus' claim here that he is "one" with the Father is only with regard to Jesus' purpose, not his literal essence. Yet, in Greek, the word "one" in this passage takes on the neuter gender and, thus, refers to "one essence." In other words, Jesus here seems to be claiming that he shares all the divine attributes of the Father. The Jews present would have had no doubts about what Jesus was saying. That is why they immediately picked up stones to stone Jesus, because he, a mere man, was clearly claiming to be God. What an audacious claim! Either Jesus knew exactly who he was, God-Incarnate, or he was quite seriously deranged! All the facts fit the former option. Moreover, if we look at the true meaning of the Greek word "one" we see that it clearly meant "oneness of nature" of the Father and the Son, implying that the two are the same in substance and equal in divine power/authority.

C.S. Lewis puts all Jesus' claims into perspective when he reminds us that he was not a Roman or Greek citizen, but a Jew among Jews. This is a critical fact as Jews were strict monotheists. Lewis writes:

Among these Jews there suddenly turns up a man who goes about talking as if He was God. Now let us get this clear. Among pantheists . . . anyone might say that he was part of God, or one with God; there would be nothing very odd about it. But this man, since He was a Jew, could not mean that kind of God. God, in their language, meant the Being outside the world who had made it and was infinitely different. And when you have grasped that, you will see that what this man said was, quite simply, the most shocking thing that has ever been uttered by human lips.[9]

> Vocab Highlight: The Greek term *homoousious* was used at the 325 Nicea Council to explain the Jesus | Father dynamic. It means to be made "of one substance."

Lewis elucidates a preeminent point: Jesus' claims were flabbergasting.

Now let us consider the three options in our trilemma, since this is indeed a powerful disjunctive syllogism to invoke once we have solidly established the initial proposition that "Jesus clearly claimed to be a divine being," that is, that Jesus truly existed and that the Gospel authors recorded his claims accurately such that these words are *not* legends. **LEGEND**

Option #1: **Was Jesus a LIAR?** This is minutely possible, but extremely unlikely, given Jesus' lofty ethical character and teachings. In my judgment, anyone who lived as Jesus lived, taught as Jesus taught, and died as Jesus died, simply could not have been a deliberate deceiver. Consider the words on Philipp Schaff as he writes about the "liar" option in his classic, *The Person of Christ*: Schaff writes:

How, in the name of logic, common sense, and experience, could an imposter — that is, a deceitful, selfish, depraved man — have invented, and consistently maintained from the beginning to end, the purest and noblest character known in history with the most perfect air of truth and reality?[10]

Option #2: **Was Jesus a LUNATIC?** Not a chance! Dr. Quentin Hyder, a renowned psychiatrist in New York, analyzed the records of Jesus' behavior, personality and teachings in his book, *Jesus: God, Ghost or Guru?* Hyder concludes that Jesus could not have been a lunatic:

A person is free to maintain that Jesus, out of honest delusion, made His claim to deity. But if one takes this position, he does so without any psychological evidence in its support and, indeed, in spite of considerable evidence to the contrary.[11]

Option #3: **Was Jesus the LORD?** Yes. This is really our only credible alternative, given the historical evidence as presented in the Gospels. Jesus indeed lived a life perfectly congruent with how a God-man would live. His pure character, bold teaching, divine miracles, compassionate ministry, and unselfish death all substantiate his incredible claims. We therefore

κύριος

The word "Kurios" or Lord is used as a NT title for Jesus 250x and was bestowed on a person who possessed great authority & power.

cannot simply call Jesus a great moral teacher. That is not an option. We must choose: liar, lunatic or Lord? Interestingly, John says he wrote his Gospel to convict us to make the right choice. In John 20:30-31, he writes:

Jesus did many other miraculous signs in the presence of his disciples, which are not recorded in this book. But these are written that you may believe that Jesus is the Christ, the Son of God, and that by believing you may have life in his name.

Jesus was not the only one convinced he was divine. Consider this utile chart which reveals all the titles assigned to Christ by NT writers:

NEW TESTAMENT TITLES ASSIGNED TO CHRIST

Title	Significance	Reference
Adam, Last Adam	First of the new race of the redeemed	I Cor. 15:45
Alpha and Omega	The beginning and ending of all things	Revelation 21:6
Bread of Life	The one essential food for life	John 6:35
Chief Cornerstone	The indispensable foundation for life	Ephesians 2:20
Chief Shepherd	Our protector, sustainer and guide	1 Peter 5:4
Firstborn from the Dead	Leads us into resurrection and eternal life	Colossians 1:18
Good Shepherd	Our provider and caretaker	John 10:11
High Priest	A perfect sacrifice for our sins	Hebrews 3:1
Holy One of God	Sinless in his nature	Mark 1:24
Immanuel (God with us)	Stands with us in all of life's circumstances	Matthew 1:23
King of Kings	The Lord, before whom every knee will bow	Revelation 19:16
Lamb of God	Gave his life as a sacrifice on our behalf	John 1:29
Light of the World	Brings hope in the midst of darkness	John 9:5
Lord of Glory	The power and presence of the living God	1 Cor. 2:8
Mediator	Brings us into God's presence	1 Timothy 2:5
Only Begotten	The unique co-eternal Son of God	John 1:14
Savior	Delivers mankind from sin and death	Luke 1:47
Son of Man	Daniel's title of the final judge of mankind	Matthew 18:11
The Word	Present with God at the creation	John 1:1

We are now at a critical juncture in our F-A-C-T acrostic regarding Christ. After examining Jesus' (1) Fulfillments of C-H-R-I-S-T prophecies, (2) Authority F-A-C-T-O-R-S and (3) Claims of Divinity, it is essential we turn to the fact that (4) Jesus' Tomb became E-M-P-T-Y, that he, in fact, rose from the dead, for the resurrection is all-important. If Jesus remains dead, then Christians need to find a new worldview. Before investigating the evidence for this miracle, however, I have  decided to add (on page 123) a brief theological essay entitled *Why should we believe in the Trinity?* for those who are curious as to why the early church adopted this doctrine. This is a key Christological issue since it relates to why Christians believe Christ to be a member of the Trinity. To show how the concept of the Trinity was solidified as an ecumenical truth-claim, I have also added the full text of the now universally accepted Nicene Creed (see page 124), a creed which, in A.D. 325, weaved the Trinity into the tapestry of ecumenical Christian orthodoxy.

TRINITY SYMBOL

Why should we believe in the Trinity?

One of the central doctrines purported by all main branches of Christendom, i.e., Roman Catholicism, Orthodoxy and Protestantism, is the doctrine of the Trinity, which states that (a) God is one, (b) that each of the three persons within the Godhead is Deity (and not inferior/superior to each other) and (c) that the oneness of God and the threeness of God are not contradictory, and even can explain why "God is love" (see I John 4:8). But why is this doctrine embraced? Where did it originate? Is it true? To answer these questions, we must turn to (1) the Bible, (2) the teaching of the early apostles and (3) ecumenical councils of the early Christian Church.

Ironically, the word "Trinity" is never used, nor is the doctrine of Trinitarianism ever explicitly taught, in the Scriptures. But, nonetheless, the biblical evidence for a holy Trinity is extremely compelling. Interestingly, Old Testament Jewish monotheism does not preclude the concept of the Trinity, since, even in Genesis 1:26, God says, "Let us make man in our image, in our likeness." With regard to the Father, we see hundreds of passages that the Father is God. No scholar challenges this. So let us focus on the Son and the Holy Spirit. With regard to the Son, the most lucid passage comes from Hebrews 1:2-3 where we read: "In these last days he [God] has spoken to us by his Son, whom he appointed heir of all things, and through whom he made the universe. The Son is the radiance of God's glory and the exact representation of his being, sustaining all things by his powerful word." With regard to the Holy Spirit, the best passage is Acts 5:4 where "lying to the Holy Spirit" is directly equated with "lying to God." In addition to these passages, we also see that early apostolic teaching (c. A.D. 33-100) clearly accepted the deity of Jesus and promoted the Trinitarian baptismal formula (which originated in Matt. 28:19).

The Bible is not the only source to which we can turn to substantiate the Trinity concept. The ecumenical councils of the early church, particularly the Council of Nicea in A.D. 325 and the Council of Constantinople in A.D. 381, confirmed that the Trinity was a fully biblical concept and, hence, should be maintained as an orthodox church teaching. In response to the heresy of Arianism, which claimed that Jesus was a created being, the Council of Nicea established what is now the most recited creed of the Christian church, the Nicene Creed (see page 124), which said that Christ was "true God of true God, not made, of one substance (or homoousia) with the Father." Likewise, in response to Macedonianism, a heresy which subordinated the Holy Spirit in much the same manner as Arianism subordinated Christ, the Council of Constantinople affirmed the deity of the Holy Spirit, saying "we believe...in the Holy Spirit, the Lord and life-giver, who proceeds from the Father, who is worshipped and glorified together with the Father and the Son." In short, Christ-followers can be confident that the Trinity doctrine is well-accepted as orthodoxy as it entirely supported by Christ's words and biblical texts. See the diagrams below.

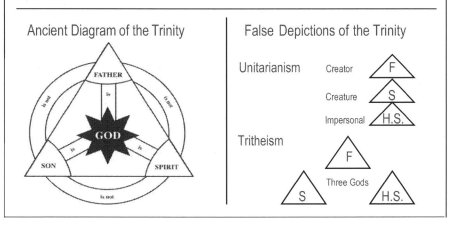

Ancient Diagram of the Trinity

False Depictions of the Trinity

Unitarianism

Tritheism

The Nicene Creed

Adopted at the Ecumenical Council of Nicea in A.D. 325

We believe in one God,
the Father, the Almighty, maker of heaven and earth,
of all that is, seen and unseen.

We believe in one Lord, Jesus Christ,
the only Son of God,
eternally begotten of the Father,
God from God , Light from Light, true God from true God,
begotten, not made,
of one Being with the Father.
Through him all things were made.
For us and for our salvation he came down from heaven;
by the power of the Holy Spirit
he became incarnate from the Virgin Mary,
and was made man.
For our sake he was crucified under Pontius Pilate;
he suffered death and was buried.
On the third day he rose again in accordance with the Scriptures;
he ascended into heaven and is seated at the right hand of the Father.
He will come again in glory to judge the living and the dead,
and his kingdom will have no end.

We believe in the Holy Spirit, the Lord, the giver of life,
who proceeds from the Father and the Son.
With the Father and the Son he is worshiped and glorified.
He has spoken through the Prophets.
We believe in one holy catholic and apostolic Church.
We acknowledge one baptism for the forgiveness of sins.
We look for the resurrection of the dead,
and the life of the world to come. Amen.

Tomb E-M-P-T-Y

Five Resurrection Evidences

Finally, to cap off our cumulative defense of the deity of Jesus Christ we must, of necessity, address the topic of Jesus' resurrection, for the resurrection is central and essential to Christianity.

In fact, Christianity as a religion stands or falls *with* the resurrection. That is, without the resurrection, Christianity completely collapses. If we can disprove the resurrection, we can dispose of Christianity entirely, for the Christian faith, and its claim to be objective truth, exists only if Jesus rose from the dead. The heart and soul of Christianity is a living Christ.

Paul the apostle makes this point abundantly clear. From the very outset of the early church, the resurrection was indispensable. In I Corinthians 15:13-17 (Amplified Bible), Paul writes:

But if there is no resurrection of the dead, then Christ has not risen; And if Christ has not risen our preaching is vain it amounts to nothing and your faith is devoid of truth and is fruitless (without effect, empty, imaginary and unfounded). We are even discovered to be misrepresenting God, for we testified of Him that He raised Christ.

It is interesting to note that Jesus himself also "put all his eggs in one basket" so to speak when it came to the resurrection. All four Gospels, in Matthew 16:21, Mark 8:31, Luke 9:22 and John 14:28, reveal how Jesus made a clear claim that he would indeed rise on the third day. Consider Luke's rendition of Jesus' prophecy. Speaking to his disciples in Luke 9:22, Jesus predicts four events that will happen to him. Jesus says:

The Son of Man must suffer many things and be rejected by the elders, chief priests and teachers of the law, and he must be killed and on the third day be raised to life.

So, the resurrection is indeed indispensable. That said, what evidence do we have for this miracle, if any? Are Christians forced to blindly accept the resurrection event, or is there any solid evidence, both internal and external, surrounding each of the Gospel accounts which confirm that Jesus indeed rose from the dead as he himself had prophesied?

They put him to death by hanging him on a tree; but God raised him on the third day.

Suffice it to say, apologists possess five main resurrection evidence categories. I have summarized the main points of each category through the acrostic E-M-P-T-Y, a mnemonic device which will show that Jesus' tomb was indeed E-M-P-T-Y on Easter morning due to the fact he had resurrected. These five evidence categories break down as follows:

E	—	Eyewitnesses of the Risen Jesus
M	—	Movement of the Security Stone
P	—	Preaching of the First Apostles
T	—	Turin's Shroud & Its 3-D Imagery
Y	—	Yes – It's the Most Cogent Option

E — Eyewitnesses of the Risen Jesus

According to the apostle Paul in 1 Corinthians 15:3-8, more than 500 people were eyewitnesses to Jesus' resurrection. In fact, Paul reminds his readers that the majority of these individuals were still alive! Consider Paul's exact wording in the text. He writes:

For what I received I passed on to you as of first importance: that Christ died for our sins according to the Scriptures, that he was buried, that he was raised on the third day according to the Scriptures, and that he appeared to Peter, and then to the Twelve. After that, he appeared to more than five hundred of the brothers at the same time, most of whom are still living, though some have fallen asleep. Then he appeared to James, then to all the apostles, and last of all he appeared to me also.

Although this number of 500 is large and is not corroborated by the Gospel portraits, this does not mean 1 Corinthians 15 is fictitious. Drs. Gary Habermas, William Lane Craig and Craig Blomberg and other biblical experts have pointed out that 1 Corinthians 15:3-8 is, in fact, one of the earliest and best authenticated passages in the NT in that it was based on an early Christian creed which predated Paul's conversion.[12] Scholars know this because Paul uses parallelism and a stylized content in 1 Corinthians 15 in order to pass on the "oral tradition" he had received after he had been blinded by Jesus himself on the road to Damascus and subsequently converted to be an apostle of Christ (see Acts 26:12-23). Dr. Blomberg describes how Paul likely encountered this early Christian creed:

Artistic depiction of the Apostle Paul being blinded by Jesus in Acts 9:8

If the Crucifixion was as early as **A.D.** 30, Paul's conversion was about 32. Immediately Paul was ushered into Damascus, where he met with a Christian named Ananias and some other disciples. His first meeting with the apostles in Jerusalem would have been about **A.D.** 35. At some point along there, Paul was given this creed, which had already been formulated and was being used.[13]

The creed found in 1 Corinthians 15 is a vital one to study, particularly since it is so early and can help provide insight into the number of eyewitnesses who encountered the risen Jesus. When we carefully examine the creed, these individuals are listed: Peter, as noted by his Aramaic name *Cephas*; the twelve disciples; over 500 believers; James the brother of Jesus; and Paul. Thus far, the number is now up to 514. Yet the Gospels note that women also served as eyewitnesses of the resurrection, including Mary Magdalene, Mary the mother of James, Salome, Joanna, and other unnamed women (see Luke 24:10). Counting these five female eyewitnesses gives us a running tally so far of 520.

That said, Luke also adds Cleopas and another disciple, perhaps his wife, to the list of witnesses when they met Jesus on the Road to Emmaus (see Luke 24:18-35). The additional two witnesses increase the total to 522. But there is probably more, particularly since Matthew and Luke add two other times when numerous witnesses saw the risen Jesus at the same time. In addition, Matthew 28 denotes an occasion where the risen Jesus taught a large crowd in Galilee when he provided the Great Commission (vs. 16-20). While 11 disciples are mentioned here, the text also leaves open the possibility that Jesus communicates to a group as he notes that some among them doubted. Moreover, in Acts, Luke records the ascension of the risen Jesus which was encountered by a large group that witnessed this from the Mount of Olives near Jerusalem. Given that this was a public event, many others may have seen Jesus. And the tally does not stop there. Some have argued that it is possible the NT could refer to over 1000 witnessing the risen Jesus given the possibility that women may have not been included in the 500 number delineated in 1 Corinthians 15 and given the large groups of unidentifiable numbers who witnessed Jesus on separate occasions (such as at the Ascension). In short, when we scrutinize 1 Corinthians 15 and related passages, we see a solid case for the resurrection emerge.

Dr. Gary Habermas, the world's top expert on the resurrection and author/editor of over 15 books on the subject, says the following regarding the veracity and vital significance of 1 Corinthians 15:

The importance of the creed in 1 Corinthians 15:3ff. can hardly be overestimated. No longer can it be charged that there is no demonstrable early, eyewitness testimony for the resurrection or for the other most important tenets of Christianity, for this creed provides just such evidential data concerning the facts of the gospel, which are the very center of the Christian faith.[14]

What is even more remarkable, though, than the fact that Jesus appeared to over 500 people in 1 Corinthians 15 is the fact that the first recorded eyewitness of the risen Jesus was a woman, specifically Mary Magdalene, who is described as a woman of ill-repute (see Matt. 28:9, Mark 16:9, Luke 24:10 and John 20:1). Now, in the modern world, this would mean absolutely nothing, since, in most places, women are seen as equal to men. But in the first century context, the mentioning of a woman would have been incredibly significant. Allow me to explain why the mentioning of Mary Magdalene as a first witness (in all four Gospels!) totally authenticates all the Gospels' resurrection accounts. To do so, we must study that era.

Sadly, women in first-century Jewish culture were not considered competent witnesses. They were not even allowed to testify in court. This fact is confirmed by Josephus (cf. page 97). Thus, if a Gospel writer desired to deceptively convince others that Jesus resurrected, even though he knew this was false, the writer *never* would have stated that women saw Jesus first — no way. In fact, in the first century, this would be the *last* thing a deceiver would do, given how women were looked upon. That is precisely why, in Mark 16:10-11, we read that Mary Magdalene "went and told" the disciples Jesus was alive and "that she had seen him," but they "did not believe it." Era norms governed their attitude.

The "Mary Magdalene" statue by Donatello is one of the most famous expressions of female emotion in Western Art.

In short, when considering the diverse witnesses to whom Jesus revealed himself, according to the NT, it is abundantly clear that Jesus wanted a diversity of male and female individuals from multiple walks of life to be thoroughly persuaded he was alive. Printed below is a 12-part summary of the various individuals and groups to whom Christ appeared after the resurrection:

After his resurrection, Christ Jesus appeared to:

- **Mary Magdalene by the tomb (John 20:10-18)**
- **Mary and the other women (Matthew 28:1-10)**
- **Peter (1 Corinthians 15:5)**
- **Two men on the road to Emmaus (Luke 24:13-35)**
- **Ten disciples (Luke 24:36-49)**
- **Eleven disciples in a room (John 20:24-31)**
- **Seven disciples by the Sea of Galilee (John 21)**
- **All the disciples (Matthew 28:16-20)**
- **500 people at once (1 Corinthians 15:6)**
- **James (1 Corinthians 15:7)**
- **All the disciples at the Ascension (Acts 1:4-8)**
- **Saul on his way to Damascus (Acts 9:1-9)**

Jesus was clearly not in hiding after his arose. In fact, when we look at the Gospel data, we see Jesus revealed his presence in at least seven locations, which the map below outlines. Clearly, Jesus wanted to be seen and heard. He also wanted to transform his apostles so that they could in turn proclaim the reality of the resurrection to the rest of the human race. Interestingly, each of Jesus' eyewitnesses was willing to suffer a brutal martyr's death for him. Why would they do this? Because each Christ-follower knew that Jesus he was/is the risen Lord and Savior.

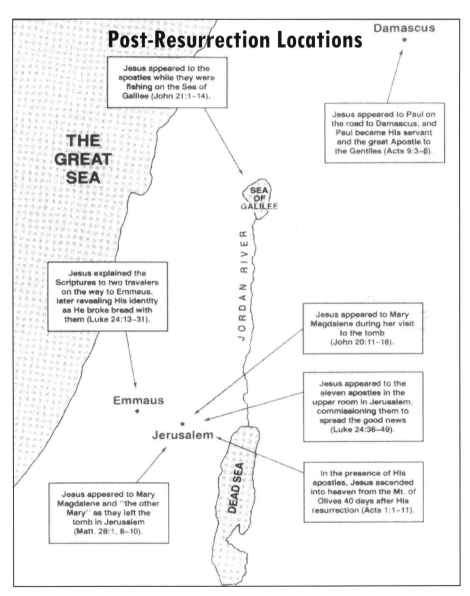

Post-Resurrection Locations

Jesus appeared to the apostles while they were fishing on the Sea of Galilee (John 21:1-14).

Damascus

Jesus appeared to Paul on the road to Damascus, and Paul became His servant and the great Apostle to the Gentiles (Acts 9:3-6).

THE GREAT SEA

SEA OF GALILEE

JORDAN RIVER

Jesus explained the Scriptures to two travelers on the way to Emmaus, later revealing His identity as He broke bread with them (Luke 24:13-31).

Jesus appeared to Mary Magdalene during her visit to the tomb (John 20:11-18).

Jesus appeared to the eleven apostles in the upper room in Jerusalem, commissioning them to spread the good news (Luke 24:36-49).

Emmaus

Jerusalem

DEAD SEA

In the presence of His apostles, Jesus ascended into heaven from the Mt. of Olives 40 days after His resurrection (Acts 1:1-11).

Jesus appeared to Mary Magdalene and "the other Mary" as they left the tomb in Jerusalem (Matt. 28:1, 8-10).

M — Movement of the Security Stone

Before any eyewitness ever saw or talked to the risen Jesus, however, three security precautions were put in place to ensure that no person disturbed Jesus' body after his brutal crucifixion:

Security Precaution #1: Matthew 27:60 records that Joseph of Arimathea (the tomb owner) "rolled a big stone in front of the entrance" to the tomb. Mark 16:4 records that this stone was actually "very large" and that when Mary Magdalene (and others) went to the tomb to anoint Jesus' body on Sunday, the stone "had been rolled away" already. The query we must ask is – who exactly did the rolling?

Security Precaution #2: In Matthew 27:66, we read that a Roman seal was also placed over the rolling stone. Such a practice was common in that day to protect graves from vandals. So anyone trying to move Jesus' stone would have had to break the seal and face the wrath of Roman law, which meant death.

Security Precaution #3: Jesus had publicly predicted he would rise three days after his death (see Luke 9:22). So the Jewish priests asked Pilate (see Matt.27:63-66) if they could also post guards at Jesus' tomb to prevent Jesus' disciples from stealing the body. Pilate authorized this guard request.

Yet despite these precautions, the Gospels tell us that (a) Jesus' stone was rolled back, (b) the tomb seal was broken and (c) the guard got scared and went AWOL (see Matt. 28:11), having to be bribed with "hush money" (see Matt. 28:12). Given the Gospel data, we have two scenarios as to how Jesus' tomb became empty: Either (1) someone was strong enough to move the stone <u>and</u> scare off an elite Roman guard to steal the body, or (2) Jesus resurrected as he predicted. We must choose.

Above: Based on the numbers that first-century Rome used in posting guards, we know that — at minimum — four Roman soldiers would have guarded Jesus' tomb. Roman soldiers were fierce fighting machines. A soldier's basic equipment included a crested helmet, breastplate, short sword, shield and lance. If they abandoned their post, the penalty imposed on them was immediate death. Brutal job.

Left: This picture of a typical tomb rolling stone, a safe-guard against grave robbers, is from a first-century rock-cut tomb found in the Shephela region of Israel. Such a stone is similar to what Joseph of Arimathea would have used to guard Jesus' rock-hewn tomb in Luke 23:53 — stout security.

ⓟ — Preaching of the First Apostles

Interestingly, no one doubted Jesus' tomb's *emptiness*. Different explanations were propagated, but it was an established fact and the silent testimony to the resurrection that has never been refuted. Dr. Paul Althus has sagaciously pointed out the vital importance of the factuality of the empty tomb during the infancy period of Christianity. He writes:

In Jerusalem, the place of Jesus' execution and grave, it was proclaimed not long after his death that he had been raised. The situation *demands* that, within the circle of the first community, one had a reliable testimony for the fact that the grave had been found empty. The resurrection kerygma [proclamation] could have not been maintained in Jerusalem for a single day, for a single hour if the "emptiness" of the tomb had not been established as a fact for all concerned.[14]

Consider the story the Jewish priests concocted to explain the empty tomb. We have already seen that these priests bribed the tomb guards who had left their post in fear (see Matthew 28:2-4). Now let's see why this bribe was made. Matthew 28:11-15 records the account:

Some of the [tomb] guards went into the city and reported to the chief priests everything that had happened. When the chief priests had . . . devised a plan, they gave the soldiers a large sum of money, telling them, "You are to say, 'His disciples came during the night and stole him away while we were asleep.' If this report gets to the governor [Pilate], we will satisfy him and keep you out of trouble." So the soldiers took the money and did as they were instructed.

But the preaching of the first apostles told a vastly different story. They proclaimed that the reason Jesus' tomb was empty was because he was alive. They had seen his body with their own eyes. Consider what happened in the lives of two of the Lord's apostles, Peter and Paul.

Preacher #1: Peter went from cowardly denier to eloquent preacher, boldly proclaiming in Acts 2:32 that "God has raised this Jesus to life, and we are all witnesses of the fact." Then, Acts 2:41 records that "those who accepted [Peter's] message were baptized, and about 3000 were added to their number that day." Peter was a man on fire. What is to explain his remarkable transformation if not for a literal resurrection? Just as Peter had cowardly denied Jesus 3x, so Jesus, after his resurrection, re-instated Peter 3x in John 21:15-19, and, undoubtedly, this divine encounter had an enormous impact. His life had been utterly transmogrified.

Peter's Symbol

Preacher #2: Paul is second prime example of an utterly transformed life. Paul (formerly Saul) persecuted early Christians (cf. Acts 9:1-2), even saying in Gal. 1:13 that he tried to destroy the church. That's why he approved of Stephen's stoning in Acts 8:1. Yet Paul claims Jesus appeared to him and changed him on a road trek to Damascus (cf. Acts 9:5). Can any other reason explain Paul's radical conversion? No. Ultimately, Paul wrote 50,190 of the 179,011 words in the NT, or 28%.

T — Turin's Shroud & Its 3-D Imagery

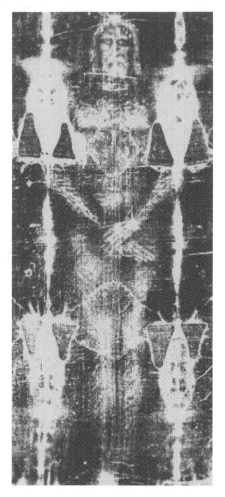

Our fourth evidence area for Christ's resurrection is "tangible" — the Shroud of Turin — which is now located in the Cathedral of St. John the Baptist in Turin, Italy where it has been kept secure since 1578.

Some skeptics might scoff when reading that I've included this, for they may have heard media reports in 1988 that three separate radiocarbon labs said Turin's Shroud was a 14th-century relic. But consider the case I present below for the shroud with a critical mind. I was a skeptic once also. But now I firmly believe the Shroud of Turin is, in fact, the authentic burial cloth of Christ.

Before I unpack evidence for the shroud's authenticity, allow me to say from the outset that this evidence, although compelling, is *not essential* to our defense of Jesus' resurrection. It adds greatly to our cumulative case, to be sure, and is worth investigating, but it is not a necessary component. That is, nothing in the Christian faith "depends" on the shroud to be true. That said, I believe the Shroud of Turin is 100% authentic based on the preponderance of evidence. In fact, I believe this evidence is so overwhelming that the Shroud is undeniably the burial cloth of Jesus, and that his very resurrection is what captured the image shown above.

For those unfamiliar with what the Shroud of Turn is, allow me to first offer a brief description. The Shroud of Turin is a 4.6 x 1.1 piece of linen which bears the image of a 6'-tall, crucified Semitic man in his early 30's who is in a state of rigor mortis, possessing all the same wounds associated with Jesus' death as described in the Gospels. And when I say all the same wounds of Christ, I mean *all* the same wounds, including a pierced scalp, a serious beating, contusions on the knees, two nail wounds in the wrists and in the feet, and postmortem blood flow from a chest wound. What is most striking about the Shroud of Turin is that it seems to have been produced by a light or heat scorch from a dead body in rigor.[16]

As the official Shroud of Turin Research Project (STURP) reported in 1981: "No pigments, paints, dyes, or stains have been found on the fibrils [of the shroud]."[17] In fact, we now know the shroud is a type of photographic negative caused by heat or light, proceeding from a dead body, "picturing" this body onto a cloth which itself was unwrapped. That is why, when the first photo images of the shroud were taken in 1898 by Italian photographer, Secondo Pia (right side), people were shocked to see that the photo-negative of the shroud (see page 132) portrayed lucid, three-dimensional imagery of a crucified dead man with all the characteristics described above. Fascinatingly, this 3-D image was not affected by the intense heat of a fire that  nearly destroyed it in 1532, meaning that it is thermally stable![18] Moreover, even with modern tech, scientists have no idea how to recreate the image. Its non-directionality is, to date, unexplainable.[19]

Other than the shroud's remarkable 3-D imagery, are there any substances located *within* the fibrils of the shroud that substantiate its authenticity? Yes! We now know a great deal about the substances contained within the shroud because, in 1978, the Roman Catholic Church allowed the Shroud of Turin Research Project (or STURP), a group of elite scholars from the U.S., to test, analyze, photograph, and x-ray the shroud over a five-day period from October 8-13. After 120 continuous hours of around-the-clock examination, which included the taking of thousands of photographs, x-rays and spectra, the most in-depth series of tests ever performed on the shroud to date, STURP found that, in addition to the 3-D image, the shroud contains (a) human blood, (b) plant pollen and (c) soil. These items point to a cloth which must have been in Palestine at one time, and which contains bloodstain patterns consistent with a severely beaten, crucified man. Consider these three key facts:

Fact #1: The bloodstains on the cloth, which indeed perfectly match the wounds of Jesus' beating and crucifixion as described in the Gospels, are not an artist's pigment or dye but real AB-type blood, and these bloodstains, amazingly, were applied to the shroud cloth *prior* to the formation of the 3-D image.[20] This fact alone rules out forgery, since a forger would have had to "paint" with real blood first, then use light energy to scorch an anatomically perfect 3-D image which perfectly matched-up with the bloodstains, an impossible feat. Theologically, it makes sense Jesus would incarnate with AB+ blood (which only 3% of humans possess), since AB+ blood is not only a universally receptive type but a universal donor type, meaning it can be transfused into any person. Even via his blood, no sinner is excluded from being taken up into Jesus' divine life. But blood is not the only strong evidence for the shroud's authenticity.

Fact #2: The pollen grains located inside the shroud's fibrils originate from 58 species of plants, 17 of which are indigenous to Europe, where the artifact has been stored for seven centuries. So, the majority of the pollen grains are indigenous (some exclusively) to the environs of Palestine.[21]

Fact #3: And we can narrow the geography even further. The dirt found near the bare feet of the "man in the shroud" is consistent with the rare calcium carbonate soil of Jerusalem, an incredible fact since a forger, if there was one, must have anticipated modern-day soil analysis.[22]

Moreover, when the constituency and design of the shroud cloth is considered, the case for authenticity grows. The shroud was made with a herringbone twill with a 3:1 weave, a common first-century Palestinian weave. Its flax fibrils contain entwisted cotton fibrils of the species Gossypium herbaceum, a rare species found in the Middle East, but not in Europe.[23] So everything about the shroud points to first-century Jerusalem.

That said, what about the aforementioned 1988 media story which reported the shroud had been dated to the 14th century? Did this debunk the shroud as being a forgery? Indeed, in 1988, three top radiocarbon labs from Arizona, Oxford and Zurich were allowed by Cardinal Ballestrero, Archbishop of Turin, to examine small Shroud samples and date these using the best methods. After the laboratories' radiocarbon analysis was forwarded, Cardinal Ballestrero made an official  statement to the worldwide press on October 13, 1988 (see photo above), saying "the three laboratories performing the carbon dating of the shroud determined an approximate 1325 date for the cloth."[24]

After this announcement, global headlines branded the shroud as being a fake created by a 14th-century forger. But can we trust these 1988 findings? Perhaps each lab generated (in good faith) an inaccurate result due to uncontrollable factors. After studying this topic in depth, I am now convinced this is what occurred, that the labs were not able to set an accurate date due to unseen factors present at the microscopic level.

Specifically, the presence of microorganisms covering the shroud linen explains why radiocarbon-dating cannot be trusted. Dr. Leoncio Garza-Valdes, a biochemist, was the first to note this fact. In 1993, he determined that a "Lichenothelia varnish," or bioplastic coating, had accumulated on the shroud and thus contaminated the 1988 radiocarbon dating, since this 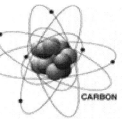 coating was not affected by the cleaning procedure used by the three radiocarbon labs.[25] This theory has since been supported by many scholars, including Dr. Harry Grove, who examined in 1994 a portion of the shroud's threads and determined these indeed had a substantial bioplastic coating.[26] Radiocarbon dating is not accurate in such cases.

If the reader has not yet been persuaded about the shroud's authenticity, I have summarized below three feats of genius that a forger must have accomplished to create his masterpiece, based on the data:

#1 The forger was able to create, in a photographic negative manner, an anatomically photographically perfect 3-D human image centuries before photography was even invented. He did this by using a yet unknown medium and unknown technique, and was not able to check his work close up as he progressed, since to discern his 3-D man, he would have to work at least 30 to 40 feet away.

#2 The forger also must have first used real AB blood to paint the bloodstains of the 3-D "man in the shroud" image before he even created the corpse image. This means that the forger must have placed the blood in an anatomically perfect position in perfect anticipation of where he wanted his "corpse" to appear. The forger, in making the bloodstains, was also able to duplicate blood flow patterns in perfect forensic agreement to blood flow from the wrists at 65° from vertical, identical to what crucifixion causes.

#3 The forger was also clever enough to link his work to the exact time and place of the Gospel accounts by (a) making his man possess a pony-tail, sidelocks and a beard style consistent with a Jewish male of the first century, (b) by incorporating dirt from the bare feet of the man in the shroud consistent with the calcium carbonate soil of Jerusalem, (c) by dabbing the linen with pollens indigenous only to the environs of Jerusalem, (d) by making the body of his hoax nude (against all medieval artistry) in order to conform to genuine Roman crucifixion and (e) accurately illustrating (unlike medieval representations) the fact that the nails of Roman crucifixion were placed through the wrists rather than the hands.[27]

But it gets even better! Another relic corroborates the shroud. Caution: this is mind-blowing. Scientists have proven that the shroud's head blood stains possess a 100% *identical* alignment with the blood stains present on a relic called the *Sudarium of Oviedo*, a cloth said to have been placed on Jesus' face following his crucifixion. If the Sudarium is authentic, then 100% the Shroud must be also as the two relics are inextricably linked by blood type and blood alignment, since the Sudarium's blood stains indeed *precisely match-up* with all the stains present on the Shroud face, a synchronicity that is totally impossible to fake or artificially fabricate.

That said, if the Shroud of Turin is somehow a creation of the 14th century and not a genuine artifact of the first century, we have before us the work of the greatest genius ever. In fact, this medieval forger was such an expert in blood biochemistry, forensic pathology, human anatomy, plant botany, photography, and 3-D computer analysis that he has, to date, completely foiled all efforts of 21st-century science to reproduce his masterpiece (along with the perfectly synchronized Sudarium face covering). Indeed, the forger's yet unknown technique baffles even 21st-century computer and laser experts, since they, with access to these tools, have yet to be able to do what he must have done.

Based on the above data, I am convinced that the Shroud of Turin was placed over Jesus' corpse and that the 3-D, thermally stable, photographic negative image on the shroud (made *over* the bloodstains) was produced by the energy of Jesus' corpse rising to life. To date, not one person, no artist, scientist, or computer expert has been able to reproduce an identical 3-D image to that found on the Shroud of Turin. I believe such a feat cannot ever be done for one basic reason, namely, the Shroud "pictured" for us a one-time historical event, the miraculous resurrection of Jesus Christ.

Y – Yes – It's the Most Cogent Option

Our last resurrection evidence to consider is the fact that no theory, other than a literal resurrection, has been able to adequately account for the historical data. Yes – resurrection is the most cogent option. But let us see why exactly. Outside of the Christian option, four theories have gained prominence to explain why the so-called "myth" of Jesus' resurrection was perpetuated. These are the hallucination theory, myth-maker theory, conspiracy theory and swoon theory. Of course, when we include Christianity, five theories in total represent all the logical options as to how the resurrection claim could have originated:

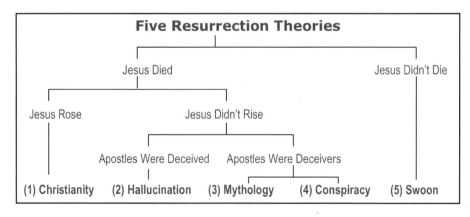

Five Resurrection Theories

- Jesus Died
  - Jesus Rose
    - (1) Christianity
  - Jesus Didn't Rise
    - Apostles Were Deceived
      - (2) Hallucination
      - (3) Mythology
    - Apostles Were Deceivers
      - (4) Conspiracy
- Jesus Didn't Die
  - (5) Swoon

Now let us examine each of the four secular alternatives above to determine each theory's credibility. In so doing, we must ask one question: Are any of these theories more credible than the Christian option, namely the belief that Jesus supernaturally rose? Let us see.

Theory #1: First, we have the _hallucination theory_. This theory purports that the early apostles only "thought" that they had seen the risen Christ, but in fact were hallucinating! This seems to defy logic since two people will never see the exact same hallucination. Paul says in the early creed of 1 Corinthians 15:3-8 that up to 500 people saw the risen Christ, so the hallucination theory faces a gigantic hurdle.

REBUTTAL: Now it is true that psychologists do know that some individuals, such as schizophrenics, do in fact experience hallucinations on occasion, but these hallucinations are always "private" events and they occur in one place at one time. Yet in the Gospels we see not only many eyewitnesses to the resurrection, but a great variety of times and places. Consider Jesus' appearances as recorded in the Gospels. One was an early Sunday morning appearance to Mary Magdalene, one was

an appearance on the road to Emmaus, and one was an appearance by the lake. Plus, hallucinations do not eat, as Jesus did (see Luke 24:42-42), nor can they be touched, as Jesus was touched (see Matthew 28:9; Luke 24:39; John 20:27). These facts totally debunk the hallucination theory! It is not credible.

Theory #2: The second theory to consider is the _mythology theory_, which purports that the Gospel authors simply wrote down false history. Whether intentionally or unintentionally, these writers (it is claimed) perpetuated myths, including the resurrection myth. Some argue that the Gospel accounts were sort of like "fish" stories gone wild and thus they present inaccurate accounts. But did this occur with the Gospels? Did they become embellished "fish stories"? No. We examined an entire book chapter (chapter 2) dedicated to addressing this critical issue. That said, I am quite confident that the Gospels do not contain myths.

REBUTTAL: Let us review four key points from chapter 2 to construct a sound rebuttal here: (1) We already saw that we can be confident that the Gospels we have today are the same Gospels originally written, i.e., distortion did not occur; (2) The Gospels also possess telltale marks of eyewitness description; they include vivid details and self-damaging material; (3) Moreover, the Gospels do not contain anachronisms; the authors accurately linked their accounts to first-century events. This is evidenced by the fact that the Gospels have been corroborated by contemporary secular historians, such as Josephus, Tacitus and Pliny, and by archeological discoveries, such as those found corroborating the names and positions of Pontius Pilate and Caesar Augustus. (4) Finally, there was simply not enough time for myth to seep into the Gospel records. Except for the Gospel of John, no reputable biblical scholar disputes the fact that the Synoptics (and the letters of Paul) were written before the destruction of Jerusalem in A.D. 70, well within the lifetime of eyewitnesses to Christ. Moreover, Jesus' prophecy of the destruction of Jerusalem maintained an apocalyptic element, meaning that the recording of his prophecy must have occurred before A.D. 70. In short, the Gospels are reliable historical documents, and hence, the "mythology" theory of the Christ's resurrection is simply not credible.

Theory #3: The third resurrection theory we need to scrutinize is the _conspiracy theory_. This theory argues that the disciples conspired to steal Jesus' body and then tell the world that he had actually risen, and were even willing to die for this lie! Those who entertain this stolen-body conspiracy theory must suppose that a group of disciples, who days before had run off scared, confronted a heavily armed Roman guard, snuck past them to roll back a large stone, and then successfully stole and carted off Jesus' corpse. Then, over the next three decades, these liars endured incredible torture and martyrdom, all to spread what they knew to be false throughout the known world. Interestingly, the first people to perpetuate the conspiracy theory were actually the chief priests of Jerusalem during Jesus' time.

After the resurrection event, some of the soldiers who had been guarding the tomb left their post and went to the chief priests to report what had happened. Matthew 28:12-15 records the scene:

When the chief priests had ... devised a plan, they gave the soldiers a large sum of money, telling them, "You are to say, 'His disciples came during the night and stole him away while we were asleep.' If this report gets to the governor, we will satisfy him and keep you out of trouble." So the soldiers took the money and did as they were instructed. And this story has been widely circulated among the Jews to this very day.

REBUTTAL: The chief priests knew definitively that what they were perpetuating here was a lie. If anybody should be labeled as conspirators, it was the Jewish priests, for they also knew well that the three security precautions they had put in place , namely the rolling stone, the official Roman seal, and the Roman security guard, would have made it impossible for Jesus' disciples (or anyone else for that matter) to be able to steal Jesus' body. Dealing with the rolling stone, for one, would have been laborious. Based upon first-century models and textual information, two Georgia Tech engineering professors have calculated that Jesus' rolling stone probably weighed about two tons and could only be rolled back by a team of strong men.[28] That is why the women, on their way to the tomb, wondered, "Who will roll the stone away from the tomb?" (cf. Mark 16:3). The nature of liars is also a factor to consider here. Simon Greenleaf, a Harvard law professor who for decades taught law students how to determine whether a witness is lying, says: "It was impossible that they [the disciples] could have persisted in affirming the truths they narrated, had not Jesus actually risen."[29]

Theory #4: Finally, we must consider the swoon theory. This theory is often called the *resuscitation theory* since it argues that Jesus didn't really die on the cross (even though he was beaten and crucified) but that Jesus merely fainted, or "swooned," from exhaustion and lack of blood. A man named Venturini was the first person to propose the swoon theory and it was later a popular hypothesis with 18th-century rationalists. According to the theory, Jesus was mistakenly buried alive, and when he regained consciousness, he walked out of his tomb and appeared to his disciples; they couldn't believe mere resuscitation revived him, so they insisted that Jesus had resurrected from the dead.

REBUTTAL: However, this theory contradicts all we know from the Gospels about Jesus' brutal passion. Consider the historical facts about Roman crucifixion. Jewish historian, Josephus (cf. page 97), who was an advisor to Titus during the siege of Je many crucifixions and called them "the most wretched deaths."[30] Cicero called it "the most cruel and hideous of tortures."[31] After the verdict of crucifixion was issued, it was customary to have a prisoner whipped by a flagrum, a Roman whip that possessed a sturdy handle to which were attached long strips containing sharp, jagged pieces of bone and lead. The Jews by their law were limited to 40 lashes, so they would only give 39 in case they miscounted. But the Romans had no such limit; so Jesus, when he was tortured with the flagrum, may have been hit more than 39x. Eusibius, a third-

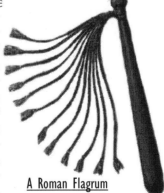

A Roman Flagrum

century historian, this about flagrams: "The sufferer's veins were laid bare, and the very muscles, sinews, and bowels of the victim were open to exposure."[32] The 2004 Mel Gibson film, *Passion of the Christ*, depicts Jesus' flagram whipping accurately. It was excruciatingly brutal.

After the whipping, a man condemned had to then carry his own horizontal crossbar to the place of execution. This piece of wood, called a patibulum, weighed over 100 pounds and was strapped to the victim's shoulders. We see in the Gospels that Jesus became too weak to carry his patibulum, so Simon from Cyrene was forced to do it (see Luke 23:26). Upon reaching the execution site, the victim was then nailed or bound by ropes to a cross. In Jesus' case, they used long iron spikes. Contrary to inaccurate medieval paintings, we now know the Romans drove these spikes through the wrists, not the hands, as hands would tear.

Crucifixion could last up to three days. In Jesus' case, it lasted six hours (see Luke 23:44-46). When Romans soldiers sought to hasten death, a victim's legs were broken below the knees so that they could no longer press up to grasp for air. But in Jesus' case, his legs were not broken (a Psalm 34:20 prophecy) because the soldiers "saw he was already dead" (see John 19:33). To make certain, one of the soldiers thrust a spear into Jesus' side. As John 19:34 records, "immediately there came out blood and water," a clear forensic sign that watery fluid had built-up around the pericardium, indicating Jesus had indeed already died. Thus, Jesus did not die the usual crucifixion death by suffocation, but actually of heart failure due to fluid constriction. According to Roman law, Pilate would not have been able to turn over Jesus' body to Joseph of Arimathea unless the five executioners present (i.e., four soldiers and centurion commander) had certified Jesus' death.[33] Ergo, the swoon theory is absolutely absurd.

Consider Josh McDowell's outstanding commentary on the irrationality of the swoon theory in his 1981 book, *The Resurrection Factor*:

The [swoon] theory would have to say that: (1) Jesus went through six trials – three Roman and three Jewish; (2) was beaten almost beyond description by the Roman flagrum; (3) was so weak He could not carry His own patibulum – the wooden cross bar; (4) had spikes through his hands and feet as he was crucified; (5) the Romans thrust a sword into His side and eyewitnesses said, "Blood and water came out," a sign of death; (6) four executioners confirmed His death – they must have all been mistaken; (7) 100-plus pounds of spices and a gummy substance were encased around his body – He must have breathed through it all; (8) He was put into a cold, damp tomb; (9) a large stone was lodged against its entrance; (10) a Roman guard was stationed there, and (11) a seal was placed across the entrance. Then an incredible thing happened, according to this theory. The cool damp air of the tomb, instead of killing Him, healed Him. He split out of His garments, pushed the stone away, fought off the Roman guards and shortly thereafter appeared to His disciples as the Lord.[34]

Obviously, this theory ignores the brutality depicted by the Gospel accounts. Indeed, if the swoon theory were true, it would be more miraculous than the resurrection itself. And yet many individuals continue to purport the ludicrous theory. Dr. Hugh J. Schonfield is a modern example. In the 1960s, his controversial book, *The Passover Plot*, played a clever variation on the swoon theory. According to Schoenfield, Jesus believed he was the Messiah and therefore plotted a very detailed plan to arrange what appeared to be a miraculous resurrection. Jesus is said to have taken into his confidence Joseph of Arimathea and an unknown "young man." The plan was for Jesus to be buried by Joseph and then appear alive at a later date. Thus, Schoenfield concludes that Jesus planned his own 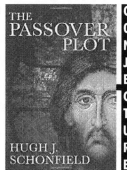 arrest, trial, and crucifixion and arranged for himself to be drugged on the cross (at the time the vinegar was offered) so that he could feign death and then recover. But Jesus' plot was thwarted when, unexpectedly, a Roman soldier thrust a spear into his side. Jesus regained consciousness, but then eventually died. The unknown "young man" Jesus chose was then mistaken as Jesus by an emotional Mary and misidentified as Christ by confused disciples. Neither Joseph nor the young man ever cleared up the error, so, according to Schonfield, the resurrection story remained alive among the disciples and Jesus' followers.

However, Schoenfield's Passover Plot has been totally discredited, since it superimposes conjecture and fabricated details. In fact, the only cogent explanation for the empty tomb and the eyewitness accounts is this Christian one, namely, that Jesus rose as he had predicted he would.

Granted, although it is true that a superficial reading of the Gospel resurrection accounts suggests there may be discrepancies between the authors, a closer examination reveals a remarkable degree of unanimity. All four Gospels had the same basic tale to tell. The main witnesses who first saw the empty tomb were a group of women and, immediately after their discovery, they seem to have scattered in order to take the news to different people. So it is not surprising that the Gospel accounts vary in detail. It would be more surprising if they did not. The variation shows that the writers collected evidence from more than one source, which makes the overall agreement of the four accounts even more impressive.

Consider the apparent discrepancy of the women at the tomb. Skeptics point to the fact that the Gospels seem to possess disagreement as to which women went there. Luke mentions that Mary Magdalene, Joanna, Mary the mother of James, and other "women from Galilee" went to the tomb (see Luke 24:9), while John singles out Mary Magdalene (see John 20:1). Yet, in John 20:2, Mary Magdalene says: "They have taken the Lord out of the tomb and we don't know where they have put him!"

The "we" here recorded by John obviously implies that other people (most likely women) were with Mary Magdalene. In contrast to Luke and John, Matthew 28:1 says that "Mary Magdalene and the other Mary went to look at the tomb." Yet just because Matthew does not mention the other women from Galilee (like Luke had done) does not mean these women were not present at the tomb.

Likewise, when we carefully examine the apparent discrepancy of how many angels were at the tomb, we see that a harmony can be found. Although Luke 24:4 and John 20:12 record that two angels were at the 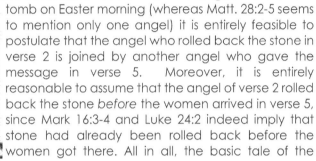 tomb on Easter morning (whereas Matt. 28:2-5 seems to mention only one angel) it is entirely feasible to postulate that the angel who rolled back the stone in verse 2 is joined by another angel who gave the message in verse 5. Moreover, it is entirely reasonable to assume that the angel of verse 2 rolled back the stone *before* the women arrived in verse 5, since Mark 16:3-4 and Luke 24:2 indeed imply that stone had already been rolled back before the women got there. All in all, the basic tale of the Gospel accounts is the same: Jesus' tomb was empty, angels announced this fact to women, and Jesus appeared alive to many different eyewitnesses on at least seven occasions (cf. map on page 129).

Given the "emptiness" of the tomb and the fact the early apostles and skeptics (like Saul), believed they had seen the risen Jesus, have we "proved" the resurrection? No. But we have indeed conclusively shown that the resurrection option is the most cogent vis-à-vis all alternatives. That is, this option is much easier to accept than to reject, even though we cannot prove it 100%. Dr. Gregory A. Boyd explains this point well in his 1995 award-winning book, *Cynic Sage or Son of God*. Boyd writes:

Admitting that the tomb was empty and that many early disciples believed they witnessed the resurrected Lord doesn't itself prove that Jesus actually rose from the dead. Historical reasoning necessarily stops short of this. Affirming the historical resurrection, therefore, is fundamentally an act of faith. But admitting this much *does* render this act of faith very reasonable. Indeed, if a "leap" is required to affirm Jesus' resurrection, it is far less than the "leap" required to deny it.[35]

Now let us summarize in five concise points what we have learned about the undeniable historical evidence for Jesus' radiant resurrection. These facts point to only one sound conclusion: Jesus is still alive. He may have died once, but death's sting could not hold him (Acts 2:24).

Five Resurrection Facts Summarized

#1 – The "emptiness" of Jesus' grave was not disputed by any of Jesus' enemies and is thus a sound historical fact recorded in reliable historical documents. Since the tomb guards told the Jewish leaders that Jesus' tomb had become vacant, the leaders concocted a lie that Jesus' disciples had "stolen" his body, even though these leaders knew that security barriers had been put in place to keep this very thing from occurring.

#2 – The fact that the Gospels report that women discovered the empty tomb is both remarkable and surprising, since, in that culture and time period, women were considered unreliable witnesses. If the Gospel writers wanted to fabricate a legend about Jesus' rising, they therefore never would have written accounts that women saw the risen Jesus FIRST – no way!

#3 – The fact that 1 Corinthians 15:3-8 has been to shown to be an early creed of the church bolsters the resurrection claim. Paul writes over 500 were eyewitnesses of the risen Jesus.

#4 – The evidence for Jesus' numerous post-resurrection appearances did not develop gradually over many years, but rather it is an indisputable fact that the resurrection was the central proclamation of the church from the very beginning. Indeed, the radical change in the lives of deniers such as Peter and skeptics such as Paul as well as the miraculous emergence of the church in the very city where the crucifixion took place is inexplicable unless we conclude the resurrection was real.

#5 – Apart from the resurrection option, there is simply no cogent explanation as to how Jesus' tomb became vacant and why skeptics – like Paul and James – had experienced a sudden conversion, even being willing to die for their new-found faith. The fact that all secular resurrection theories fail to account for the evidence shows the resurrection to be a cogent claim.

Is the Christian Bible actually the Word of God?

Now that we have demonstrated the cogency of the ecumenical Christian belief that Jesus was in F-A-C-T God-incarnate, we can turn our attention, briefly, to defending the Christian Bible. But before doing so, we need to understand the concept of the *biblical canon*. For the reader unfamiliar with term *canon*, the word actually comes from the root word "reed" (English word *cane*; Hebrew word *ganeh* and Greek word *Kanon*). The reed was used as a standard measuring rod and thus eventually came to mean "standard." As applied to the Christian Bible, the word canon means "an officially accepted list of books" or the "standard" by which Christians measure and evaluate all doctrines of faith and practice.

The belief that the canon of the Bible is God's Word is technically not an ecumenical belief per se since Protestants and Catholics disagree considerably as to what actually constitutes the complete canon of Scripture. Nonetheless, we can make a sound case for the Bible, since, apart from the *Deuterocanonical books* that were pronounced canonical by the Roman Catholic Church (RCC) at the A.D. 1546 Council of Trent (yet are still rejected by most Protestant groups), all branches of Christendom do accept a minimum of 66 biblical books as authoritative. It is this universally-accepted canon of 66 books — 39 from the OT and 27 from the NT — that we can indeed soundly defend in an ecumenical manner. Pictured below is a useful infographic which depicts the genre organization of the 66 universally accepted books of the Christian Bible:

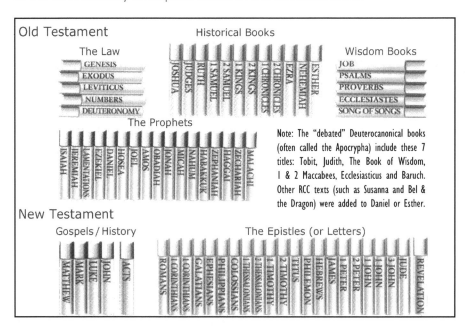

Why wait till this point in our apology (defense) to address the issue of the Bible? One key reason: All credible apologists first demonstrate the divinity of Christ *before* progressing to deal with the authority of Scripture, since this is the only way to construct a sound argument for Scripture. Allow me to explain. We cannot use the Bible to prove the Bible, for this would employ fallacious circular reasoning. It would be like saying: "I believe the Bible is true because it says it is true." This is circular reasoning and should be avoided whenever we try to substantiate a proposition.

But we *can* firmly establish, as we have done in the last two chapters, that there exists compelling historical and literary evidence to conclude that Jesus was indeed the God-man. And based on this fact of history, and the words that Jesus himself used to talk about Scripture, we can build a sound case that is not circular. Interestingly, using this sound approach, we technically *do not* have to believe the Bible to be God's Word to draw the sound conclusion that Jesus is the Lord of the Universe. Many Christian apologists miss this key point. That is, the conclusion of Jesus' deity can be arrived at from solid historical evidence. And it is from Jesus' deity that we, in turn, can build a sound and solid case for the 66 canonical books of the Christian Bible.

Basically, a sound argument for the 66 books can be constructed using six basic propositions: (1) The Gospels are trustworthy and reliable historical documents; (2) Jesus clearly claimed to be God in at least four places in these documents; (3) Historical data, such as the factualness of the empty tomb, validates Christ's claims; (4) As the God-man, Jesus spoke with divine authority; (5) Jesus considered the OT to be God's Word as evidenced by Matthew 5:17-18 where he says that he has not come to "abolish the Law or the Prophets"; (6) In John 14:26, Jesus the Holy Spirit to his disciples (many of whom became NT authors) and claims that Holy Spirit will "remind" them of "everything." So, with this argument, instead of beginning with Bible and assuming it to be God's Word, we start with the divine authority of Christ who teaches it is God's word.

This approach, which makes acceptance of the authority of the Bible dependent on a prior commitment to Jesus, is in full agreement with Jesus' own teaching, since Jesus promised in John 7:16-17 that those who follow God will be able to verify the truthfulness of God's revelation. Jesus says: "My teaching is not my own. It comes from him who sent me. If anyone chooses to do God's will, he will find out whether my teaching comes from God or whether I speak on my own." In his best-selling book, *Answers to Tough Questions*, well known apologist Josh McDowell offers an excellent summation as to why we, based on Jesus' divine authority, can soundly trust that God played a role in creating both the Old and New Testament. McDowell captures this point exceedingly well. He writes:

Since Jesus considered the Old Testament to be the Word of God (Matthew 15:1-6, 5:17-18) and promised his disciples, who either wrote or had control over the writing of the New Testament books, that the Holy Spirit would bring all things back to their remembrance (John 14:26), we can insist, with sound and accurate logic, that the Bible is God's Word. This is not circular reasoning.[36]

When we add this argument to the facts that (1) the Bible shows a remarkable thematic unity, viz., the redemption of fallen humanity by Christ, despite being written by 40 different authors in three languages across three continents over 1500+ years, and (2) the fact the Bible has been published more times in more languages and read by more people than other book, we see a solid case emerge, one that shows that a divine hand was indeed at work in the development of this revelation. Ken Ham, founder of Answer-in-Genesis, calls the Bible "the history book of the universe." And this is a great title, for through this *unique opus* God has revealed his divine nature, his plan of salvation, and our eternal destiny.

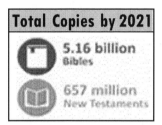

Total Copies by 2021
5.16 billion Bibles
657 million New Testaments

A Brief Summary

To sum up this chapter on Christological apologetics, pertinent for skeptics and individuals who deny the orthodox doctrine of Jesus' deity (e.g., Jehovah's Witnesses, Mormons, etc.), we can state the following five summative points re: the undeniable F-A-C-T of Jesus' divine nature:

(1)   We saw that Jesus fulfilled over 60 major messianic C-H-R-IS-T prophecies, including his Clear Davidic Lineage, Humble Bethlehem Birth, Royal Jerusalem Colt Ride, Internal Betrayal by a Friend, Suffering while Lots Cast, and Tomb Corpse Resurrection. There is no possible way a human Jesus could have orchestrated all these fulfillments as each was out of the purview of his control.

(2)   We also saw that Jesus possessed seven divine powers, or authority F-A-C-T-O-R-S, that only a God-man could possess. Jesus *Forgave Sins, Accepted Worship, Controlled Nature*, Taught with *Authority, Ordered Demons, Raised the Dead* and audaciously proclaimed that he alone would *Save Humankind*. Either Jesus really performed these remarkable feats or the Gospels are fabricating fairy tales. But we already saw that the Gospels are credible and reliable historical documents. So we can soundly surmise that Jesus' divine miracles were indeed facts of history and recorded as such by honest eyewitnesses and evangelists.

(3)   In addition to laying claim to prophetic fulfillments and possessing God-man authority, Jesus also clearly claimed to be divine, specifically to be (a) the Messiah, (b) God's Son, (c) the divine I AM and (d) one with the Father. With regard to these claims, we only have three options from which to choose. Either Jesus was a LIAR, a LUNATIC or the LORD as he made these divine claims. We cannot simply call Jesus a good moral teacher, for he did not leave that label to us! We must choose: Liar, Lunatic or Lord? As we saw, our most credible option is clearly the latter, that Jesus is indeed the Lord of this universe and one true hope for humankind.

(4)   We also investigated five resurrection evidences, each of which pointed to the F-A-C-T that Jesus' tomb was E-M-P-T-Y on Easter Sunday. We looked at the Eyewitnesses of the Risen Jesus, the Moved Security Stone, the Preaching of the First Apostles, Turin's Shroud & Its 3-D Imagery and the fact that the resurrection theory is really Your Most Cogent Option, given all of the historical data. Given the evidence, it simply takes more faith for someone to deny the resurrection event than to affirm it. Faith fits the facts. And the facts, taken together, say undeniably that Jesus is eternally alive.

(5)   Finally, we saw that, based on the solid case we have for the authority of Jesus as God, we can forge a credible apology for the authority of the Bible (at least for the 66 books of the biblical canon that are universally accepted within Christendom). Such a case is cogent since, instead of initially assuming the Bible to be inspired and true, which leads to circular reasoning, we base its truthfulness in Christ as Truth, and Christ backs the Bible's veracity.

All in all, we have provided solid unassailable evidence to substantiate Jesus' own claims that he was/is a divine being. And this is no surprise, for if God were to become a man, then we would expect the evidence to reveal this. It does. We would also expect any God-man to make a lasting effect on humanity. And this is what Christ has done. The great historian, Kenneth Latourette, cites this key fact: He writes: "As the centuries pass, the evidence is accumulating that, measured by His effect on history, Jesus is the most influential life ever lived on this planet." [37]

Now that we have established a cogent case for Christ's divine nature, we must turn our defense of universal Christianity toward the universal gospel message that Christ came to establish on Earth in the first place, the kerygma proclamation. It is here where our apologetics will merge into evangelism, where our propositional facts *about* Christ will point to the soundness of placing personal faith *in* Christ.

"The devil would gladly give a Bible to every man and promote obedience to its commands if in exchange we would surrender to him the Gospel [kerygma]."

— Paul David Washer

THE DEVIL'S BARGAIN

OKAY

BUT...

KERYGMA

Kerygma

"I am not ashamed of the gospel for it is the power of God unto salvation for all who believe."

— Paul the Apostle in Romans 1:16

Pictured above is a carving that I found in Rome's catacombs in 1993 which depicts the two most well-known and powerful symbols of Christianity — the FISH & CROSS — each of which encapsulated the ancient Christian kerygma (or Christianity's early gospel proclamation), specifically who Jesus was (e.g., the Greek word for fish formed an acrostic for Jesus-Christ-God's-Son-Savior) and what Jesus did (e.g., the cross represented the fact that Jesus had died as a propitiation for the sins of humanity so that all could be invited to find new and eternal life).

Why exactly was this word *kerygma* chosen to be the title of a final chapter in a handbook on apologetics? Is the kerygma an essential, ecumenical concept? To offer a complete answer as to why a careful study of the kerygma is 100% fitting and apropos to apologetics, let us address four questions re this fourth core topic in our Diamond of Truth diagram: (1) What is the Christian kerygma exactly? (2) Where is kerygma's content found specifically? (3) What is the

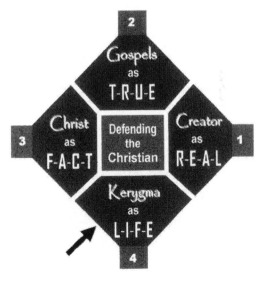

main purpose of the kerygma? (4) Does the kerygma of the NT *make sense* as a 21st-century proclamation? As we address these questions, we will we see that the kerygma is not only a central ecumenical Christian truth-claim, but a message vital to the final destiny of mankind.

#1 – What is the Christian kerygma exactly?

Simply put, the kerygma was the basic evangelistic message proclaimed by the earliest Christian apostles. More completely, it was the proclamation of the death, resurrection, and exaltation of Jesus which attempted to (a) lead one to an evaluation of Jesus as both Lord and Christ, (b) confront one with the necessity of repentance and (c) promise the forgiveness of sins and unending life, since Christ himself is risen. The kergyma was thus the same as the gospel message, although the term kerygma emphasized the "manner" of delivery as well as the message.

To explain, in the ancient world, a king often made known his decree by means of a *kerux*, the kingdom's official herald. This hand-picked servant, a person who often served a close confident, would travel throughout the kingdom boldly announcing to citizens whatever the king wished to make public. In the same manner, Peter, Paul and the early apostles were essentially "keruxes" for a much greater kingdom, that of God. As commanded by the risen King Jesus, their message, the Christian kerygma, was to be authoritatively preached to all who would listen; in fact, all humanity was to be the target audience. As Acts 1:8 (Amp) states, the apostles were to be Jesus' "witnesses in Jerusalem and all Judea and Samaria and to the ends (the very bounds) of the earth."

When we analyze the kergyma, it is evident Christ's resurrection played the central role in the drama of redemption. The kerygma in fact always focused on the resurrection. This supernatural miracle in history authenticated the works and words of Jesus and constituted the basis

Early Christian Symbol of Resurrection

Early Christians adopted the symbol of the PEACOCK to represent resurrection and immortality. This idea had its roots in a Greek legend that peacock flesh did not decay.

for Christian immortality. Without the resurrection, everything fell apart. So, for early Christian preachers, the kerygma was a living, active message, the declaration that Christ was truly risen, and by that great act of God, Christ as the chosen Messiah had secured salvation for humanity.

#2 — Where is the kerygma found specifically?

The best examples of the kerygma proclamation can be drawn from two biblical sources: (1) the speeches of Peter in the Book of Acts and (2) the speeches of the apostle Paul. Two speeches in particular, Peter's Pentecost speech in Acts 2:14-41 and Paul's "Unknown God" speech to the Athenians in Acts 17:21-53, provide lucid illustrations of how the early kerygma was specifically proclaimed. Let us examine each separately. As we do, the kerygma's essentiality will become apparent.

Speech #1:   First, let us consider Peter's most famous speech in Acts 2, which was delivered on the Day of Pentecost and took the form of a Jewish chiasmus, which was a common rhetorical structure for organizing ideas in which a reversal of the order of words amidst parallel phrases was used. Consider below the reverse-parallel structure of Peter's sermon as displayed in its distinctive chiastic layout.[1] From a literary perspective, the chiasmus is quite elegant, containing a total of 10 parallel lines (as marked by the letters A to J):

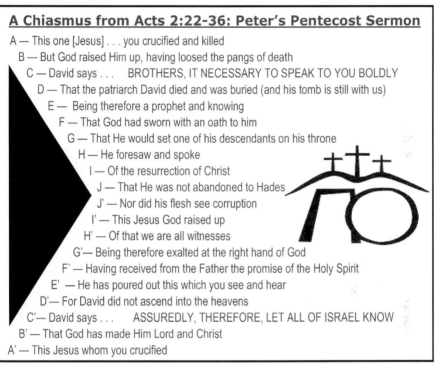

A Chiasmus from Acts 2:22-36: Peter's Pentecost Sermon

A — This one [Jesus] . . . you crucified and killed

B — But God raised Him up, having loosed the pangs of death

C — David says . . .   BROTHERS, IT NECESSARY TO SPEAK TO YOU BOLDLY

D — That the patriarch David died and was buried (and his tomb is still with us)

E — Being therefore a prophet and knowing

F — That God had sworn with an oath to him

G — That He would set one of his descendants on his throne

H — He foresaw and spoke

I — Of the resurrection of Christ

J — That He was not abandoned to Hades

J' — Nor did his flesh see corruption

I' — This Jesus God raised up

H' — Of that we are all witnesses

G'— Being therefore exalted at the right hand of God

F' — Having received from the Father the promise of the Holy Spirit

E' — He has poured out this which you see and hear

D'— For David did not ascend into the heavens

C'— David says . . .   ASSUREDLY, THEREFORE, LET ALL OF ISRAEL KNOW

B' — That God has made Him Lord and Christ

A' — This Jesus whom you crucified

In Acts 2:37, when Peter finished his chiastic sermon, the crowd cried: "What shall we do?" They felt forced to respond when confronted with the logic of the apostle's claim that, by the resurrection of Jesus, "God has made him both Lord and Christ" (Acts 2:36). Peter responds, telling them to "repent and be baptized in the name of Jesus for the forgiveness of sins" (Acts 2:38). And 3000 people did so on that day (see Acts 2:41). They could not help but believe in Christ given Peter's words. Craig S. Keener points out the radical cost of Peter's call for people to be "baptized" in the name of Jesus, particularly for the Jews in the audience:

Because baptism was a sign of conversion to Judaism normally reserved for pagans, Peter's demand [in Acts 2:38] would offend his Jewish hearers and cost them respectability. He calls for a public, radical testimony of conversion.[2]

The adjacent 1994 Jerusalem photo of me standing near Second Temple ruins shows the likely location of the temple grounds where Peter stood to proclaim his Acts 2 sermon. It is incredible how Acts 2:41 records that "those who accepted [Peter's] message were baptized, and about 3000 were added to their number that day." These stone steps, which descend from the south wall of the temple, can indeed host a crowd of

over 5000. In fact, archeologists have uncovered pools at the base of these steps, dating from Jesus' era, which were likely used for the Acts 2:41 baptisms. What a prime location for the kerygma message to be proclaimed. And what an incredible day for Peter, God's kerux.

Speech #2: We observe a second paragon of kerygma preaching in Acts 17:21-53. Here, Paul the apostle is traveling on his second of three missionary journeys and this journey brings him to Athens, the ancient world's center of art, philosophy, literature and science. Distressed to see that Athens was full of man-made idols, Acts 17:17 says Paul "reasoned in the Synagogue and in the marketplace day by day" some Epicurean & Stoic philosophers were impressed enough to invite Paul to the Areopagus, a place where men gathered for debate and discussion. Paul stood before those who had gathered and offered one of his most famous NT speeches:

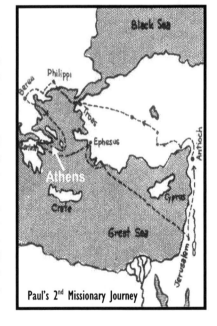

Paul's 2nd Missionary Journey

Men of Athens! I see that in every way you are very religious. For as I walked around and looked carefully at your objects of worship, I even found an altar with this inscription: **TO AN UNKNOWN GOD.** Now what you worship as something unknown I am going to proclaim to you. The God who made the world and everything in it is the Lord of heaven and earth and does not live in temples built by hands. And he is not served by human hands, as if he needed anything, because he himself gives all men life and breath and everything.

As polytheists, Greeks were careful to acknowledge the existence of unknown gods, lest they miss one. Paul here, after beautifully using the theme of "THE UNKNOWN GOD" to introduce to the Athenians the one true God, elaborates on the resurrection, which always was the essential part of the kerygma. Paul exclaims that God "has set a day when he will judge the world with justice by the man [Christ] he has appointed" and that God "has given proof of this to all men by raising [Christ] from the dead" (vs. 31). Verse 34 then says that a few men "believed" Paul's words.

#3 — What is the main purpose of the kerygma?

From the immediate reaction of the Jerusalem crowd to Peter's sermon and the Athenians to Paul's "Unknown God" speech, we see that the main purpose of the kerygma was (and still is) not to construct a dull recital of facts, but to serve as a catalyst for a dynamic confrontation between the Holy Spirit and the sinful heart, to convict people to repent of sin and embrace the lordship of Christ. When confronted with its message, the kerygma forced the hearer to make a choice about Christ. Neutrality was not a valid option. Even in the 21st century, who can resist the compelling logic of the resurrection as it leads to the undeniable conclusion that Jesus was/is the true risen Lord. The kerygma thus bore an infinitely vital message. The apostles knew this. To repent and trust in Christ was to enter, for eternity, into the kingdom of God. In short, the ultimate goal of the kerygma was not a sophisticated theology but a new and transformed life, a life "born again" unto God. In fact, the kerygma's central declaration was that, in Christ, a new order of reconciliation and eternal life had entered into history. This, in turn, caused the rapid growth of the church as people, upon hearing the kerygma, were compelled to repent and believe in Christ. After making this choice, most were even willing to suffer martyrdom for the cause of Christ, particularly since they knew that their sojourn of eternal life had already begun on their "born again" day (see adjacent figure which explains this).

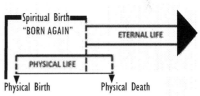

So important was this role of the kerygma that some scholars, such as Stephen Neil in *The Interpretation of the New Testament*, have argued, in contrast with some form critics, that the preservation of the early kerygma (and not the addressing of concerns of the early church) was the main purpose behind the creation of the Gospel accounts. Neil writes:

The original aim of Gospel-writing seems to have been not so much the edification of the church . . . as the maintenance in its purity of the original missionary proclamation.[3]

Now that we have examined the content and purpose of the kerygma, we need to determine if its message still makes sense today. Is the Christian kerygma a relevant proclamation for a 21st-century world?

#4 – Does the kerygma make sense in the 21st century?

As we turn to this final section, we consider the easy-to-memorize truism below, our final Diamond of Truth acrostic, one which summarizes the evangelistic message of the kerygma, particularly its underlying *bottom line* that, through Christ, all people can possess a future of new and unending L-I-F-E in him. As Christ said of his own mission, "I have come that [all people] may have life and have it to the full" (John 10:10). The kerygma points to the L-I-F-E Christ offers through these four motifs:

The biblical kerygma proclaims:

DoT Acrostic #4

Love, Godly, Beget Incarnate Breath, since

Imperfection, Sinful, Wrought Human Death; so

Forgiveness, At Calvary, Christ attained, that

Eternal Life, God's Gift — Thru F-A-I-TH — We Gain.

Let examine each of the four L-I-F-E statements above and see if we can show that the kerygma, or early gospel proclamation fully squares with 21st-century reason, for if the kerygma of ecumenical Christianity is not relevant to the modern world, then we need a new message. As we examine the four gospel themes above, I have added a four-part heart diagram that Christian readers can use to pictorially represent. and more deftly explain. the four main parts of the Christian gospel. This diagram is basic, to be sure, but its message of L-I-F-E is extraordinarily profound.

L Love, Godly, Beget Incarnate Breath

Gospel Truth #1   (Draw a Heart Shape)

Love is at the heart of the gospel, the motive behind the kerygma and coming of Christ. Consider these texts: (1) John 3:16 says: "For God so loved the world that gave his one and only Son..."; (2) Romans 5:8 says: "But God demonstrates his love for us in this: While we were sill sinners, Christ died for us"; (3) And in 1 John 4:8 we see that "God is love," as if to say that love constitutes the core of God's character/nature.

Ergo, the first foundational truth behind the gospel message is the beautiful fact that God loves humanity. We are a special part of creation. Indeed, it appears that the central motive behind God's initiation of our salvation is that He deeply loves humans as His children. But what kind of love are we talking about here? The Greeks knew well that there are many different forms of love, such as sexual love (or eros), friendship love (or philia), and family love (or storge). But how does God love human beings? The Greek word used for "love" in the texts above is "agape." What is this?

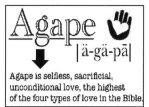

Agape is selfless, sacrificial, unconditional love, the highest of the four types of love in the Bible

Agape love is pure, godly, unselfish love where the "other" is most important; it is not at all self-centered, nor is it ever proud or impatient. It is always exemplified by kindness and forgiveness. In the NT, agape forms the very essence of God's being. In short, God is a giving God; he wants to share himself and his love with creation. He desires to bless others. And his love, according to the NT, knows no bounds. The hymn, The Love of God, by Frederick M. Lehman, captures, with sublime poetry, the immensity of the agape of God. The hymn says: "Could we with ink the ocean fill, and were the sky of parchment made, were every stalk on earth a quill and every man a scribe by trade, to write the love of God above would drain the ocean dry, nor could the scroll contain the whole, though stretched from sky to sky." Beautiful imagery of unfathomable love.

But what does God's agape nature explain about our world? Everything! In fact, when we fully grasp God's agape nature, we will see that it explains the reason for our creation. Follow this logic. Although God does not need humans, because God's nature is agape, He nonetheless desires to give love. He could have created robots to love, but robots cannot freely return love. So. it makes sense that God created humans to be the objects of his love, free beings granted the free volition to return (or not return) love. Consider Genesis 1:16: "Then God said, "let us make man in our image, in our likeness." So, we are unique creatures made in God's likeness. And this means that we, like God, can freely love others and God.

It is thus not at all surprising that, in Matthew 22:37-38, when Jesus was asked to disclose what was the greatest OT commandment, he said: "Love [agape] the Lord your God with all your heart and with all your soul and with all your mind. This is the first and greatest commandment." So. although God does not need our love, he does desire it and is infinitely deserving of it. In sum, God's agape nature explains not only the reason for Christ's Incarnation (and the kerygma proclamation), but the very purpose of human creation and why humans are each commanded to love. Even in the 21st century, this fact makes sense. We all need to give/receive love.

Imperfection, Sinful, Wrought Human Death

Gospel Truth #2   (Break Heart w/ Line)

Although God immeasurably loves us, God does not at all love the sins we commit. The Bible speaks to this issue as our common disease. Sin breaks God's heart, for it causes a relational schism between people and God. As we saw, Peter's Acts 2 sermon assumed that people needed to be forgiven, but forgiven of what? The answer is sin. When we commit sinful acts and defile God's perfect holiness, we become persona non grata and totally *unfit* to enter a heavenly realm which emanates only beautiful righteousness and divine perfection.

The great Methodist, John Wesley, once defined a sinful act as a "voluntary transgression of a known law of God." This is accurate, but not complete. Sin is actualized on a much deeper level. Sin ultimately boils down to foolish pride and self-centeredness, of putting oneself on the throne instead of God, of preferring one's own ideas to God's truth, of choosing the satisfaction of one's own will to God's will, of loving oneself more than God. As such, sin manifests itself as idolatry (Gal. 5:19-20), as trespass (Romans 5:15), and/or as enmity to God (James 4:4). In short, sin's essence is placing something else in God's place; it is not just mere disobedience; it is anything that "falls short" of God's empyreal perfection.

And we are all guilty! Romans 3:23 exclaims: "For all have sinned and fall short of the glory of God." What does "fall short" mean? It implies that whenever we sin, we become "less than" what we were purposed to be as humans: perfect. Now, often when we commit a sinful act, we say, "Well, I'm only human." But this is a misguided idiom, for, when we sin, we technically become "less than" what God originally intended us to be. To be fully human is to be like Christ, totally without sin. He is the perfect spiritual model for us, the new Adam (see Rom. 5:5-21). So, sin is still "*ad rem*" today.

The Bible is clear about the penalty for sin. Romans 6:23 says: "For the wages of sin is death." This death-penalty was issued in Genesis 3:19. As a result of Adam & Eve's sin, God said to them: "Dust you are and dust you shall return." Ergo, sin is our #1 quandary. It is the reason that (without Christ) we cannot live with God forever. We go back dust. Yet God did provide a cure for our death dilemma. Christ took our penalty. In 2 Cor. 5:21, we read: "God made him [Jesus] who had no sin to be sin for us so that we might become the righteousness of God." So, there is "good news" for us. Our sin debt has been paid in full. James M. Boice aptly notes this essential truism:

For the good news is not just that God became man, nor that God has spoken to reveal a proper way of life for us, nor even that death, the great enemy, is conquered. Rather, the good news is that **SIN** has been dealt with (of which the resurrection is proof); that Jesus has suffered its penalty for us as our representative, so that we might never have to suffer it; and therefore all who believe in him can look forward to heaven.[4]

One of the traits of our era, however, is that many fail to see the full gravity of sin. The gospel clearly states that we are lost and in need of God's forgiveness. Yet the gospel becomes at best an *irrelevant message* if we are not convinced of this reality. So do not be fooled! Just look at the moral evil and depravity that is present in our world today. Sin is rampant! My words here ring true. Sin is our #1 problem; we do need a Savior! So let us never become naïve to the seriousness of sin. Jesus paid too high a price for us; he suffered and gave his very "life as a ransom" (Matt. 20:28), he offered himself as the "atoning sacrifice for our sins" (I John 2:2), so that we might find new life. As John Chrysostom once wisely noted, "By the cross we know the gravity of sin and the greatness of God's love for us."[5]

Forgiveness, At Calvary, Christ Attained

Gospel Truth #3   (Sketch Cross Image)

So let us now turn to the cross of Christ, for the Bible is clear that it is only through Jesus' death on the cross that we can possess forgiveness of sins. In the Bible, to be forgiven of sin is likened to being "saved" from sin, therefore, biblically-speaking, forgiveness and salvation are basically synonymous. The New Testament (NT) uses the Greek word "soteria" to describe salvation; the word means simply to rescue or to deliver someone. And from what does God deliver us? Answer: The just punishment of mankind's fall into sin — eternal death and destruction.

The NT actually presents a multitude of word pictures to describe God's *divine rescue project* for humanity. That is, in the NT, salvation is depicted as a multifaceted concept. This is evidenced by the fact that NT authors use **FIVE BEAUTIFUL METAPHORS** to describe what Christ attained for us *through the cross of Calvary*. So let us unpack each metaphor below. As we do, we shall see that each biblical "word picture" captures a unique aspect / facet / dimension of the one ultimate reality that God's salvation was designed to actualize, a reality that even today squares with reason.

Metaphor #1:   REGENERATION — To Become a New Creature

The first NT metaphor we can consider together is regeneration. We find this image in John 3:1-17 where Jesus converses with Nicodemus. John 3:2 says that Nicodemus secretly "came to Jesus at night," most likely because Nicodemus was a ruling member of the Pharisees, a religious sect that violently opposed Jesus. Jesus' words must have had a profound affect on Nicodemus since, in John's Gospel, we see Nicodemus later stand up for Jesus at the Jewish ruling council (7:50) and even help prepare Jesus' body for burial (19:39). But what did Jesus say? What gripped Nicodemus?

After Nicodemus admitted he believed Jesus must be from God, Jesus said, "I tell you the truth, no one can see the kingdom of God unless he is born again." Jesus was speaking to a religious leader, but he knew humanity's spiritual condition. His use of "born again" was, of course, not meant to be taken literally, as Nicodemus first naïvely thought (see 3:4), but spiritually. Jesus knew all humans need a change that penetrates the heart and dismantles the dominion of sin, a change that replaces self-centeredness with a new center of gravity. After using the "born again" metaphor, Jesus then summarized the gospel in what is now the most iconic verse in human history, John 3:16, a verse that pastor/author Max Lucado says bears "the numbers of hope." Nifty adage.

$$3 \colon 16$$

The Numbers of Hope

Regarding hope, Alexander Pope, the famed English poet, once hoped he could improve and thus was overheard to say, "O Lord, make me a better man," to which his astute colleague replied, "Alexander, it would be easier to make you a new man!" Regeneration does this. It is the divine act of making the repentant believer a new person who is "born of God" (1 John 5:4) and considered a "new creature in Christ" (2 Cor. 5:17).

Metaphor #2:   REDEMPTION — To Go from Enslavement to Freedom

A second metaphor used in the New Testament concerns the concept of redemption. The word "redemption" comes from the Hebrew word meaning "to tear lose, to rescue" and is used in the Old Testament to describe the practice of one called a kinsman redeemer, the person who came to a relative's aid by purchasing back land that had been lost to the family.[6] God is said to be the kinsman redeemer of Israel since he is the one who tears Israel loose from her oppressors and restores her to her proper owner, God Himself. The idea of redemption was thus common in the OT.

People in NT times also knew well the concept of redemption. Prisoners were often released from jail by a payment of a ransom; slaves too would often be purchased by a generous man and set free. Jesus' words would have thus made complete sense to a first-century audience when he said in Matthew 20:28, "The Son of Man did not come to be served, but to serve, and to give his life as a ransom for many." In summary, we see that just as land could be bought back by a kinsman redeemer, just as a prisoner's debt could be cancelled, just as a slave could be bought and set free, so God has paid the purchase price for humanity, with the very blood of Christ, so that we can be set free from the oppression of sin. As 1 Peter 1:18-19 proclaims, "For you know that it was not with perishable things such as silver and gold that you were redeemed from the empty way of life handed down to you from your forefathers, but with the precious blood of Christ, a lamb without blemish or defect." What a precious truth.

Metaphor #3:   JUSTIFICATION — To Be Declared Not Guilty

A third metaphor to study is justification. Justification takes us to a courtroom scene; it was a legal term used in the courts of the first century to describe the situation when a judge (whose verdict was final) declares a prisoner not guilty. As applied by NT authors to describe salvation, justification expresses the judicial action of God as judge according to which sinners are acquitted and reinstated as God's children. Sinners are, in effect, declared "not guilty" By God. It is not that our guilt is in doubt. Not at all! A penalty must still be pronounced; God's perfect justice must be served. And here is where Christ enters the drama of divine court justice.

In the courtroom, Christ is our self-sacrificial advocate. In effect, Christ stands up and says, "I will accept in their stead the punishment that is due." And, on the cross of Calvary, this is precisely what occurred.   God judged his own Son. To allow humans to be declared righteous, Christ endured sin's penalty. In effect, then, God acts as both judge — i.e., he punishes sin through Christ — and justifier, since he forgives anyone who has faith in Christ. Romans 5:18 says this well: "Just as the result of one trespass was condemnation for all men, so also the result of one act of righteousness [Christ's death] was justification that brings life for all men." Powerful simile.

Metaphor #4:   PROPITIATION — To Be Protected from God's Wrath

A fourth salvation metaphor used in the NT is propitiation. We are not too familiar with this concept in our day. Yet, as evangelist Mark McCloskey points out, "propitiation was a common religious word in biblical times, used in relation to heathen religious rites to win the favor of the gods or to avert the impending wrath and disfavor of the gods."[7] Early Christian writers adopted the concept for their own use to describe how Christ's work on the cross had dealt with the righteous wrath of God toward all who have sinned. Propitiation thus describes the facet of our salvation which lifts us away from God's perfect judgment and places us instead under the protection and safety of the cross; believers in Christ are no longer objects of God's wrath, but recipients of God's divine mercy. All wrath fell on Christ.

In effect, Jesus' blood atones [makes payment for] what was once offensive to God. As 1 John 4:10 puts it, "This is love: not that we loved God, but that he loved us and sent his Son as an atoning sacrifice [propitiation] for our sins." And this sacrifice is really the core of the gospel. As James Denney echoes 1 Peter 2:24, "The simplest truth of the gospel and the profoundest truth of theology must be put in the same words, 'He bore our sins.' "[8] Piercing words.

1 Peter 2:24
He himself bore our sins in his body on the tree...; by his wounds you have been healed.

Metaphor #5: RECONCILIATION — To Go from Enemy to Friend

Finally, NT writers describe our salvation as one of reconciliation, where a relationship of animosity has been changed into one of harmony. Whereas once we were enemies of God, we now can be called friends. In the NT, mankind's reconciliation to God is made possible only by the cross. All of God's just grievances against us were settled through Christ's death on the cross. In Romans 5:8-10, Paul explains it well: "But God demonstrates his own love for us in this: While we still sinners, Christ died for us. Since we have now been justified by his blood, how much more shall we be saved from God's wrath through him! For if, when we were God's enemies we were reconciled to him through the death of his Son, how much more, having been reconciled, shall we be saved through his life!" Flawless logic.

As a result of God's action through Christ, we can indeed go from being God's enemy to God's friend. It is remarkable to note that God left a tangible sign of this fact as evidenced by what occurred immediately after Jesus' death. The temple veil was ripped in two. Matthew 27:50-51

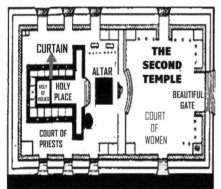

FACT: The curtain which separates the "Holy of Holies" from the lesser Holy Place (see arrow) was torn in two upon Jesus' death, signifying that, from that moment onwards, all humanity would be able to enjoy direct access to God's forgiveness & presence.

records the event: "And when Jesus cried out again in a loud voice, he gave up his spirit. At that moment, the curtain in the temple was torn in two from top to bottom." But what did this tearing event symbolize? Christ's sacrifice, the temple's Holy of Holies, the place said to be inhabited by God alone, was no longer restricted. All people could now enter. Prior to this veil tearing miracle, once a year, on Yom Kippur, the Day of Atonement, only the Jewish high priest was allowed to enter the Holy of Holies to atone for the sins of all Israel in order that reconciliation might follow. Yet, after the propitiation effectuated on the cross of Calvary, God allows direct access. As Craig Keener comments on the supernatural tearing of the veil, "by the cross God provides access for all people into his presence."[9] See sidebar to view where the tear occurred.

According to NT writers, this was also a once-for-all event. As Hebrews 9:12 reads, Christ "went once for all into the Holy of Holies of heaven, not by virtue of the blood of goats and calves [by which to make reconciliation between God and man], but His own blood, having found and secured a complete redemption." So, Christ's cross had eternal efficacy.

To sum up, through the cross, we can indeed be reconciled to God, protected from His wrath, justified and redeemed through Christ's blood, and **Matthew 27:51** born again to a new spiritual life. All these metaphors make sense. They are clear and cogent. They square with reason and experience. And they accurately describe the one salvific reality that God himself initiated and actualized. Now all the obstacles preventing us from having a healed and intimate relationship with God have been removed, except for one, our freedom. We as free beings still must *agree* to accept God's gifts of regeneration, justification and redemption; we must choose to embrace His reconciliation. And this serves as a perfect segue to our next Gospel truth. We must all ultimately accept God's gift of salvation by F-A-I-TH.

Eternal Life, God's Gift – Thru F-A-I-TH – We Gain

Gospel Truth #4   (Add Eternity Sign)

We are never forced to embrace salvation, i.e., to be redeemed, justified, atoned, regenerated, and reconciled, because we are free. Although God does offer eternity to every person, for he has indeed secured eternal life for all humanity through Christ, we must still accept God's offer. That is, we may be saved by grace, but God does not force His grace umbrella over anyone. Each soul must walk under this umbrella;  there is a synergy required. As Ephesians 2:8 says, we are saved by grace through faith. Faith is thus the force which makes grace become operative.

But what is faith exactly, this supposed door to grace? Why do we have to possess faith to be in possession of God's grace and gift of eternal life? If God's grace (unmerited favor) is big enough to save everyone, and we do not deserve salvation, so why are all not saved? Shouldn't we be universalists (like Carlton Pearson) and believe that, ultimately, because of God's great love for humankind, all will eventually be saved? After all, does not 2 Peter 3:9 say that "God desires that none should perish, but all come to repentance." The answer we can give here is this: not all are saved because not all want to be saved. Some simply refuse to ever repent, that is, to "turn away" from the path of sin and self. And God won't force faith.

Although God commands us to love, He also respects our volition, so He never forces us to love. We have to *choose* to believe. Jesus himself addresses this point clearly. Consider Jesus' potent words in John 3:16-18:

For God so loved the world that he gave his one and only Son, that whoever believes in him shall not perish but have eternal life. For God did not send his Son into the world to condemn the world, but to save the world through him. Whoever believes in him is not condemned, but whoever does not believe stands condemned already because he has not believed in the name of God's one and only Son.

So, the NT is clear that we must have faith to draw near to God and to become His reconciled children. John 1:12 confirms this: "Yet to all who received him, to those who believed in his name, he gave the right to become children of God." As children, we inherit a free, beautiful gift, that of eternal life, an end-state for humanity that God always intended to actualize. However, since "without faith it is impossible to please God" (Heb. 1:16), humans must understand that God himself linked saving "faith" to eternity.

The Egyptian "ankh" sign was adopted by Coptics to symbolize eternity in Christ.

But what does faith entail exactly? In the NT, faith (like salvation) is also multi-faceted; it involves FOUR BIBLICAL MOTIFS. To possess F-A-I-TH, the NT indicates we must, of our own volition, do the following activities:

F	-	Forsake Sin & Repent
A	-	Accept Christ as Lord
I	-	Increase Love for God/Others
TH	-	Think & Act Christ-like

As faith is the essential key to unlocking saving grace, and thus eternity, let us now carefully probe each biblical faith theme. As we do, we shall see that each motif operates not separately but jointly.

F — Forsake Sin & Repent

Humble Contrition

The first element of faith is repentance. In Acts 2, Peter ended his sermon by commanding his audience "to repent and be baptized in the name of Jesus for the forgiveness of sins." In the Bible, "to repent" meant not just to be contrite and "turn away" from sin (although this is vital), it literally meant to put on a change of mindset, to embrace a change in the whole personality from a sinful course of action to a path pleasing to God. True repentance is thus accompanied by a true change in character. Repentance is such an important aspect of conversion that it is often stressed rather than belief, as when Christ said that there is joy in heaven among the angels over one sinner who repents (Luke 15:7). Repentance and belief in Christ are in fact inseparable, which is why, in Acts 11:18, Luke could describe the conversion of the Gentiles to Christ as God granting them "repentance unto life." Repentance is thus requisite to authentic faith.

But why do we need to repent? To many the word "repentance" is antiquated and irrelevant. But make no mistake. Repentance is an act of vital importance, for when we repent, we do three things that God demands. First, we recognize exactly what we are before God: sinners who fall short of his glory. Second, we show a genuine sorrow for sin, for repentance without sorrow becomes hollow. Third, we demonstrate to God our willingness to turn 180 degrees from sin and embrace God's way of life. In effect, when we repent, we deny our self-will and allow Christ to rule our hearts. Jesus himself cites this paradox of "denying" oneself in order to find true life. In Luke 9:23-24, he says, "If anyone would come after me, he must deny himself and take up his cross daily and follow me. For whoever wants to save his life will lose it, but whoever loses his life for me will save it." In other words, if we want to follow Christ, we must first "repent" of everything (attitudes, behavior, etc.) that puts ourselves on the throne instead of God; we must surrender. Rev. Jim Elliot, the great missionary to Ecuador, knew well this important spiritual truth. Just before his martyrdom by the Acua Indians, Elliot wrote: "He is no fool to lose what he cannot keep only to gain what he cannot lose." Elliot was a hero of faith.

A — **Accept Christ as Lord** ⟶

Sand-Drawn on CMI Scuba Trip to Palau in 2019

Yet repentance of sin is not enough; we must also believe in the reality of the person who conquered sin. The second vital motif of F-A-I-TH is that we must accept Christ as Lord. We must confess who he really is. Romans 10:9 spells this out plainly: "That if you confess with your mouth, 'Jesus is Lord,' and believe in your heart that God raised him from the dead, you will be saved." Yet such a confession must also lead to a change of heart. According to the NT, we must allow Christ to take control; we must allow him to establish a home in our hearts. I own a T-shirt which says, "Under New Management," and this is exactly what occurs when we surrender to Jesus' lordship. No longer do we place ourselves on the throne; Jesus becomes King. You see, the gospel is not just information about Christ, it is his mandate to step into his kingdom; it is a demand that we repent and embrace Christ as Creator and risen Lord, for that is who he is. Even the fallen angels know this truth and shudder (see James 2:19).

I — **Increase Love for God/Others** ⟶

Celtic Trinity Love Symbol

A third truth about faith is that it necessitates love. Life is really all about love! As Pastor Rick Warren points out in his best-selling book, *The Purpose-Driven Life*, "because God is love, the most important lesson he wants you to learn on earth is how to love. It is in loving that we are most like him, so love is the foundation of every command he has given us."[10]

Jesus indeed says the two greatest commands are to love God and our neighbor (Matt. 22:37-40). So, love is vital to faith. In fact, 1 John 4:8 says, "Whoever does not love does not know God." Fortunately, our agape love is never wasted because its value does not rest on reciprocity. That said, its value is nonetheless all-important. *The Message Bible* beautifully translates Paul on this point in 1 Cor. 13:3. He proclaims: "No matter what I say, what I believe, and what I do, I'm bankrupt without love." *I am the vine, you are the branches —John 15:5*

TH --Think & Act Christ-like

Finally, we must understand that faith is not just a one-time prayer of commitment. The NT is clear that one who has faith will, as a natural consequence, bear fruit in what they do. Jesus points this out clearly. He says, "I am the vine; you are the branches. If a man remains in me and I in him, he will bear much fruit" (John 15:5). Likewise, the Book of James is clear that genuine faith automatically yields virtuous action. James 2:14-19 captures the necessary link between faith and deeds. James writes:

What good is it, my brothers, if a man claims to have faith but has no [works]? Can such faith save him? Suppose a brother or sister is without clothes and daily food. If one of you says to him, "Go, I wish you well; keep warm and well fed," but does nothing about his physical needs, what good is it? In the same way, faith [or mere belief] by itself, if it is not accompanied by action, is dead. But someone will say, "You have faith; I have [works]." Show me your faith without deeds, and I will show you my faith by what I do. You believe that there is one God. Good! Even the demons believe that — and shudder!

Perhaps an explanatory commentary will help clarify a common misconception here. Some have argued that James stands in conflict with the apostle Paul when the latter asserts that we are justified by "faith alone" (see Romans 4). Actually, the two stand in full agreement, as both men say that faith in Christ will ultimately produce good works. James use of the word "works" differs from Paul. For James, "works" are works of faith, the outworking of true spirituality. But Paul see James' idea of works as the "fruits of the Spirit." When Paul uses the term "works," he, unlike James, has in mind works righteousness, the attempt by man to establish his own righteousness.

faith WITHOUT ACTION IS DEAD
James 2:17

Ergo, saying James and Paul are in conflict is baseless. Paul, like James, consistently called for Christians to be Christ-like in all that they think, do, and say (see Ephesians 4:13). And this is no surprise. As pastor Rick Warren points out, we were "all created to be like Christ."[11] This is one of the main purposes of existence, as Christ is the paragon of perfection. That said, God's ultimate goal for us is not comfort, but character/soul development, so that we honor Christ as Lord and gain maximal spiritual maturity. Does this mean all moral struggles cease? No. Faith is a journey.

Although the Holy Spirit surely helps us cultivate godly virtue, we must still consistently seek to be "transformed" by the "renewing of our minds" (Rom. 12:2) so that we develop godly habits and live as God intended. That said, life struggles take on new meaning in this light, for we are each meant to grow in our soul-building trek. Like a tree, growth is part of our "telos" (p.51).

To sum up this F-A-I-TH section, we can conclude that it makes sense to embrace Jesus as he offers humanity the best way to live. As we saw, many blessed things happen when we choose to follow Christ. We become children of God (John 1:12); our sins our forgiven (Eph. 1:7); we become new creatures in Christ (2 Cor. 5:17); we have peace with God (Rom. 5:1); we receive the gift of eternal life (John 3:16). How could anyone say "no" to these blessings? That said, we should not embrace Christ out of selfishness just to attain  benefits. We should accept Christ's lordship because *it is true*. Nonetheless, these points show that Christ, out of all options, is the most appealing. And he lovingly says "whosoever will" may come (Rev. 22:17), for all are invited.

A Brief Summary

Now that we have examined all facets of the biblical kerygma, the basic gospel message, we can review these five summary points:

(1)   First, we observed that the kerygma was the gospel proclamation preached by Christ's first apostles. These apostles acted as "keruxes" (or messengers) for the heavenly kingdom of God. Christ's resurrection and lordship was the kerygma's primary focus.

(2)   Next, we saw that the best examples of the early kerygma appear in the speeches of Peter and Paul, particularly in Acts, where each of these keruxes for Christ explain how God has acted in the world through Christ. We saw that Peter proclaimed in Jerusalem that "God has made him [Jesus] both Lord and Christ" (Acts 2:36). Likewise, Paul stood up Athens' Areopagus and used the city's UNKNOWN GOD idol as a bridge to proclaim that the true God "has set a day when he will judge the world with justice by the man [Christ] he has appointed" and that God "has given proof of this to all men by raising [Christ] from the dead" (Acts 17:31).

(3)   We also saw that the kerygma's purpose was not to offer a recital of theological facts, but to serve as a catalyst to bring about a dynamic confrontation between the Holy Spirit and the sinful heart, to convict people to truly repent and to follow Christ. When confronted with the kerygma, then, one was forced to choose: embrace or deny Jesus as Lord. Neutrality was not an option.

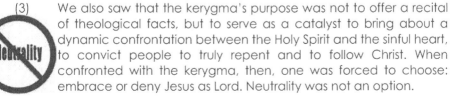

(4)   We saw that the ecumenical gospel message of Christianity, as articulated by NT writers, still makes sense today; the gospel squares with modern reason and experience: (1) It makes sense that God initiated salvation (and created us) out of agape love and that this giving-type of love is the motive behind the kerygma; (2) It makes sense that, since sin separates us from God and causes all of us to "fall short" of God's perfection, death is our just penalty; (3) It makes sense that only a perfect God-man, like Christ, could take our penalty and be our substitute. Via his cross/resurrection Jesus indeed brought real salvation to humankind, a salvation characterized by the NT as regeneration, redemption, justification, propitiation and reconciliation; (4) It makes sense that, as a result of Christ's action, we can, if we possess F-A-I-TH in Christ, experience a peaceful and joyful life on this Earth and, yes, even an eternal life in God's forever family. In sum, this Gospel's soundness is irrefutable.

(5)   Finally, we saw that saving F-A-I-TH involves four inter-related biblical motifs. To accept God's gift of salvation, we must (1) Forsake sin and repent, (2) Accept Christ as Lord, (3) Increase our love for God and others and (4) THink and act Christ-like. The NT is clear that genuine faith is the force that makes saving grace become operative, for God does not force anyone to surrender to him. We attain God's gift of grace only through F-A-I-TH.

All in all, since the kerygma message ultimately addresses the all-important subject of our final and future destiny, that is, where we will spend eternity, I believe it is fitting to close this chapter on the Christian gospel with the wise and discerning words of C.S. Lewis. Lewis writes:[12]

Christianity is a statement which, if false, is of no importance and, if true, of infinite importance. The one thing it cannot be is moderately important.

Lewis is absolutely right. Christ is either totally *true* or totally *false*; he is either worthy of worship or 100% worthless. No neutrality exists. All must decide – God-man or corpse? – for eternal life itself is what is at stake. With that in mind, take some time now to review on page 167 each of the 12 acrostics we studied, and make a goal to be able to deftly present each one, especially the kerygma L-I-F-E poem and sketch. Why? Simple. Every believer has a duty to preach the gospel, the good news that Christ is indeed the author of all existence and the guarantor of our eternal life.

Review of "Diamond of Truth" Acrostics

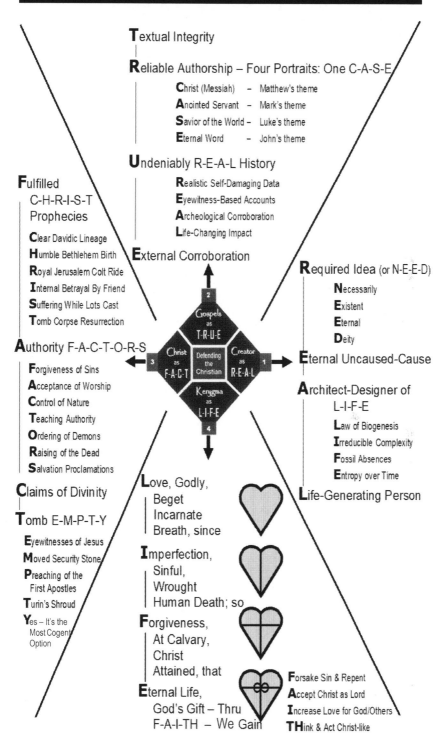

Textual Integrity

Reliable Authorship – Four Portraits: One C-A-S-E
- **C**hrist (Messiah) – Matthew's theme
- **A**nointed Servant – Mark's theme
- **S**avior of the World – Luke's theme
- **E**ternal Word – John's theme

Undeniably R-E-A-L History
- **R**ealistic Self-Damaging Data
- **E**yewitness-Based Accounts
- **A**rcheological Corroboration
- **L**ife-Changing Impact

External Corroboration

Fulfilled C-H-R-I-S-T Prophecies
- **C**lear Davidic Lineage
- **H**umble Bethlehem Birth
- **R**oyal Jerusalem Colt Ride
- **I**nternal Betrayal By Friend
- **S**uffering While Lots Cast
- **T**omb Corpse Resurrection

Authority F-A-C-T-O-R-S
- **F**orgiveness of Sins
- **A**cceptance of Worship
- **C**ontrol of Nature
- **T**eaching Authority
- **O**rdering of Demons
- **R**aising of the Dead
- **S**alvation Proclamations

Claims of Divinity

Tomb E-M-P-T-Y
- **E**yewitnesses of Jesus
- **M**oved Security Stone
- **P**reaching of the First Apostles
- **T**urin's Shroud
- **Y**es – It's the Most Cogent Option

Required Idea (or N-E-E-D)
- **N**ecessarily
- **E**xistent
- **E**ternal
- **D**eity

Eternal Uncaused-Cause

Architect-Designer of L-I-F-E
- **L**aw of Biogenesis
- **I**rreducible Complexity
- **F**ossil Absences
- **E**ntropy over Time

Life-Generating Person

Love, Godly,
Beget
Incarnate
Breath, since

Imperfection,
Sinful,
Wrought
Human Death; so

Forgiveness,
At Calvary,
Christ
Attained, that

Eternal Life,
God's Gift – Thru
F-A-I-TH – We Gain

- **F**orsake Sin & Repent
- **A**ccept Christ as Lord
- **I**ncrease Love for God/Others
- **TH**ink & Act Christ-like

(Diamond center:)
- 2 — Gospels as T-R-U-E
- 3 — Christ as F-A-C-T
- Defending the Christian
- 1 — Creator as R-E-A-L
- 4 — Kerygma as L-I-F-E

"If Christianity was something we were making up,
of course we could make it easier. But it is not. We cannot
compete, in simplicity, with people who are inventing religions. How
could we? We are dealing with Fact. Of course anyone can
be simple if he has no facts to bother about."

– C. S. Lewis

Conclusion

In the last four chapters, we saw emerge an irrefutably compelling case. We also saw why this book's title is apropos: Faith fits the facts indeed. What final conclusion can we now draw? It is this: Although like all truth-claims we cannot prove Christ with 100% certainty, we can dauntlessly assert that Christianity's central ecumenical truth-claims are *undeniably cogent*. Christ is 100% credible.

This sound conclusion now forces us toward a personal verdict, to choose a specific road that makes *rational sense* out of all the apologetics evidence for Christ and *personal sense* out of all we experience in life. We cannot remain neutral about Christ given his claims and salvific work. Indeed, given the totality of philosophical, historical, scientific, literary and archeological evidence for ecumenical Christianity, we have only four paths before us. We can follow (1) the path of disbelief and skepticism, (2) the path of agnosticism; (3) the path of mental assent (which even the demons possess), or (4) the path of personal faith. I contend that this last option, personal faith in Christ, is the most *intellectually satisfying* and  *personally fulfilling* road we can traverse, as it is a path and way of life guaranteed by the Way, the Truth and the Life, Jesus himself. Fortunately, Jesus does not call us to take a blind leap of faith. Ultimately, there exists both a *personal* and *evidential* component to faith. Faith fulfills the heart's desire for peace and love as well as the mind's desire for cogency, soundness, and truth.

On a personal level, Jesus wants you to take a "leap of faith" towards him, to fully trust in him. After his resurrection, Jesus said a remarkable thing to Thomas, the disciple who doubted. In John 20:29, Jesus said: "Because you [Thomas] have seen me, you have believed; blessed are those who have not seen, and yet have *believed*." The kerygma, which we discussed in chapter 4, calls us to repent and believe in the lordship of Christ for the forgiveness of sins. In Romans 10:9, Paul summarizes what a person must do, saying, "That if you confess with your mouth, 'Jesus is Lord,' and believe in your heart that God raised him from the dead, you will be saved." So a faith-leap we are asked to take. Yet our faith-leap is not at all blind or irrational. As we saw throughout this book, the cumulative case for the veracity of Christ and the ecumenical truth-claims of Christianity is incontrovertibly convincing. Faith in Christ fits all the facts.

Dr. Clark Pinnock in *A Case for Faith* offers a sound observation about *personal faith* and *cumulative evidence*. He crafts a compelling summation to what this handbook has promulgated from beginning to end. He writes:

I am convinced that . . . the Christian message fits the facts. It is not a pre-supposition that has to be accepted on authority or a self-evident truth that needs no argument; it is a solid truth claim that can be tested and verified across the whole range of human experience. It meets our existential needs, makes sense out of our religious intuitions, stands up under rational scrutiny, corresponds with the historical evidence and speaks to today's moral necessities.[1]

Pinnock is right. Throughout this book, we were able to construct a cogent case for ecumenical Christianity which can be verified across a whole range of human knowledge and experience. Now it is time for you to respond to the apologetics you have studied. You must make a choice. Which of the four paths above do you want to traverse? Neutrality is gone.

If you are not a Christian, would you consider embracing Christ and his invitation to receive new and eternal life? Here is a sample prayer that Rev. Dr. Billy Graham cites in his 1977 book *How to Be Born Again*. It is a simple sinner's prayer that Dr. Graham said he had prayed with literally millions of people in hundreds of crusades on every continent:

Oh God, I acknowledge that I have sinned against You.
I am sorry for my sins. I am willing to turn from my sins.
I now openly receive & acknowledge Jesus Christ as my Savior.
I confess Him as Lord. From this moment on, I want to live
for Him and serve Him. In Jesus' name. Amen.[2]

If you are already a Christ-follower, do you desire to share Christ? Would you consider using the 12 acrostics of this book to more effectively present the truth of Christ to skeptics and agnostics, to lovingly convince others that faith fits the facts? If so, here are five practical tips to keep in mind as you seek to use this book to engage in dialogical apologetics:

Tip #1: Establish *rapport* with a person first. Don't just unload a bunch of data. Develop a relationship of mutual respect. Offer to disclose your testimony.

Tip #2: Use the appropriate base in the Diamond of Truth, as every person lies at a different stage of belief. Some will want to desire to discuss God's existence first, while others will be ripe for the gospel message.

Tip #3: Use, if possible, the *12 acrostics* we studied; these will help you recall and more easily explain ecumenical apologetics to those willing to dialogue.

Tip #4 : Keep points concise and offer *cogent reasons* in a courteous manner. You may be the first witness who has ever planted a seed in a one's life.

Tip #5: Always offer an invitation to receive Christ. You never know how a person might respond. Properly done, an invitation is not offensive since it expects a positive answer, but always allows for a way out.

Regarding tip (1), offering a personal faith testimony is often more impactful than invoking apologetics arguments, since many people desire down-to-earth authenticity. Regarding my own personal faith journey, I can vouch that, although my life issues did not end when I surrendered to Christ, he did bestow fruits of the Spirit which helped me transcend the mundane trials of this earthly realm and gave me a peace that his promise to prepare a special place for me will come true (John 14:3)—a place where I can flourish in his forever family, where I can forever feel flawless joy, where my fierce craving for eternal fulfillment and meaning can forever be satisfied.

Allow me to elaborate on the idea of satisfaction, for although most people would desire eternal satisfaction if such could be effectuated, most also traverse through life totally unsatisfied. When the Rolling Stones came out with the popular song "(I Can't Get No) Satisfaction" in 1965, it rang true and became a number one hit, as indeed many in the 1960's had experienced that no amount of money, fame, power, sex, drugs or rock-n-roll could bring ultimate satisfaction to the human heart. As discussed in chapter one, the main reason for this is that, inexplicably to science, the heart (one's sentient essence) bears 10 core attributes that only humans possess, *personal* attributes such as conscious self-awareness, abstract reasoning, emotive capacity, creative artistry, free will, linguistic ability, moral conscience, worship desire, altruistic capability and, in relation to satisfaction, a deep longing for eternity, a yearning that is not only ubiquitous and indelible in humans, but one intentionally set by God "in the human heart" (see Ecclesiastes 3:11).

HE HAS MADE EVERYTHING
BEAUTIFUL
IN ITS 🕐 TIME
HE HAS ALSO SET
Eternity
IN THE
HUMAN HEART
Ecclesiastes 3:11

That said, within each heart's undying quest to discover eternal verity, meaning, and significance, all man-generated options are found to be totally deficient, including naturalism, humanism, and all man-concocted religions, as each ideology is simply a harbinger of the same pointless destiny, namely, humanity's desolate future fate of inexorable annihilation. Each view is thus incapable of quenching the thirst for eternity which resides in every human spirit. Naturalism uses science as its pathfinder, but in the end can offer only a heartless, finite, something-from-nothing Cosmos, one barren of any bona fide meaning and fated for a cold cataclysmic demise where max entropy is reached in circa 100 quintillion years. Humanism too tries to fabricate meaning in philanthropy, patriotism and/or self-actualization, but can offer humanity only a totally finite, flawed, here-by-chance species, one plagued by epistemic and ethical relativity and destined for a desolate, hopeless, forlorn future of annihilation. Religions also have all tried to capture eternal Truth and vouchsafe satisfaction but, in the end, they are more-often-than-not fraught with rigid intolerance and judgmentalism and rife with rank hypocrisy, ritualism and fraud. Then Christ appears in human history and offers humanity an enduring and thriving eternity, one of absolute satisfaction, of veracious meaning, of flawless existence — all freely available to whosoever will come and embrace his gift of grace.

Indeed, through his salvific work, Christ, the Cosmos' true Creator, is the *only* wellspring who can quench humanity's insatiable thirst for eternal meaning. Why?—Because he is the *author* of both eternity and meaning. Ergo, all who place their trust in Christ can have perfect confidence that their quest to touch eternity can and will find both (a) temporary fulfillment within this present, fallen, sin-corrupted world and (b) final consummation in the perfect, wholly redeemed, eschatological world which Christ, from the beginning of time itself, always intended to actualize and maintain.

Make no mistake. Christ's heavenly realm will be a faultless world of eternal substantiality, a world where free beings from every tribe will conjointly flourish and always choose only what is good, where entropy, sin, suffering and death will bear no more sting, where sacred worship and creativity shall thrive in perpetuity, and where life will be forever marked only by robust love, joy, serenity, beauty and bliss, all in the endless and holy presence of the one loving Creator known by a myriad of fitting, exquisite epithets: Emmanuel (God with us), the great "I AM", the Lion and the Lamb, the Word of God, the Alpha and the Omega, the Chief Cornerstone, the King of Kings & Lord of Lords.

With the beauty of the heavenly realm in mind and considering the practicability of tips #2 and 3 above, I implore my fellow believers in Christ to utilize this handbook's apologetics-driven Diamond of Truth and its 12 mnemonic devices to better present the truth of Christ in person-centered dialogues, since nowadays sound apologetics is requisite to effective evangelism. Why? Because apologetics reveals that the Christian

The early church's Chi Rho cross created this acrostic: "I am the Alpha & Omega."

worldview is indeed undeniably credible and true. When a person's mind has been convinced of the lordship of Christ, their heart's desire is not far behind.

That said, to close out this manuscript, I sincerely pray that *all* who have read this work will come to the sound conclusion that Jesus is exactly who he claimed to be, the Way, Truth and Life, the loving Creator of the cosmos and all-sufficient Redeemer of humankind. If we do not recognize this fact now, the apostle Paul indicates that someday *all* of us will be forced to acknowledge this fundamental truth of reality. So why not start today? Why not surrender to the Lord Jesus Christ now and embrace the undeniable reality which we have championed throughout this handbook, that only Christ can explain humanity's true origin, purpose and destiny, and that, because of His incarnation, "faith fits the facts." To be sure, the Bible exhorts that "now is the day of salvation" (see 2 Cor. 6:2). So do not wait. Jesus is the Lord! This is an unassailable, irrefutable fact. In fact, every human is said to be destined to confess this key fact one day, either in the glory of heaven, or elsewhere. On that point, Philippians 2:12 elegantly makes the following beautiful conclusion:

Therefore, God exalted him to the highest place and gave him a name that is above every other name, that at the name of Jesus every knee will bow, in heaven and on earth and under the earth, and every tongue will confess, that Jesus Christ is Lord to the glory of God the Father.

To God Be the Glory Indeed!

CONCLUDING QUOTE & POEM TO CONTEMPLATE:

"Although evidence is potent, ultimately, the best apologetics that a Christ-follower can ever promulgate is the sublime witness of their life, a life marked by the honoring of the Creator above all else, and the fulfilling of His requirements as stated in Micah 6:8 — to always do justice, and to love kindness, and to walk humbly with God, namely, the God incarnated in Jesus Christ, humanity's true Creator, Redeemer & King of Kings."

— Rev. Dr. David J. Carlson

One Solitary Life: An Anonymous Poem

Here is a man who was born in an obscure village, the child of a peasant woman.
He grew up in an obscure village. He worked in a carpenter shop until he was thirty,
and then for three years he was an itinerant teacher. He never wrote a book.
He never held an office. He never owned a home. He never had a family.
He never went to college. He never traveled, except in his infancy, more than two
hundred miles from the place where he was born.
He never did one of the things that usually accompanies greatness.
He had no credentials but himself. While he was still a young man, the tide of popular
opinion turned against him. His friends ran away. One of them denied him.
He was turned over to his enemies. He went through a mockery of a trial.
He was nailed upon a cross between two thieves. His executioners gambled for the only
piece of property he had on earth, his seamless robe.
When he was dead, he was taken down from the cross and laid in a borrowed grave
through the courtesy of a friend.
Twenty wide centuries have come and gone, and today he is the centerpiece of the
human race and the leader of all human progress.
I am well within the mark when I say that all the armies that ever marched,
all the navies that ever were built, all the parliaments that ever sat, and all the kings
that ever reigned, put together, have not affected the life of man upon this earth
as powerfully as has this One Solitary Life.

Appendix

Having been a part of hundreds of dialogues across seven continents, I have observed that, even though it is difficult to deny the cogency of ecumenical apologetics, one common objection to the Christian worldview always surfaces — the problem of evil. So, it is vital for Christians to know how to cogently address this often-raised topic. I have thus added this Appendix to address this hot-button issue. The quandary associated with evil, and its relation to Christianity is often worded as follows:

Exactly how can it be that the supposedly perfect, all-good (omni-benevolent) and all-powerful (omnipotent) God of Christianity can sit back and allow such tremendous moral evil and physical suffering to occur every day in our present world?

Owls & Evil: As owls can peer keenly through the dark, many past cultures have associated owls with evil acts & the occult as members claim they have secret hidden knowledge.

To address this difficult question, I have crafted below a theodicy, or a vindication of God with respect to evil, one which provides a sound solution to the problem of both moral & physical evil by arguing that (1) the Christian God has voluntarily chosen to limit his own omnipotence by giving created beings genuine and irrevocable power to commit evil and (2) that this present world is actually for God a necessary means toward actualizing the best of all possible worlds, a world in which all evils, in the end, will be destroyed. As this essay is abstract, the reader should digest it slowly, especially since it adds to our case that the ecumenical Christian worldview is completely cogent.

A Sound Theodicy to Answer the Problem of Evil

The problem of evil posed by the above question is nothing new; skeptics of the Christian God have been bringing up this quandary — in various ways — for centuries. The 18th-century skeptic, David Hume, was the first modern philosopher to phrase the problem of evil in a concise form. Borrowing from words first espoused by the Greek philosopher, Epicurus (340 – 271 B.C.), Hume wrote the following query:

Is God willing to prevent evil, but not able? Then is he impotent? Is he able, but not willing? Then is he malevolent? Is he both able and willing; whence then is evil?[1]

Hume's questions describe what has come to be known as the logical problem of evil, specifically the logical tension that arises when we combine the following three concepts: (1) God's omnipotence (his power), (2) God's omnibenevolence (his goodness) and (3) the presence of evil. In propositional form, the problem can be stated as follows:

(1) If God were all-powerful (omnipotent), he could prevent evil.
(2) If God were all-good (omnibenevolent), he would not desire evil.
(3) Yet there exists the constant presence of genuine evil in the world.

All three propositions cannot all be true. If proposition (3) is true, then either proposition (1) and/or (2) must be false. As a result, the theist is caught in a logical quagmire. J.L. Mackie posits the enigma this way:

The problem is this: God is omnipotent; God is wholly good; and yet evil exists. There seems to be some contradiction between these three propositions, so that if any two of them were true the third would be false. But at the same time all three are essential parts of most theological positions; the theologian, it seems, at once must adhere and cannot consistently adhere to all three."[2]

Is there any solution to this quandary? Yes! To construct a cogent "theodicy" (i.e., a vindication of God with respect to evil), we must understand that proposition (1), as currently stated, is not accurate. Technically, God is not currently "all-powerful" in the sense that every decision made in the cosmos is under the purview of divine control. We exist too. God created us to share himself with us. Ergo, proposition (1) needs to be appropriately "modified" if the logical problem of evil is to be solved. We must show why omnipotence & evil are not mutually exclusive.

To do this, we must accurately define the idea of omnipotence. Dr. Millard Erickson in his textbook *Christian Theology* defines omnipotence as God being "able to do all things which are proper objects of his power."[3] This is accurate, yet the clause "proper objects of his power" needs clarification. The consensus of Christian thinkers from Thomas Aquinas to C.S. Lewis has been that omnipotence does not mean that God can do *anything*. For example, an omnipotent being cannot perform an act that is 100% logically contradictory, such as squaring a circle. This does not mean something exists that God cannot do! He *can* do absolutely everything "doable." Ergo, God's inability to, say, create a "square circle" is not a result of him being limited by intrinsic conditions in his nature. Rather it is his inability to make the logically absurd. Square circles cannot

exist. Interestingly, on that point, the phrase "square the circle" evolved into an English idiom meaning "to do an impossible task."

Dr. Richard Rice makes this point well, stating that "it implies no deficiency in divine power to say that God cannot do the logically impossible, not because the logically impossible lies beyond God's power but because it is not anything *doable*."[4] James Sterba enhances this point when he espouses the following: "Nor could an omnipotent being perform actions which, though logically possible in themselves, would be logically

TOO HEAVY

impossible for an omnipotent being to perform. For example, while I can forge an object I cannot lift or love a person I can't understand, it is logically impossible for an omnipotent being to do either,"[5] As C.S. Lewis once opined, "non-sense does not cease to be non-sense when we add the words God can before it." So, we need to be careful when we talk about omnipotence.

That said, although we have appropriately defined the concept of omnipotence by pointing out its logical limitations, this definition by itself has not sufficiently resolved the problem of evil. The definition above only tells us, by negation, what omnipotence is not. To find a cogent solution to the logical problem of evil, we must determine exactly what omnipotence is. To do this, let us examine again the proposition we have said is false: "If God is all-powerful (omnipotent), then he could prevent evil." How can we claim that this statement is inaccurate? The answer lies in seeing that the "then" part of the proposition is what is false, not the "if" part. God is all-powerful, yes, but he is still unable to prevent evil in this present world. Why? Because omnipotence can bear a two-pronged meaning,

J.L. Mackie was the first modern philosopher to point this out in a clear manner. Mackie writes that "we must distinguish between first order omnipotence (O1), that is, *unlimited power to act*, and second order omnipotence (O2), that is, *unlimited power to determine what powers to act things shall have*. Then we could say that God all the time has O1, but if so no beings at any time have powers to act independently of God. Or we could say that God at one time had O2 and used it to assign independent powers to act to certain things [like humans], so that God thereafter did not have O1."[6] What Mackie is getting at here is that we simply cannot consistently ascribe to any continuing being omnipotence in an inclusive sense. God either possesses O1 or O2, but he cannot possess both types of omnipotence at the same time.

The theodicy-related implications of Mackie's qualification explain how the logical problem of evil may be resolved. These implications are two-fold: (1) By creating free beings, God has actualized his second order omnipotence (O2) at the expense of his first order omnipotence (O1). This means that God, in choosing to grant free beings the power to make free decisions has, in short, produced a cosmos where God allows for free creatures which he cannot control. God has "voluntarily" chosen to limit his omnipotence so that these beings can possess power; (2) Although God can at any time take back this power — i.e., bring back O1 — he cannot take it back without wiping out all beings he initially bestowed with power. In short, God does intrinsically have *unlimited* power to act, but he chooses to relinquish this power by granting other beings power. Why does he do this? Because God wants children who can worship and share in his glory, children who are capable of freely returning godly love.

The Bible asserts this view that God desires to live with free humans as his children. In Matthew 25:34, Jesus claims that one day he will say: "Come, you who are blessed by my Father; take your inheritance, the kingdom prepared for you since the creation of the world."

All in all, in positing the above implications of God's O1 and O2 orders of omnipotence, we can see how the logical problem of evil may be resolved. God, in this present state of affairs, by granting others power to actualize evil, cannot subsequently prevent the potential for evil to occur. Although he might *ultimately* be able to do this — e.g., heaven will have no evil — he cannot do this in this present world. Why? Because, in this world, God has chosen to relinquish his unlimited power to act; God created this world to possess the possibility of evil. In fact, logically speaking, as long as there is a world of free creatures who at times do what is evil, the use of God's power will be limited to the degree that he has allowed these creatures to possess power. Such a limitation, in turn, demonstrates the falsity of the proposition, "If God is omnipotent, he could prevent evil," for evil is not something preventable in a world where its potential always exists. Because this is true, we cannot blame God for evil. Evil is never actualized by God. It is always caused by free created beings. Although one could argue validly that God is the *ultimate* cause, since he allowed for the possibility of evil, he certainly is never the *direct* cause. Free creatures, viz., humans and fallen angels, are entirely to blame.

God is also not the direct cause of any "physical evils" that rock our world either (e.g., earthquakes, tsunamis, floods, disease, etc.), since we can account for such physical evils via five factors: (1) Some physical evils are a necessary consequence of free choice. For example, if a man gets drunk and drives, he has the potential of killing someone in a car accident; (2) Some physical evil is the result of the free choice of demons. For example, we see that Job was attacked by the devil (see Job 1) and Paul said that "a thorn was given me in the flesh, a messenger of Satan, to harass me" (see 2 Cor. 12:7); (3) Some physical evils are, in fact, necessary components of a physical world. For example, if one chooses to live in a place that could easily flood if city levies break, he/she should not be surprised when such occurs, for nature is operating by physics laws God set-up. Nature is neutral; it does not know a person resides in a flood-prone city; (4) Some physical evils serve as a moral warning. When a man is down physically, there is a good chance he will look up spiritually. As C.S. Lewis one opined, "God whispers to us in our pleasures, speaks in our conscience, but shouts in our pains: it is His megaphone to rouse a deaf world."[7] Indeed, God may often allow the megaphone of sickness to occur for our own benefit. For example, a cough and shortness of breath could be God's kind way of warning a smoker that worse ailments are soon on the horizon.

PAIN CAN SHOUT

(5) Finally, the Bible claims that the entire creation was drastically affected by the fall of man into sin; physical evil is essentially connected with moral evil. In Romans 8:19-22, Paul writes: "The creation waits in eager expectation for the sons of God to be revealed. For the creation was subjected to frustration, not by its own choice, but by the will of the one who subjected it, in hope that the creation itself will be liberated from its bondage to decay and brought into the glorious freedom of the children of God. We know that the whole creation has been groaning as in the pains of childbirth right up to the present time." Suffice it to say, though it is difficult to ascertain why dysteleo- logical (i.e., meaningless) physical evils occur, like those that kill innocent children, we must also realize that our moral fall in the Garden of Eden also caused this physical world to become imperfect. Everything is now dying and running down.

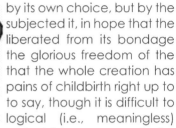

But one quandary remains: Wouldn't a perfect God create a perfect world? Why is this world so flawed? Cannot God instantly create a world with free beings who always choose the good? The answer is no. As Alvin Plantinga has pointed out in positing the concept of "trans-world depravity," it is possible that, no matter what possible free-creature-filled world God could actualize, eventually, sometime down the road, a free being would choose evil.[8] If God wants free creatures, evil may be a necessary evil! That said, such a fact does not lead to finite godism, a worldview made popular by Rabbi Harold Kushner in the 20th century in which God is finite. God is not, to any degree, impotent as Kushner claims. Ultimately, the final outcome of evil is guaranteed. Like a perfect chess player, God will always win, for this world is not the end of the drama. If it were, life would indeed be a sick joke, for final justice would never be served for the horrible atrocities that occur in this life. But, as Rev. 20:14 indicates, evil will one day be destroyed, for God has both the desire and power to do it. That is, we can rest assured that God will indeed one day actualize the best of all possible worlds, a place Rev. 21:1 calls the "new heaven and new earth." God always intended to create this world, a place where free beings will always choose the good. Yet even an all-powerful God could not instantly actualize this world. Allow me to explain.

I would propose that this present world, a world where free beings have the potential to choose or not to choose the good, is a *necessary means* to achieving a world where free beings will always choose the good. That is, it appears that we need a character-building world where the possibility of evil exists, before we can enter a perfect world where no evil exists. Many scholars have come to see the cogency of this line of reasoning. For example, the world-renowned philosopher and former University of Birmingham theology professor, John Hick, takes the approach that, in this present world, evil bears a unique "soul-making" function for all human beings who commit it and experience it.

For Hick, God wants us to progressively develop into Christ-like beings over time. As Hick writes, "Men may eventually become the perfected persons whom the New Testament calls 'children of God,' but they cannot be created ready-made as this."[9] In a similar vein, Norman Geisler, a genius in philosophy and theology who authored dozens of textbooks, also once elucidated a unique this-world-has-a-purpose theodicy. Geisler writes: "This is not the best of all possible worlds, but it is the best of all possible ways to achieve the best of all possible worlds."[10]

I believe Hick and Geisler both make extremely compelling points. This present world appears to have a special function. How can I appreciate heaven if I have no reference point to which to compare it? How can I fully comprehend righteousness if I have no idea of what evil is? As Geisler puts it, "A sinless heaven is better than an evil earth, but there was no way for God to achieve a sinless heaven unless He created beings who would sin and did sin in order that out of their sin He could produce the best world where beings could sin but would not sin. An imperfect moral world is the necessary precondition for achieving the morally perfect world."[11]

In sum, we can rest assured that the all-powerful, all-good God who made this universe, will one day actualize the best of all possible worlds. Evil will be no more. This present world is simply a necessary means toward that inevitable end. And what an end it will be! Even death shall be destroyed (see Rev. 20:14) and we will be able to forever live in peace. Speaking of the end times, the apostle John in Revelation 21 provides us with a beautiful eschatological vision of what the "new heaven and new earth" will be like. John writes the following in verses 1-5:

Then I saw a new heaven and a new earth, for the first heaven and the first earth had passed away, and there was no longer any sea. I saw the Holy City, the new Jerusalem, coming down as a bride beautifully dressed for her husband. And I heard a loud voice saying, "Now the dwelling of God is with men, and he will live with them. They will be his people, and God himself will be with them and be their God. He will wipe away every tear from their eyes. There will be no more mourning or crying or pain, for the old order of things is passed away. He who was seated on the throne said, "I am making everything new!"

Notes

Preface

1. Gregory A. Boyd and Edward K. Boyd, *Letters from a Skeptic* (Wheaton: Victor Books, 1995), 11.
2. David K. Clark, *Dialogical Apologetics* (Grand Rapids: Baker Books, 1993), 122.
3. Ibid, 123.
4. Ibid, 112.

Introduction

1. The Random House College Dictionary — Revised Edition (1982).
2. Ron Carlson and Ed Decker, *Fast Facts on False Teachings* (Eugene: Harvest House, 1994), 7.
3. Clark, 100.
4. Ibid.
5. Barry Huddleston, *The Acrostic Summarized Bible* (Grand Rapids: Baker Books, 1990), 3.
6. Clark, 89.
7. Rev. Dimanche's homily was preached in December 1999 at Brent International School located in Subic Bay Freeport, Philippines.
8. Billy Graham's *Foreword* appeared in Bill Bright's *Witnessing Without Fear* (Nashville: Thomas Nelson, 1993), 7.
9. Immanuel Kant, *The Critique of Pure Reason*, trans. Norman Smith (New York: St. Martin's Press, 1965), 173.
10. Roderick M. Chisholm, *Theory of Knowledge* (London: Prentice-Hall International, 1989), 16.

Creator

1. A portion of Anselm's *Prologion* can be found in William I. Rowe & William J. Wainright, *Philosophy of Religion: Selected Readings* (New York: Hartcourt Brace Jovanovich, 1973), 103-05.
2. Norman Malcolm, "Anselm's Ontological Arguments," *Philosophical Review* (January 1960).
3. See Alvin Plantinga, *God, Freedom and Evil* (Grand Rapids, MI: Eerdmans, 1977), 112.
4. Peter Kreeft & Ronald K. Tacelli, *Handbook of Christian Apologetics* (Downer's Grove, IL: InterVarsity Press, 1994), 51.
5. S.A. Bludman, "Thermodynamics and the End of a Closed Universe," *Nature* 308 (1984): 322.
6. Paul Davies, *The Last Three Minutes* (London: Weidenfeld & Nicolson, 1994), 18.
7. Walt Brown, *In The Beginning* (Phoenix: Center for Scientific Creation, 2001), 24.
8. Paraphrased from William Paley, *Natural Theology* (1802).
9. David Hume, *Dialogues Concerning Natural Religion*, ed. Norman K. Smith (Indianapolis: Bobbs-Merrill, 1947), 170.
10. This commentary is printed on the back cover of *Darwin's Black Box*. (see note 11 below).
11. Michael J. Behe, *Darwin's Black Box* (New York: Simon & Schuster, 1998), 39.
12. Scott M. Huse, *The Collapse of Evolution* (Grand Rapids: Baker Books, 1993), 115.
13. Dr. Paul Brand & Philip Yancey, *Fearfully and Wonderfully Made* (Grand Rapids: Zondervan, 1980), 45.
14. Michael Denton, *Evolution: A Theory in Crisis* (Bethesda: Adler & Adler, 1985), 334.
15. Brown, 3. Note: This citation covers both the second and third illustrations shown concerning DNA capacity.
16. Elizabeth Mitchell, "Dinosaur-Bird Confusion" (July 30, 2011). https://answersingenesis.org/dinosaurs/feathers/dinosaur-bird-confusion/
17. Bodie Hodge offers this argument in *War of the Worldviews*, a 2005 Answers-in-Genesis publication co-authored by Ken Ham & other scholars.
18. Huse, 114.
19. Ibid, 110. Note: The "Wanted" cartoon shown was derived from Huse.
20. Duane Gish, *Acts and Facts* (El Cajon, CA: Institute for Creation Research, 1985).
21. Phillip E. Johnson, *Darwin on Trial* (Downers Grove: InterVarsity Press, 1991), 146.
22. The bacterial flagellum diagram is from D. Voet & J. G. Voet, *Biochemistry* (New York: John Whiley and Sons), 1259.
23. Behe, 70.
24. Huse., 92. The human eye diagram has been reproduced based on Huse's original model, page 93.
25. Charles Darwin (1872), *Origin of Species* (New York: New York University Press, 1988), 151.
26. Ibid, 154.
27. Huse, 71.
28. Ibid.
29. Hugh Ross, "Astronomical Evidences for a Personal, Transcendent God," in *The Creation Hypothesis*, ed. J. P. Moreland (Downers Grove: InterVarsity Press, 1994), 160.
30. Ibid.
31. Ibid, 160-163.
32. Bernard J. Carr, "On the Origin, Evolution and Purpose of the Physical Universe" in *Physical Cosmology and Philosophy*, ed. John Leslie (New York: Macmillian, 1990), 134.
33. Hugh Ross, *The Creator and the Cosmos* (Colorado Springs: NavPress, 1994), 114.

34. Paul Davies, *The Cosmic Blueprint* (New York: Simon and Schuster, 1988), 203..

35. C..S. Lewis, *Mere Christianity* (New York: The Macmillan Company, 1952), Bk. III, chap. 10, 120.

36. Gregory A. Boyd and Edward K. Boyd, *Letters from a Skeptic* (Wheaton: Victor Books, 1995), 51.

37. Ron Carlson and Ed Decker, *Fast Facts on False Teachings* (Eugene: Harvest House, 1994), 17.

Gospels

1. With regard to this NT chart, I am indebted to the lecture notes of Dr. Robert H. Stein (my seminary professor in Gospel studies).

2. Robert H. Stein, *The Synoptic Problem: An Introduction* (Grand Rapids: Baker Books, 1987), 218.

3. Craig S. Keener, *The IVP Bible Background Commentary* (Downer's Grove: InterVarsity Press, 1993), 41.

4. Gregory A. Boyd and Edward K. Boyd, *Letters from a Skeptic* (Wheaton: Victor Books, 1995), 90.

5. Frank Colquhoun, *Four Portraits of Jesus* (Downer's Grove: InerVarsity Press, 1984), 2.

6. F.F. Bruce, *The Books and the Parchments* (Westwood, NJ: Fleming H. Revell, 1963), 178.

7. Bruce Metzger, *The Text of the New Testament* (Oxford: Oxford University Press, 1968), 34.

8. Don Bierlie, *Surprised by Faith* (Lynnwood: Emerald Books, 1992), 35.

9. Bruce, 178.

10. F.F. Bruce, *The New Testament Documents: Are They Reliable?* (Downers Grove: InterVarsity Press, 1960).

11. Ibid, 15.

12. Joel B. Green and Scot McKnight, editors, *Dictionary of Jesus and the Gospels* (Downers Grove: InterVarsity Press, 1992), 514.

13. David Alexander and Pat Alexander, editors, *Eerdman's Handbook to the Bible* (Herts, UK: Lion Publishing, 1973), 550.

14. Bruce, 31.

15. Gregory A. Boyd, *Jesus Under Siege* (Wheaton: Victor Books, 1995), 105.

16. Millar Burrrows, *What Mean These Stones?* (New York: Meridian Books, 1956), 1.

17. Gary Habermas, *Ancient Evidence for the Life of Jesus* (Nashville: Thomas Nelson, 1984), 152-53.

18. Boyd, 85.

19. Justo L. González, *The Story of Christianity* (San Francisco: HarperCollins, 1984), 27.

20. Robert Grant, *Historical Introduction to the New Testament* (New York: Harper and Row, 1963), 302.

21. William Whiston, Translator, *The Complete Works of Josephus* (Grand Rapids: Kregal Publications, 1981), VIII.

22. González, 130.

23. I am indebted to Holy Land tour guide, Mr. Tony Boyadgion, for his informative 1994 verbal expose re: Josephus.

24. Bruce, 46.

25. E.M. Blaiklok, *The Acts of the Apostles* (Grand Rapids: Eerdmans, 1959), 89.

26. William M. Ramsay, *The Bearing of Recent Discovery on the Trustworthiness of the New Testament* (London: Hodder & Stoughton, 1915), 222.

27. González, 34.

28. Ibid, 40.

29. Clark Pinnock, *Set Forth Your Case* (New Jersey: The Craig Press, 1968), 58.

Christ

1. Josh McDowell, *More Than a Carpenter* (Wheaton: Tyndale House, 1977), 102.

2. Peter W. Stoner and Robert C. Newman, *Science Speaks* (Chicago: Moody Press, 1976), 106-112..

3. Timothy J. Dailey, *Mysteries of the Bible* (Lincolnwood: Publications International, 1998), 179.

4. *Mishna*, Third Tractate, "B. Pesachim," 4; Tractate 'J. Sabbath," Chapter IX, Par. 3.

5. I am indebted to Holy Land tour guide, Mr. Tony Boyadgion, for his informative 1994 verbal expose re: Herod's temple.

6. Josh McDowell, *Evidence Demands a Verdict* (San Bernardino: Here's Life Publishers, 1972), 103.

7. C.S. Lewis, *Mere Christianity* (New York: Macmillan Publishing Company, 1952), 40-41.

8. William Lane Craig, *The Son Rises: Historical Evidence for the Resurrection of Jesus* (Chicago: Moody Press, 1981), 140.

9. C.S. Lewis, *Miracles* (New York: Macmillan Publishing Company), 54-55.

10. Philip Schaff, *The Person of Christ* (New York: American Tract Society, 1913), 94-95.

11. Jon A. Buell and O. Quentin Hyder, *Jesus: God, Ghost or Guru?* (Grand Rapids: Zondervan, 1978), 102.

12. An excellent discussion as to why 1 Corinthians 15 is an early Christian creed can be found on pages 43ff., 280ff. and 308ff. of Lee Strobel's *The Case for Christ* (Grand Rapids: Zondervan Publishing House, 1998) where Mr. Strobel interviews Dr. Craig Blomberg, Dr. William Craig and Dr. Gary Habermas, respectively.

13. Ibid, 44. Blomberg makes this assertion while being interviewed by Strobel.

14. Ibid. Note: In Chapter 13, Strobel asks Habermas if there are any alternative theories to the resurrection. He mentions that one theory is that Jesus's appearances were legendary and another theory is that they were hallucinations. In response, Habermas explains that the legend theory cannot explain why early eyewitness accounts of Jesus exist or why 1 Corinthians contains a creed written by Paul before the gospels existed.

15. Paul Althus' erudite comment is cited by Wolfhart Pannenburg, *Jesus — God and Man*. Translated by L.L. Wilkins & D.A. Priche (Philadelphia: Westminister Press, MCMLXVIII), 100.

16. Gary Habermas and Antony Flew, *Did Jesus Rise From the Dead? The Resurrection Debate*. Terry L. Miethe, Editor (San Francisco: Harper & Row, 1987), 28.

17. Shroud of Turin Research Project (STRP), "Text," New London, CT (October 1981), 1.

18. Ian Wilson, *The Blood and the Shroud* (London: Orion Books, 1999), 235.

19. Habermas, 28.

20. Wilson, 104.

21. Ibid, 120.

22. Ibid, 124.

23. Ian Wilson, *The Shroud of Turin* (New York: Doubleday & Company, 1978), 54.

24. Ian Wilson, *The Blood and the Shroud* (London: Orion Books, 1999), 8.

25. Ibid, 380.

26. Ibid.

27. I am indebted to Ian Wilson for all facts related to the three "feats" listed. Both of Wilson's works above were used to create this summary.

28. Josh McDowell, *The Resurrection Factor* (Nashville: Thomas Nelson, 1981), 54.

29. Simon Greenleaf, *An Examination of the Testimony of the Four Evangelists by the Rules of Evidence Administered in the Courts of Justice* (Grand Rapids, Baker Book House, 1965. Reprint of 1874 edition. New York: J. Cockroft and Co.), 29.

30. Flavius Josephus, *De Bello Judaico*, 7.202, 203.

31. Cicero, *V in Verrem*, 64.

32. Eusebius, "The epistle of the Church in Smyrna," *Trials and Crucifixion of Christ*, A.P. Stout, ed., Cincinnati, Standard Publishing, 1986.

33. Will Durant, *Caesar and Christ* (New York: Simon & Schuster, 1944), 572.

34. McDowell, 98.

35. Gregory A. Boyd, *Cynic Sage or Son of God* (Wheaton: Victor Books/ A BridgePoint Book), 293.

36. Josh McDowell, *Answers to Tough Questions* (San Bernadino, CA: Here's Life Publishers, 1980), 148.

37. Kenneth Scott Latourette, *American Historical Review*. LIV, January, 1949 quoted in McDowell's *Evidence Demands a Verdict*.

Kerygma

1. I am indebted to both Kenneth Bailey and Craig S. Keener (see Gospels #3 above; page 329) for their outlines of Peter's Pentecost chiasm.

2. Craig S. Keener, *The IVP Bible Background Commentary* (Downer's Grove: InterVarsity Press, 1993), 329.

3. Stephen Neill, *The Interpretation of the New Testament*, page 274 cited in a class handout produced by Dr. Robert H. Stein.

4. James M. Boice's quote is cited by Lee Strobel & Gary Poole, *Experiencing the Passion of Jesus* (Grand Rapids: Zondervan,, 2004), 49.

5. Ibid, 50.

6. Frank Gaebelein, ed., *The Expositors Bible Commentary*, Vol. 9 (Grand Rapids: Zondervan, 1976), 157.

7. James Denney, *The Death of Christ* (Chicago: InterVarsity Press, 1951), 157.

8. Mark McCloskey, *Tell It Often, Tell It Well* (San Bernadino, CA: Here's Life Publishers, 1986), 23.

9. Keener, 128.

10. Rick Warren, *The Purpose-Driven Life* (Grand Rapids: Zondervan, 2002), 123.

11. Ibid, 171.

12. C.S. Lewis's well known quote is cited by many authors as it reveals there is indeed a limit on the number of options we have before us.

Conclusion

1. Clark Pinnock, *A Case for Faith* (Minneapolis: Bethany, 1980), 119.

2. Billy Graham, *How to be Born Again* (Waco: Word Books, 1977), 202.

Appendix

1. Epicurus (341-270 B.C.) was quoted by David Hume in his *Dialogues Concerning Natural Religion*, ed. Henry D. Aiken (New York: Hafner, 1948), 66.

2. J.L. Mackie, "Evil and Omnipotence," *Mind* 64 (1955), 200.

3. Millard Erickson, *Christian Theology* (Grand Rapids: Baker Book House, 1983), 416.

4. Richard Rice, *God's Foreknowledge and Man's Free Will* (Minneapolis: Bethany House Publisers, 1985), 54.

5. James Sterba, "God, Plantinga and a Better World," *International Journal for the Philosophy of Religion* 7 (1976), 446.

6. Mackie, 211.

7. C.S. Lewis, 81.

8. Alvin Plantinga, *God, Freedom and Evil* (New York: Harper & Rowe, 1974), 66.

9. John Hick, *Evil and the God of Love* (New York: Harper & Rowe, 1966), 255.

10. Norman Geisler, *Philosophy of Religion* (Grand Rapids: Zondervan Publishing House, 1974), 326.

11. Ibid.

Apologetics-in-Action

Given that I have been fortunate to be able to dialogue with others about the verity of Christ across every continent on Earth, I have included (on the next three pages) snapshot portraitures of some of my fondest memories where meaningful apologetic conversations took place near iconic global destinations as I sought to serve Christ with efficacy as either an itinerant apologist or U.S. Navy chaplain spanning 1989-2021. If a picture paints 1000 words, then the main take-away intended to be gleaned from inclusion of these global images is to remind all Christian readers that *every* Christ-follower, in whatever places he or she might reside and/or travel, has been commissioned by Christ to not only be salt and light in a dark world (see Matt. 5:13-16), and to not only go into all the world and preach the Gospel kerygma (Mark 16:15), but to always be prepared to provide a logical defense regarding the truth of Christ (1 Peter 3:15). Ergo, it is vital Christ-followers hone the indispensable skill of being able to effectuate practical and wise apologetics-in-action. This handbook is meant to serve as a user-friendly guide to assist in that venture.

Apologetics Done via Dialogues on 7 Continents

"My globetrotting has taught me one undeniable fact—that we're all part of one human race & eternity resides in each of our hearts."-D.J.C.

Giza Pyramids & Sphinx - Cairo, Egypt

Taj Mahal Mausoleum - Agra, India

Ancient Colosseum - Rome, Italy

82 Flag Patches

Corcovado - Rio, Brazil

King George Island - Antarctica

Great Wall of China - PRC

Angkor Wat – Siem Reap, Cambodia   Al-Khazneh Temple – Petra, Jordan

Great Barrier Reef – Australia   Notre Dame – France   Niagara Falls – N.Y. | Canada

"Blue Cave" Dive – Okinawa, Japan   Arab Qtr. – Old City Jerusalem, Israel

CMI's mission/motto is *Championing Christ & His Agape Love*. With an apologetics/charity focus, CMI's vision is to globally impact 1M+ for Christ by 2050. CMI's "Apologetics 101: Faith Fits the Facts" seminar, which is based on this handbook, is a practical, dynamic, world-class training for academic audiences & church congregations. To book the seminar and/or contact CMI, please visit caseintl.com.

Apologetics Done via U.S. Navy Chaplain Ministry

Baptism at the Marine Corps Recruit Depot San Diego   Okinawa Beach Wedding   Somali Refugees Rescued by CG-57 in Gulf of Aden

CCTV Night Photo of CG-57 Transiting Panama Canal   Chaplain Corps Emblem   Shipboard Shot of Welcome Sign at Suez Canal, Egypt

Photo of Welcome Sign at Karachi Navy Base, Pakistan   Rappelling with Marines   Visting Remote Naval Facility Diego Garcia, BIOT Atoll

Preaching at Combat Zone Base Chapel   Doing a COMREL at a Bahrain Orphanage   Baptizing USMC Dependent in the Jordan River

Disclaimer: The views & images expressed in this publication are those of the author and do not reflect the official policy or position of the U.S. Navy, Department of Defense, or the U.S. Gov't.

Made in the USA
Coppell, TX
13 September 2022